# NO BAD KIDS

## The Positive Parenting and Modern Parenting Guide

### Samuel Pattinson

© **Copyright 2020 by Samuel Pattinson - All rights reserved.**

This document is geared towards providing exact and reliable information in regards to the topic and issue covered. The publication is sold with the idea that the publisher is not required to render accounting, officially permitted, or otherwise, qualified services. If advice is necessary, legal or professional, a practiced individual in the profession should be ordered.

- From a Declaration of Principles which was accepted and approved equally by a Committee of the American Bar Association and a Committee of Publishers and Associations.

In no way is it legal to reproduce, duplicate, or transmit any part of this document in either electronic means or in printed format. Recording of this publication is strictly prohibited and any storage of this document is not allowed unless with written permission from the publisher. All rights reserved.

The information provided herein is stated to be truthful and consistent, in that any liability, in terms of inattention or otherwise, by any usage or abuse of any policies, processes, or directions contained within is the solitary and utter responsibility of the recipient reader. Under no circumstances will any legal responsibility or blame be held against the publisher for any reparation, damages, or monetary loss due to the information herein, either directly or indirectly.

Respective authors own all copyrights not held by the publisher.

The information herein is offered for informational purposes solely, and is universal as so. The presentation of the information is without contract or any type of guarantee assurance.

The trademarks that are used are without any consent, and the publication of the trademark is without permission or backing by the trademark owner. All trademarks and brands within this book are for clarifying purposes only and are the owned by the owners themselves, not affiliated with this document.

**THE WHOLE BRAIN CHILD** ............................................................................ 8

**INTRODUCTION** ............................................................................................ 9

**CHAPTER 1: EARLY DEVELOPMENT OF BRAIN** ................................. 11
   1.1 Brain Development before Birth ............................................................. 13
   1.2 Stages of Brain Development ................................................................. 17

**CHAPTER 2: INTEGRATION IN BRAIN** ................................................... 22
   2.1 Where Integration Occurs in Brain? ....................................................... 22
   2.2 Functional Imaging of Mind ................................................................... 25
   2.3 Brain and Body Integration .................................................................... 29

**CHAPTER 3: REVOLUTIONARY STEPS TO NURTURE CHILD'S DEVELOPING MIND** ..................................................................................... 33
   3.1 Nurturing Baby's Mind through Reading and Learning ........................ 34
   3.2 Nurture Child's Mind through Trust, Confidence, and Love ................ 36
   3.3 Twelve Innovative Strategies to Nurture Child's Brain ......................... 39
   3.4 Research Study on Nurturing Child's Brain through Mother's Love ............................................................................................................... 42
   3.5 Nurturing Child's Imagination ................................................................ 43

**CHAPTER 4: CHANGES IN BRAIN** ........................................................... 46
   4.1 Research and Discovery of Neuroplasticity ........................................... 47
   4.2 How Brain Changes with Age ................................................................ 49
   4.3 What Happens to Brain as we Age ......................................................... 54
   4.4 Aging Slows down the Brain .................................................................. 61
   4.5 Effects of Aging Brain on Thinking ....................................................... 63

**CHAPTER 5: PARENTING ROLE IN NURTURING CHILD'S BRAIN** .......................... 69
   5.1 Effect of Parenting on Development of Child's Brain ........................... 70
   5.2 Parenting Styles ...................................................................................... 74
   5.3 Effects of Negative Parenting Style on Child's Brain ............................ 78

**CHAPTER 6: WAYS TO IMPROVE BABY'S BRAIN DEVELOPMENT** 82
   6.1 Developing Cognitive Skills in Children ............................................... 82
   6.2 Improving Cognitive skills through Games ........................................... 86
   6.3 Cognitive Nurturing in Early Childhood ................................................ 87

**CHAPTER 7: IMPACT OF EXTERNAL SURROUNDING ON BRAIN DEVELOPMENT** 91
   7.1 Early Childhood Experiences Effect Brain for Long Term .................. 92
   7.2 Environmental Impact on Child's Brain Development .......................... 95
   7.3 Brain Development Affected By Poverty .............................................. 98
   7.4 Development Affected by Technology .................................................. 99

7.5 PLAY DEPRIVATION CAN DAMAGE THE CHILDHOOD DEVELOPMENT OF THE BRAIN .................................................................................................. 105

**CHAPTER 8: IMPORTANCE OF NURTURING CHILD'S MIND ............................ 107**
    8.1 CHILDREN DEVELOP CYNICISM AT EARLY STAGE ................................. 108
    8.2 IMPACT OF CYNICISM ON CHILD'S LIFE ............................................. 111
    8.3 IMPORTANCE OF NURTURING CHILD'S MIND AT EARLY STAGE ........... 113

**9: CONCLUSION ........................................................................................... 115**

**DANISH WAY OF PARENTING ...................................................................... 118**

**INTRODUCTION ........................................................................................... 121**

**CHAPTER 1: OUR DEFAULT SETTINGS (P.A.R.E.N.T) ...................................... 123**
    1.1 AN EPIDEMIC OF STRESS .................................................................... 124
    1.2 EXAMINING OUR "DEFAULT SETTINGS" ............................................. 126

**CHAPTER 2: PLAY ........................................................................................ 129**
    2.1 P IS FOR PLAY ..................................................................................... 129
    2.2 INTERNAL VS. EXTERNAL LOCUS OF CONTROL ................................. 132
    2.3 PLAY AND COPING SKILLS ................................................................. 136
    2.4 TIPS FOR PLAY ................................................................................... 140

**CHAPTER 3: AUTHENTICITY ........................................................................ 142**
    3.1 A IS FOR AUTHENTICITY .................................................................... 142
    3.2 PARENTING WITH AUTHENTICITY .................................................... 144
    3.3 THE DANISH WAY OF AUTHENTIC PRAISE ........................................ 145
    3.4 THE KEY TO LIFELONG LEARNING AND SUCCESS ............................. 147
    3.5 TIPS FOR AUTHENTICITY ................................................................... 150

**CHAPTER 4: REFRAMING ............................................................................ 153**
    4.1 R IS FOR REFRAMING ........................................................................ 153
    4.2 REALISTIC OPTIMISM ........................................................................ 155
    4.3 THE EXPERTISE OF REFRAMING ........................................................ 157
    4.4 HOW REFRAMING WORKS WITH CHILDREN .................................... 159
    4.5 THE DANISH WAY OF REFRAMING ................................................... 164
    4.6 TIPS FOR REFRAMING ....................................................................... 167

**CHAPTER 5: EMPATHY ................................................................................ 169**
    5.1 E IS FOR EMPATHY ............................................................................ 169
    5.2 THE TRUTH ABOUT EMPATHY .......................................................... 174
    5.3 THE RESPONSIBILITY OF PARENTS .................................................... 176
    5.4 THE POWER OF WORD ...................................................................... 179
    5.5 TIPS FOR EMPATHY ........................................................................... 183

## CHAPTER 6: NO ULTIMATUMS ............................................................. 185
- 6.1 N Is for No Ultimatums ................................................................ 185
- 6.2 Four Parenting Styles ................................................................... 186
- 6.3 How Danish Practice No Ultimatums at School ........................ 191
- 6.4 Avoiding Power Struggles ........................................................... 193
- 6.5 Tips for No Ultimatums ............................................................... 198

## CHAPTER 7: TOGETHERNESS AND HYGGE ................................... 200
- 7.1 T Is for Togetherness and Hygge ................................................. 200
- 7.2 Hyggge as a means of living ........................................................ 201
- 7.3 The Danish Way of Hygge ........................................................... 208
- 7.4 Tips for togetherness and hygge .................................................. 209

## 8. CONCLUSION .................................................................................. 215

## THE MONTESSORI FAMILY ............................................................... 217

## INTRODUCTION .................................................................................... 1

## CHAPTER 1: HOW MONTESSORI EDUCATION WILL SHAPE YOUR CHILD ........................................................................................................ 3
- 1.1 How did Montessori Education Develop ..................................... 13
- 1.2 Montessori Approach ..................................................................... 13
- 1.3 Differences ....................................................................................... 14
- 1.4 What Does a Montessori Classroom Look Like ......................... 15
- 1.5 Is a Montessori a Good Fit For Your Child ................................. 16
- 1.6 Special Needs .................................................................................. 16
- 1.7 What To Look On a Tour .............................................................. 16
- 1.8 Transitioning To a Traditional School ......................................... 16

## CHAPTER 2: EASY AND PRACTICAL MONTESSORI PRACTICE ..... 27
- 2.1 Produce Sensory Experience ......................................................... 28
- 2.2 Encourage Your Child to Practice Deep Concentration ........... 28
- 2.3 Practice Walking Meditation ........................................................ 29
- 2.4 Take Advantage of "THE SILENCE GAMES" ........................... 30
- 2.5 Try Age Appropriate Essential Oils ............................................. 31
- 2.6 General Montessori Resources ..................................................... 31

## CHAPTER 3: INCORPORATING MONTESSORI PRINCIPLES AT HOME ........................................................................................................ 34
- 3.1 Organize Environment .................................................................. 38
- 3.2 Emphasize Life Skill ....................................................................... 39
- 3.3 Teach Concentration ...................................................................... 40
- 3.4 Focus on Inner Motivation, Not Reward .................................... 40

3.5 Baby-proof Your Home ............................................................. 41
3.6 Use Baby Gates to Create Areas for Exploration ................. 41
3.7 Make Their Bedroom Child-Friendly ..................................... 41
3.8 Utilized Child Size Furniture .................................................. 41
3.9 Keep Books and Toys on Low shelves ................................... 42
3.10 Hang Interesting Art Work .................................................... 42
3.11 Create Seasonal Nature Trays ................................................ 43
3.12 Recommended Montessori Resources .................................. 43
3.13 Montessori Method at Home ................................................ 46

## CHAPTER 4: MIND-MINDED PARENTING ........................... 50
4.1 Help Children Develop Secure Attachments ......................... 51
4.2 Help Kids Develop Social Survey ............................................ 51
4.3 What About Cautions? ............................................................. 53
4.5 Mind-minded parenting: The takeaway ................................ 55
4.6 What is Montessori Parenting ................................................. 55
4.7 Montessori at Home and Montessori Parenting ................... 55
4.8 Ways to Montessori Parenting ................................................ 56

## CHAPTER 5: MONTESSORI PARENTING HABIT PRACTICE ........... 59
5.1 Respect Your Children as a Person ......................................... 60
5.2 Give Them Freedom But in Limits ......................................... 61
5.3 Slow Down and Give Them Space ......................................... 62
5.4 Use Big Words Even With Little Kids .................................... 62
5.5 Always Making Observation of Your Little One .................. 64
5.6 Fun Family Time with Children .............................................. 65
5.7 Montessori Child Ages .............................................................. 66
5.8 Teachers ' Position at Montessori ........................................... 85
5.9 ACCREDITED VS. NON-ACCREDITED MONTESSORI ......... 85
5.10 ADVANTAGES OF MONTESSORI EDUCATION ................ 88
5.11 DISADVANTAGES OF MONTESSORI ................................... 90
5.12 MYTHS ABOUT MONTESSORI ............................................. 94
5.13 QUESTIONS FREQUENTLY ASKED .................................... 99

## 6: CONCLUSION ............................................................................ 110
## REFERENCES ................................................................................ 112
## REFERENCES ................................................................................ 113
## REFERENCES ................................................................................ 114

# The Whole Brain Child

*Guide to Raising a Curious Human Being and Revolutionary Strategies to Nurture Your Child's Developing Mind*

**Samuel Pattinson**

# Introduction

A Whole-Brain Child is a ground-breaking approach to the rearing of children with main criteria that supports active and flourishing development of the brain, which will ultimately lead to calmer, and happier babies. The "upstairs brain," which takes emotional decisions and balances, is under construction until the mid-20s. And, particularly in young children, the right brain and its emotions tend to rule over the left brain's reasoning. No wonder children quietly throw tantrums, fight, or sulk. By applying these results to day-to-day parenting, you can turn every outburst, disagreement, or anxiety into an opportunity to transform your child's brain and foster critical development.

Parents are often experts on the bodies of their children. They know Fever is a temperature over 98.6 degrees. They know how to clean a wound so that it won't become contaminated. They know the foods that will most likely leave their child wired before bedtime. But even the most loving, best-educated parents still lack basic brain knowledge. That is not surprising? Particularly when they consider the central role that the brain participates in every part of a child's life that parents care about: discipline, decision-making, self-awareness, school, relationships, etc. The brain actually decides pretty much who we are, and what we are doing. And learning how the brain changes in response to our parenting will help us grow a healthier, more resilient infant, as the brain itself is profoundly influenced by the interactions that we offer as parents. So, we want to bring you to the viewpoint of the whole mind.

We would like to clarify some basic brain concepts and help you apply your new knowledge in ways that encourage and make parenting more meaningful. They don't assume having a whole-brain child is going to get rid of all the problems that come with parenting. But by learning a few simple and easy-to-master concepts about how the brain works, you'll be able to understand your child better, react to stressful situations more effectively, and build a foundation for social, emotional, and mental wellbeing. What matters is how well you are parenting your child, and we'll provide you with simple, scientifically-based ideas that will help you establish a healthy relationship with your child that can help shape his brain well and give him the best chance for a safe, happy life.

The chapters in this book are projected to explain the development of brain in children in its early stages. How left part of the human brain is with its right part and how they are interlinked with the body. The human brain involves many revolutionary steps through which it passes, and finally, it reaches to developmental stage. During the developmental stage, the child's brain is observing every single act from his surroundings and is feeding those actions in his mind. If the child's brain is not nurtured in a right and way, he may adopt adverse effects from his surroundings, which may hurt the child throughout his whole life. This can make him a cynic and cynical person who will contribute negativity and destruction to society. The last chapter of this book is based on the importance of nurturing children's minds in a better and positive way so that he can contribute positivity and good deeds towards his society. It is essential to nurture a child's mind at a developmental stage in the right way.

# Chapter 1: Early Development of Brain

The stage of starting years in a child's life is specifically crucial for health and growth later on. Some of the critical reasons for this is how rapidly the brain develops starting before birth and continuing into early childhood. As the brain continues to grow and evolve into adulthood, the first eight years will lay the groundwork for potential success in learning, health, and life. Since birth to age 5, the brain of a child grows more in life than at any other time. And early brain development has a profound impact on the ability of a child to learn and excel in both school and life. Babies need nutrition, security, and stimulation for healthy brain development in the earliest years of experience, especially from pregnancy to age three. Recent advances in neuroscience give new evidence of the event of a baby's brain during this time. As a result, we know that babies ' brains form new connections at a fantastic rate in their earliest years–according to the Developing Child Center at Harvard University, more than 1 million every second–a pace never again repeated. In the beginning years of life, the nature of a child's interactions-positive or negative-helps to form the development of their brain. The average baby's brain is about one-quarter of the average adult brain size when he is born. Incredibly, in the first year, this doubles in size. It continues to grow to about 80 percent of adult size by age 3 and 90 percent - almost fully grown -by age 5. The brain is the human body's command center. A newborn baby has all of the brain cells (neurons) they'll have for the rest of their lives, but it's the connections between those cells that make the brain work. Brain connections allow us to move about everything, think, interact, and do just about everything. To make these relations, the early years of childhood are crucial. Every second, at least one million new neural connections (synapses) are created more than at any other time in life. Different areas of the brain, like movement, language, and emotion, are responsible for different abilities and develop at different rates. Development of the mind builds on itself, as connections eventually connect in more complex ways. This allows the child to move, speak, and think in more complicated ways. The initial years are the most significant opportunity for the brain of a child to develop the connections that they need to be healthy, able, and successful adults. In these early years, the relationships required for many relevant, higher-level skills such as motivation, self-regulation, problem-solving, and communication are formed -or not formed. For those essential brain connections to be formed later in life, it is much more difficult.

The brain is a profoundly interrelated organ and works in a richly coordinated fashion with its many functions. Emotional well-being and social skills provide a strong foundation for developing cognitive abilities, and together they are the bricks and mortar that form the foundation of human evolution. All-important prerequisites for success in school and later in the workplace and community are the physical and emotional health, cognitive-linguistic capacities, and social skills that emerge in the early years. The brain's underlying architecture is built through an ongoing process that starts before the birth of a child, and it keeps going on into adulthood. Early childhood experiences significantly impact the quality of that architecture by establishing a solid or fragile foundation for all of the following learning, health, and behavior. More than 1 million new neural connections are created every second during the first few years of life. After this time of sudden increase and concentration, connections are decreased by a process called pruning, to make brain circuits more efficient. The first to develop sensory pathways such as those for essential vision and hearing, followed by early language skills and higher cognitive functions. In a prescribed order, connections proliferate and prune, with later, more complex brain circuits built on more rapid, more uncomplicated courses.

Genes form neural relationships and life experiences in the brain-building process – including proper nutrition, security, and stimulation from caregivers talking, playing, and sensitive attention. The mixture of nature and nurture will lay the foundation for the future of a child. Research in neuroscience has shown us early childhood is a time of tremendous brain development. The young brain changes shape and size in reaction to everything the first years experienced. New environment, life experiences, careers, and relationships can all influence how the minds of children get wired. Numerous advances in brain development studies have been made in the last decade. They now realize there is much more that takes place in the first five years to influence a child's development than previously thought. This is a critical time in guiding the healthy growth and development of a child's brain. This thing should be kept in mind that the development of the brain is not a linear, step-by-step process but a life-long cascade of waves.

## 1.1 Brain Development before Birth

Most of what scientists know about the development of the fetal brain comes from studying animal brains or examining human postmortem samples. This work has provided insight into the creation of brain structure, but it does provide little clues as to how functional structures are structured. The earliest human fetal brain function investigations date back to the 1950s. In labor, when researchers placed electrodes on the abdomen of a pregnant woman and the walls of her cervix, they could detect electrical impulses that signaled fetal brain activity. Researchers and scientists started to evaluate that specific patterns of electrical activity were associated with neurological abnormalities.9 Scientists began experimenting with fMRI in the 1990s to map the connections in various regions of the brain. The fMRI measures brain activity changes related to changes in blood flow. During fMRI, the patient typically performs a task — seeing, for example, images of faces or finger tapping —

while the machine scans his or her brain. Researchers are looking for brain areas that light up during the mission. By that point, neuroscientists knew there was much more functional happening than a stimulus or task could be tested, but it was unclear how these functions could examine in a better way. Then, in 1995, a fortuitous observation was made by then-graduate student Bharat Biswal: the brain produces signals all the time, even if it is not engaged in a task. The use of fMRI to quantify these resting-state signals allowed scientists to analyze brain activity for the first time, without the subject having to tap a finger as much as possible. Researchers turned to preterm infants in the search for answers about how and when brain networks are created. Nearly 10 percent of all babies around the world are preterm born, that is before the end of the 37th week of pregnancy. Those kids are more likely to develop autism spectrum disorders, attention-deficit / hyperactivity disorder, emotional disorders, and neurological abnormalities compared with term babies. Preterm infants are also more likely to experience cognitive difficulties and problems later in life. A growing body of research suggests that changes in the way the brain is wired before or shortly after birth can cause these cognitive impairments. These first experiments by Smyser and other researchers have shown that the communication channels of the brain were active, albeit in an embryonic state, before term birth. Preterm babies allowed researchers to study the production of neural processes typically found within the womb. Researchers have found it difficult to know, however, whether the patterns they saw in these infants represented the healthy development of brain communication networks.

Human brain formation begins shortly after birth and carries on into early adulthood. During the third week of gestation (pregnancy), the fetal brain starts developing. Neural progenitor cells begin to divide and differentiate into neurons and glia, the two types of cells which form the nervous system's base. Before we get into fetal brain development science, here's a short anatomy lesson on the brain of your infant. We're familiar with five different regions, each responsible for different functions:

**Cerebrum:** This is the central part of the brain, and it's responsible for thought, remembering, and emotions. This is where the cerebral cortex lives, with its distinct lobes (including the frontal and temporal lobes).

**Cerebellum:** Area responsible for engine control.

**Brain stem:** This is the engine that powers most of the vital functions of your baby, including heart rate, breathing, and blood pressure.

**Pituitary gland:** This pea-sized gland releases hormones that are responsible for growth, metabolism, and more in your body.

**Hypothalamus:** This area covers the temperature of the body, hunger, thirst, sleep, and emotions.

### First Trimester

The neural layer of the female's fetus (think of it as the base of her baby's brain and spinal cord) develops just 16 days after conception. This grows longer and folds on itself until the fold becomes a groove, and that groove becomes a tube — the neural tunnel. Once the neural tube is closed, it bends and bulges into three parts at around week six or week 7 of pregnancy, commonly known as the forebrain, midbrain, and hindbrain. Just to the back of the hindbrain sits the section which will soon become the spinal cord of your infant. Finally, these areas spill into those five different brain regions with which we are most familiar: the cerebrum, the cerebellum, the brain stem, the pituitary gland, and the hypothalamus. All of these fetal brain regions, of course, require more time to be fully up and running.

At the same time, different neural cells develop and travel to form the very beginnings of nerves throughout the embryo. The nervous system of an unborn baby is comprised of millions upon millions of neurons; each of these small cells has itty-bitty branches branching off of them so that they can link and interact with each other. Baby's first synapses come with this, which essentially means that the baby's neurons can create and communicate initial movements in fetal like twisting and moving into the fetal position. Certain motions begin quickly, with a mother's fetus wiggling at around eight weeks to his developing limbs. By the ninth week, a thin, smooth structure emerges in the brain. The structure of the brain will change throughout pregnancy as it develops and begins to shape the characteristic folds which designate distinct brain regions. Changes in brain anatomy are indicative of significant cellular level changes. Neurons start producing the chemical signaling molecules in the different brain regions, which will allow contact between nerve cells. The fiber networks are emerging that will become the superhighway of information for the brain. The cells that make up the neocortex — the part of the brain that co-ordinates sight, sound, spatial reasoning, critical thought, and language — begin communications.

**Second Trimester**

Baby's brain directs steady contractions of the diaphragm and chest muscles during the second trimester (think of them as breathing movements). In about 16 weeks, Baby's first kick of sucking and swallowing impulses. By 21 weeks, the natural reflexes of the baby will allow him to take a few ounces of amniotic fluid every day. And all that swallowing also involves the taste of the infant, another concept that is in full gear now. The first kick of the baby can be felt by his mother in about 18 weeks of pregnancy (but don't panic if it takes a couple of weeks longer— that's normal, particularly among first-time moms). At about the same time, myelin covers the baby's nerves, protective insulation that speeds up communications between nerve cells (myelin keeps growing until the first birthday of your baby). And a further primary reflex happens at 24 weeks: Blinking. Little one's brainstem (controlling heart rate, breathing, and blood pressure) is almost fully mature at the tail-end of trimester two, sitting just above the spinal cord but below the cerebral cortex (the last region to mature). The fetal nervous system is being sufficiently developed to startle your baby from loud noises outside the womb— and may even turn his head towards the sound of your voice! Another promising development: Fetal brainwave activity includes sleep cycles at 28 weeks, including REM (the period when dreaming takes place).

**Third Trimester**

The third trimester is brimming with rapid neuronal growth and cabling. Baby's brain has approximately increased in weight over the last 13 weeks of gestation, rising from around 3.5 ounces at the end of the second quarter to about 10.6 ounces at the peak. And it also starts to look different: its once smooth surface becomes more grooved and indented. At the same moment, the cerebellum (motor control) is growing speedily— faster now than any other region of the fetal brain (it's surface area in the last 16 weeks of pregnancy increases30-fold). All of this development is excellent news for the cerebral cortex (think, recall, feel). Although this critical area of the brain multiplies during pregnancy, it only really begins to exercise nearly to the time when a full-term baby is born— and it matures slowly and progressively in the initial years of life, thanks to the enriching environment of the infant.

## 1.2 Stages of Brain Development

It continues to change all through the lifetime of the human brain. We cannot emphasize the importance of each point, and how we need to maintain and protect our growth rate of the mind from 0 to 100 and hopefully beyond. Let's look at every one of the five stages of human brain growth:

**Step 1: 0 Months to 10 Months**

Neurons and connections are increasing at a developmental stage in the mother's womb. A pregnant woman should have a healthy intake, including supplements like folic acid, B6 & B12, and should stay away from stress as much as possible, stimulate with sounds and sensations this young brain develops. Mum should avoid toxins, cigarettes, heavy metals, alcohol, and drugs. The body had been occupied with brain development until the child takes his first breath, preparing for life outside of the womb. Newborns have around 100bn neurons. It means that the average rate of brain cell development during pregnancy is about 250,000 new brain cells per minute. A child's brain at birth is about 60 percent of the size it will be when it is fully grown. The child's brain starts at about 20 cubic inches; then, in the first 90 days, after birth grows another 14 cubic inches, it comes close to doubling within the first three months. At conception, near the spinal cord is the only myelin-a fatty material that insulates the axons of your brain to help signals move faster. The brain area is responsible for core functions such as breathing, eating, and regulating heart rate.

**Stage 2: Two Years to Six Years**

Voluntary movement development, thought, cognition, frontal lobes involved in emotional development, associations, planning, working memory, and awareness. A sense of self develops, and experiences in life shape the psychological well-being. By the time the child is three years old, in terms of volume and brain cells, his brain is about 80 percent of his adult size. A three-year-old's mind is exceptionally sophisticated and maybe more [advanced] than any other animal on earth. At that point, as an adult, the brain has 200 percent more synapses. As the growth of the brain progresses, the mind of children tends to "prune" by breaking down specific synapses. Getting rid of the connections, it is not using helps the brain to concentrate its resources on the links that matter. The years leading up to the fifth birthday of a child are a part of the developmental "critical period." At this stage, experience forms the way synapses are shaped directly. Everybody's brain is adapted to their environment.

On the one hand, this means negative experiences will leave the child forever with a psychological scar. On the opposite side, it also means early intervention services, and more successful than ever attempt to reverse the effects of traumatic experiences. At age six, the brain is its adult weight and energy consumption peak at 95 percent. The caregivers must provide a nurturing environment and individualized contact daily. Harmful or harsh treatment may have future emotional consequences.

**Stage 3: Seven Years to Twenty-Two Years**

In terms of weight, teen brains appear adult-like, but they are not yet fully developed. Your body grew myelin from the back of the mind (which is responsible for the most basic functions) to the forehead (which has more complex circuits). The last area to be fully myelinated in the front lobe, which is essential for decision making, control of impulses, and empathy. The neural connections or' gray' matter are still pruning; brain wiring is continuing, the fatty tissues surrounding neurons or' white' matter are growing and helping to speed up electrical impulses and maintain connections. The prefrontal cortex is developed at the end, which involves regulating desires and making decisions. While the frontal lobe of an adult knows when to say "no" to peer pressure and threats, the ability has not yet been developed for teenagers. Parents should practice patience and provide guidance: To avoid poor choices, teens need "frontal lobe help." Adolescents, therefore, need to learn how to control careless, erratic, and irritable behavior. Do not use narcotics, caffeine, smoking, unprotected sex, and misuse of substances.

**Stage 4: Twenty-Three Years Sixty-Five Years**

Eventually, at age 22, the brain hits its peak power and lasts five more years. It is a downhill pattern afterward. Last to develop and first to go are the executive control brain circuitry that exists in both prefrontal and temporal cortices. Capacity to remember episodes is starting to decrease, processing speed slows, and less information is being processed in working memory.

Remaining mentally active, learning new things, staying physically active, and eating a very healthy diet is the best approach. Avoid drugs that change chemicals, cigarettes, alcohol, and mind. By the time you are in your mid to late 20s, your frontal lobe's brain development finally ended myelination— especially in the frontal lobes you need to assess. You will continue to shape and remove your entire life's synapses and brain cells. Still, there is one possible downside to your frontal lobe's development: mental illnesses such as schizophrenia or anxiety may now flare-up. Around 18 and 25 people are diagnosed with about 60 to 80 percent of people with major affective disorders. To be able to manifest these diseases, the frontal lobe needs to be connected to a point.

The brain slows down the production of brain cells and synapses in your 20s— plus it doesn't do as much "pruning" as it does — which is why you have a difficult time learning by the time you reach your 30s. Meanwhile, in the coming decades, your diet and exercise habits will set you up for a healthy-or forgetful-mind. Most people in their 50s begin to notice their mind slipping, starting with short-term memory. We're calling those' senior moments' and writing it off and making jokes. Nevertheless, only 5 percent of Alzheimer's diagnoses start early, so don't overlook signs that might be a sign of severe memory loss. One in ten adults age 65 and up is who Alzheimer's has. The risk doubles every five years after age 65, between the effects of biology and lifestyle. The causes of the condition aren't visible, but scientists do know that our brain cells and synapses are declining as we age. "These links go off, so the signals don't get from here to there. You look at an object, and you can suddenly no longer name it because you can't connect to the part of the brain where the name was stored.

**Stage 5: Above Sixty-Five Years**

Brain cells are damaged in critical areas such as the hippocampus, which is responsible for memory retrieval. Learn new skills, practice counseling to promote constructive feelings, exercise to improve abstract reasoning and concentration. Evite stress or include tension that decreases relaxation and exercises. Eat a healthy diet with foods to fuel one's dopamine level. By the time you reach 85, Alzheimer's risk is about 50 percent. This does not mean, however, that your memory's fate is sealed. While genetics play a part, brain-boosting behaviors and socializing can help test the mind. One method stands above the rest: "Aerobic exercise is by far the most potent thing. In a ten-year study involving more than 3,700 adults aged 60 and over, those who physically exerted the most had the giant brains and the lowest risk of dementia relative to those with the least physical activity. For those 75 and older, the protective effect was highest. Try every single day for 20 minutes of aerobics.

# Chapter 2: Integration in Brain

Integration is the process whereby information from many sources is combined. The nervous system incorporates data from different senses (vision, hearing contact, etc.), and from many other parts of the brain, each part of the brain integrates information. This process is essential for the smooth and efficient functioning of the body and its components. It's also vital to the brain's ability to collect and organize world knowledge. The nervous system can achieve this because the neurons (nerve cells) have a portion (called dendrites) designed to incorporate or integrate information. We get contacts from many other neurons we call (synapses), and they integrate the signals from them. The core CNS nervous system is responsible for processing and reacting sensory information appropriately. It consists of two main components: the spinal cord acts as a communication medium between the brain and the rest of the body. It also controls necessary musculoskeletal reflexes without brain input.

The brain is both consciously and unconsciously responsible for integrating the most sensory information and for coordinating body function. Different parts of the brain function complex tasks such as thinking and feeling as well as control of homeostasis.

The human brain has more links than the stars in the universe. As an integrated system, this topic focuses on the brain and looks at how its many linked networks achieve synchronized results, connecting the mind to the brain and body.

## 2.1 Where Integration Occurs in Brain?

There are three main functions in the nervous system: sensory input, data integration, and motor output. Sensory input is when the body, via neurons, glia, and synapses, gathers information or data. The nervous system contains excitable nerve cells (neurons) and synapses that develop between the neurons and connect them throughout the body or with other neurons to centers. These neurons act on excitation or inhibition, and although nerve cells can vary in size and position, their function is determined by their contact with each other. Such nerves transmit impulses into the brain and spinal cord from sensory receptors. The data is then interpreted utilizing data processing, which only happens in the brain. After the brain has processed the information, signals are then transmitted from the brain and spinal cord to the muscles and glands, which are called motor production. Glia cells are present in tissues, and they are not excitable but aid with myelination, ionic regulation, and extracellular fluid. The nervous system consists of two major parts, the central nervous system (CNS) and the peripheral nervous system (PNS) or subdivisions. The CNS comprises the spinal cord and the spine. The brain is the "control center" of the body. Inside it, the CNS has different centers that perform the sensory, motor, and data integration. Such centers are subdivided into lower centers (including the spinal cord and brain stem) and higher centers by effectors that interact with the brain. The PNS is an extensive system of spinal and cranial nerves linked to the brain and backbone. It includes sensory receptors that aid in the perception of internal and external environmental changes. This information is transmitted to CNS by afferent sensory nerves. Then the PNS is subdivided into the independent nervous system and the somatic nerve network. The autonomic system involuntarily regulates internal organs, blood vessels, smooth and heart muscles. The bodily has voluntary skin, bones, joints, and skeletal muscle control. The two systems work together, joining and becoming part of the CNS by way of nerves from the PNS, and vice versa.

neuronal cells, an image may be collected, which summarizes simultaneous activity across the entire brain. This provides a different yet complementary view of neural coding (see, for example, functional integration, below). Nonetheless, a drawback is that functional imaging provides neuroscientists with only an approximate indicator of the quantities of primary interest, e.g., firing rates and membrane potentials.

**Functional Analysis**

The study of usable image data includes two key themes. We represent the ongoing debate about functional specialization versus functional integration within the brain in neuroscience.

**Functional Specialization**

The first is brain 'mapping' where three-dimensional neuronal stimulation images are generated, showing which parts of the brain are responding to a specific cognitive or sensory challenge. This is also term as the examination of functional specialization and usually takes some form of Statistical Parametric Mapping (SPM) to proceed. A classic example is the recognition of the human V4 and V5, the specialized areas for color and motion processing.

SPM is a voxel-based approach to reflecting on regionally specific responses to experimental stimuli, using classical statistics and topological inferences. PET or fMRI data are first processed spatially to conform to a specified anatomical space where responses are usually classified statistically using the General Linear Model (GLM). The GLM embodies a hemodynamic response convolution model for fMRI results. This accounts for the fact that neuronal response is a delayed and dispersed version of BOLD signals. At each voxel, GLMs are fitted, and inferences are made, in a statistical sense, about which parts of the brain are active. SPM techniques use Random Field Theory (RFT) and other analytical methods, e.g., False Discovery Frequency, to accommodate the spatial complexity of the image data (and compensate for numerous statistical comparisons made). The SPM technique can also be used to identify brain regions that have a higher gray matter density Using structural evidence. This is known as Voxel-Based Morphometry (VBM) and was used to demonstrate, for example, that the posterior hippocampus, which is useful for spatial navigation, is being expanded in taxi drivers. Data can be analyzed in sensor space for MEG or EEG to furnish a crude spatial mapping of brain function.

Nevertheless, functions may be more precisely defined using methods of source reconstruction. They function by using Maxwell's equations, setting a forward model explaining how a current source in the brain propagates to become a MEG or EEG measurement. Then invert these equations using statistical inference. The averaging technique is often used to analyze data from sensory systems. To order to produce an Event-Related Potential (ERP), the data immediately following a sensory event, e.g., hearing an audible sound, is averaged over several occasions. ERP modules can then be distributed into different parts of the brain. However, other cognitive components aren't easily isolated from this ERP approach. A characterization of time-frequency may be more appropriate for these.

**Functional Integration**

Functional integration is the knowledge of knowing the working of brain regions work together to process the responses to information and effect. Although functional integration often relies on anatomical knowledge of the connections between brain areas, the emphasis is placed on how large clusters of neurons–numbering in the thousands or millions–fire together under different stimuli. The broad datasets required for such a detailed brain function image have inspired the development of several novels and general methods for statistical interdependence analysis, such as dynamic causal modeling and statistical linear parametric mapping. Such samples are usually obtained by non-invasive approaches such as EEG / MEG, fMRI, or PET on human subjects. The findings can be clinically useful by helping to define the regions responsible for psychiatric disorders, as well as determining how different activities or habits affect brain function. There is a distinction drawn in functional integration between functional connectivity and effective connectivity. It is stated that two brain regions are functionally connected when there is a high correlation between the times the two are firing, although this does not imply causality. In comparison, efficient connectivity is a summary of the causal relationship between various regions of the brain. While statistical evaluation of the functional connectivity of multiple brain regions is non-trivial, determining the causality of which brain regions have a much thornier influence on which to fire, and requiring solutions to imposed optimization problems.

Several previous fMRI studies found that spontaneous activation of functionally related brain regions occurs during the resting state, even when there is no stimulus or movement of any kind. Human subjects faced with a visual learning task experience functional connectivity changes in the resting state for up to 24 hours, and complex practical connectivity experiments have even demonstrated alteration in professional association during a single scan. Taking fMRI scans of subjects before and after learning exercise, as well as the next day, it was shown that the practice caused a change in the hippocampal activity in the resting-state. Dynamic causal modeling revealed that, although there was no learning-related improvement in any visual field, the hippocampus also demonstrated a new level of successful communication with the striatum. The mixture of fMRI with DCM on subjects achieving an understandable task allows one to delineate which brain systems are involved in different learning sorts, whether implicit or explicit and documenting these tasks for a long time leads to changes in brain activation of the resting-state.

## 2.3 Brain and Body Integration

For many, it is easier to focus on physical health because it yields tangible results. You can look at the scale, look in the mirror, or search on your move counter for your mile log. Mental & emotional wellbeing is challenging to see outwardly, which is one reason why these areas can be daunting for change. New technologies hit the marketplace faster than we can keep up. New brain areas are being discovered, and new ways of imaging the brain are becoming a reality. The notion of an intricate laboratory or medical system to track brain activity is obsolete, and technology is now available to better integrate mind & body. The question of mind and body concerns to what degree the mind and the body are different or the same thing. The intention is about mental processes, perceptions, and knowledge. The body is concerned with the brain-neuron physical aspects, and how the brain is organized. Is the subconscious part of the mind, or part of the consciousness of the body? If they're different, how do they communicate then? And which of the two is responsible for this? Several theories were put forward to understand the relationship between what we call your mind (defined as the' you' conscious thinking that experiences your thoughts) and your brain (that is, part of your body). The connection between our minds and our bodies is something we feel instinctively, but how much attention do we pay each moment to your bodily sensations? We need a more profound awareness to understand our own emotional lives and those of the people around us, achieved through the practice of mindfulness and the development of body intelligence. Human beings are artifacts of material form. We have weight, solidity, and a variety of solids, liquids, and gases. Unlike other material objects (e.g., rocks), however, humans also can make decisions and justification for their existence. We've got' minds' in short. Usually, humans are described as possessing both a (nonphysical) account and a physical body/brain. This is called dualism. Dualism is the concept that the body and mind are both separate entities. Descartes / Cartesian dualism claims that mental and physical stimuli interact in two forms. Descartes has argued that the brain at the pineal gland interacts with the body. This form of dualism or duality implies that the mind influences the body, but the body can also have an impact on the rational mind, for instance, when people act out of emotion. Most of the previous accounts had been uni-directional about the relationship between mind and body.

**Research Study on Mind-Body Connection**

It has been shown in the studies for the first time that practicing meditation in mindfulness or being involved in a support group has a significant physical impact on breast cancer survivors at the cellular level. A group working from the Tom Baker Cancer Center of Alberta Health Services and the Department of Oncology at the University of Calgary has shown that telomeres— protein complexes at the end of chromosomes — retain their duration in survivors of breast cancer who practice meditation or are active in support groups while shortening without intervention in a comparison group. While telomeres ' disease-regulating properties are not fully understood, shortened telomeres are associated with multiple disease states as well as cell aging. In contrast, longer telomeres are thought to be disease-protective. "We also know that psychosocial techniques such as mindfulness meditation can help you feel better emotionally, but now we have evidence for the first time that they can also affect key aspects of your physiology," says Dr. Linda E. Carlson, Ph.D., Principal Investigator and Research Director at the Tom Baker Cancer Centre's Psychosocial Services Division. "It was interesting that over the three months examined, we could see any difference in telomere length," says Dr. Carlson, who is also a U of C professor at the Cumming School of Medicine and Faculty of Arts, a member of the Southern Alberta Cancer Institute. "To further measure these potential health benefits, more research is needed, but this is an exciting finding that provides encouraging news."

For the duration of the research, a total of 88 survivors of breast cancer who had finished their medical care for at least three months were involved. The average age was 55, with most patients completing treatment two years ago. We also had to experience significant levels of emotional distress to be successful. Participants attended eight weekly, 90-minute group sessions in the Mindfulness-Based Cancer Recovery group that offered guidance on awareness reconciliation and gentle Hatha yoga, intending to promote present-day un judgmental knowledge. Participants were also asked to perform 45 minutes of meditation and yoga per day at home.

Members met for ninety minutes weekly for twelve weeks in the Supportive Expressive Therapy group and were encouraged to talk freely about their problems and feelings. The aims were to develop mutual support and direct women in sharing, rather than suppressing or repressing, a wide range of both challenging and constructive emotions. Placed randomly in the control group, the participants attended one, six-hour seminar on stress management. Both participants in the study had blood tested and the duration of telomeres assessed before and after the involvement. Scientists have shown a short-term impact of these interventions on the length of the telomere as compared to a control group, but it is not known whether the effects last. Dr. Carlson says another path for further studies is to see if psychosocial approaches have a positive impact beyond the study period of three months. Allison McPherson was first diagnosed in 2008 as having breast cancer. She was put within the mindfulness-based cancer recovery group when she joined the study. She says today that experience has changed one's life. "At first, she was cynical and thought it was a lot of hocus-pocus," says McPherson, who underwent a whole year of chemotherapy and many surgeries. "But she was now practicing conscientiousness throughout the day, and it encouraged her to become less aggressive, childlike towards her and others." Research participant Deanne David has also been put in the focus group. "It made a great contrast to her to be part of this," she says. "People on their cancer journey will benefit from learning more about the knowledge and interacting with others who are going through the same issues."

# Chapter 3: Revolutionary Steps to Nurture Child's Developing Mind

Everything that happens during the first five years of life can have a tremendous impact not only on how well the baby's brain is progressing right now but also on how well that baby is learning and growing over their lifetime. A reasonably straightforward matter is caring for the physical needs of your child (food, shelter, and clothing). It can be trickier to seek to provide for your child's emotional needs. While there are many types of parenting, most experts agree on some general guidelines for maintaining the emotional health of a child and laying the groundwork for emotionally healthy adulthood. Although experts say that baby brain growth is still mostly a mystery, what we know is how important a role natural parenting instinct will play in making your baby successful on the fast track. The brains of children develop quickly from birth across three ages. Growth in the brain influences all areas of development for an infant. Four main development areas exist motor (physical), language and communication, social and emotional, and cognitive. The development of the brain is a part of cognitive development. Cognitive development explains how the intelligence of a child develops, which requires the ability to think, learn, and solve problems. Such competencies impact all other developmental regions. Education and growth are essential to a child's first three years of life. Most parents are curious about how they can help develop their child's brain. The best way is to involve your child actively in everyday activities such as playing, reading, and being there when he/she is experiencing tension.

## 3.1 Nurturing Baby's Mind through Reading and Learning

Learning is one of the best ways to further the growth of a child's brain. The reading kick starts language and communication skills even before he/she can understand letters or words. Hearing words and seeing pictures in a child's mind binds the two. Reading the same books creates a connection between the words you say and the images on the screen. As a child grows, ask him/her to point out specific pictures on the website, such as "Where is the dog? "A lot of ways you can help, encourage, and support the growth of your child's brain as he/she grows up. The lecture is still the key to learning, with all of our modern technology. And while children and adults can learn by experimenting, reading is essential to getting an education that prepares one for life. Because of this, parents may think they need new electronic gadgets to help their kids learn necessary reading skills before school begins. All kids need, though, is their parents' time and attention, chatting, reading, singing, and playing with them. Reading and writing are like speaking on paper-the real prerequisite is developing keen language skills, including listening, speaking, and understanding what's being said. Children must also recognize and shape the forms of the letters used to represent language on paper. One essential skill is learning to understand and generate the native language's distinct sounds. That is called phonemic awareness. Infants can produce all the sounds of all the words in the world. When listening to human speech, their brain starts focusing in on the sounds of their style and imitate those sounds. The ability should train them down the road for phonics. Parents can promote the development of this essential skill with ease and pleasure by talking, reading, singing, and playing with their child. Plenty of warm and loving smiles, singing-like vocal inflections that imitate sounds, as well as touch and laughter will keep them focused so that they will learn how to distinguish between sounds and how to construct language together. Educators recommend using rhyming and clapping out the syllables of a word when reciting a short poem or singing a song to help them develop another ability known as phonological awareness (understanding how words are formed in exact order by a set of different sounds). As your child gets to understand what you're saying and reading and can interact with you through delivering a speech, you're at a point where you can build on that — ask open-ended questions about a story you're reading to your child and use a serve-and-return exchange to help them build up their vocabulary. In their own words, have your child tell the story, or make up their own. It helps them develop a new skill–understanding.

The next skill is the ability to recognize and write alphabet letters. This will allow them to develop the ability to read short letter naming beforehand. Show a message to your kids, say the word, then have them trace the letter on paper and write it in the air. You can also use clay to shape words, bend straws, or create a series of sandpaper letters for them to trace. The best way to learn this ability is through a multisensory approach–visual, auditory, kinesthetic (movement), and tactile (feeling by touch). Educators here refer to learning as the VAKT method. Recent research suggests early reader brains are using all four of the brain regions associated with each of these tasks. Most kids are ready for phonics, which is the next ability in early reading by the time they reach kindergarten. Many kids are prepared sooner, so concentrating on the first three skills above will make your kid for the early stages of learning how to read. Such three skills are best learned by regular and varying listening and engaging interactions with the human language. The way to go is not electronic gadgets, videos, computers, DVDs, and educational toys. Again, what works is for parents to talk, read, sing, and play with their kids. Such human interaction allows the child to be fully responsive to the stimuli, contributing to learning and maintaining new skills. While you and your child have fun and enjoy each other, there is also strong parent-child bonding that is essential for healthy emotional and social development.

## 3.2 Nurture Child's Mind through Trust, Confidence, and Love

Understanding how to trust starts at birth: babies are born entirely dependent on caregivers to fulfill their primary food, shelter, comfort, and love needs. When caregivers respond in an attentive, clear, and compassionate manner to the cries of babies and body language, these babies may feel safe and learn to trust their environment. The relationship between parent and child is the first social relationship,' Kassow says. "It teaches the child that to meet his needs, he can communicate, which transfers to form relationships later in life." From the starting age, children start to differentiate between trustworthy people and those who are not. A few researchers conducted an experiment that children aged three and four were presented with adults who had shown different names for items that the children had never seen before. Some of those names had been accurate; others had not. The four-year-olds were able to tell the exact adults from those who made lists and later searched for the honest adults, describing them as being trustworthy to the researchers. Ken Rotenberg of Keele University in the United Kingdom has found in other studies that children develop trust in response to specific experiences they have with others; this is not something they apply uniformly. "Trust is dyadic and mutual, and children have to develop unique patterns of trusting each person they meet," Rotenberg says. "So optimistic can be a disadvantage." Instead of promoting blind faith in children, Rotenberg believes that parents should focus on raising trustworthy children. "Trustworthy Children have more friends in school and are better adjusted.

Be aware of the child development stages, so you don't expect too much or too little of your child. Encourage your child to share its feelings; value those sentiments. Let your child know that pain, fear, anger, and anxiety are all felt by everyone. Try to learn the origins of those emotions. Help your child to positively express anger, without resorting to violence and promoting mutual respect and confidence. Keep your voice level down— even if you are not in agreement. Hold Channels of Communication available.

Hear out your kids. You are using words and examples that your child can understand. Foster questions. Provide convenience and assurance. Be frank. Concentrate on the positive. Express your willingness to discuss any subject. Look at your skills in problem-solving and coping. Do you set a good example? If you are frustrated by the feelings or actions of your infant, or if you cannot control your frustration or rage, seek help. Encourage the strengths of your kids and recognize limitations. Set goals based on the talents and desires of the child— not the expectations of another. Feast on successes. Do not compare your child's abilities to those of other kids; appreciate your child's uniqueness. Pass time with your child regularly. Foster independence and self-worth for your child. Help your child tackle the ups and downs in life. Express confidence in the ability of your child to manage challenges, and address new experiences. Discipline with constructiveness, fairness, and consistency. Using training as an instructional tool and not as physical punishment. All kids and families are different; learn what works for your kid. Express support for positive behaviors. Help your child learn from its mistakes. Give unconditional love to your child. Teach others the importance of excuses, cooperation, tolerance, empathy, and consideration. Don't expect perfectness; parenting is a tough job.

A good relationship is built on confidence, security, and love. Taking advantage of these three principles is essential to a healthy relationship with your teenager. Even though your child is getting more participative in her peer relationships, it is still vital for you to be attentive to her needs and be there to direct and help her. Parents are considered the first teacher of their child, and their relationship with her forms the cornerstone of its emotional and social growth.

Reset standards and limits. Take out some time and have a conversation with your child about your values, rules, and expectations regularly and the reasons behind them helps give her a blueprint of proper behavior. You can start doing this by explaining your household rules and ensuring you are consistently adhering to them. For starters, curfew during the middle-school years is becoming a big issue. It is significant to describe the reasons why you set this specific curfew time to your child and discuss the implications of failing to meet this deadline. If she violates her curfew, be sure to follow through and let her bear through the results and outcomes, as this can be helpful for her in developing a sense of responsibility and accountability. The same goes for expectations relating to the school. When she fails to take an exam, ask her what happened. Allow her to articulate her reasons for her acts and help her understand how she can change such habits, such as through timely analysis of more or completing homework. Try making these interactions as healthy as possible, and at the moment. Middle-schoolers have a meager moral ability to lecture.

The most crucial primary foundation for both intellectual and social growth is to nurture emotional relationships. Relationships cultivate comfort, affection, and enjoyment at the most basic level; furnish security, physical safety, and disease and injury protection; and provide basic nutritional and housing needs. Relationship "regulatory" factors (for example, protecting children from over-or under-stimulation) help children stay calm and alert for new learning. When relationships are secure, empathetic, nurturing, children learn to be intimate and empathetic, and ultimately communicate their feelings, reflect on their desires and develop their relationships. Relationships also teach children which actions are and which are not acceptable. As the behavior of children in the second year of life becomes more nuanced, they know from the facial expressions, tone of voice, movements, and vocabulary of their careers what kind of behavior contributes to approval or disapproval. Patterns are built up between children and careers by giving-and-taking. But emotions, wishes, and self-image also come into being along with behavior. For relationships, the emotional tone and implicit gestures are essential to who we are and what we lean.

## 3.3 Twelve Innovative Strategies to Nurture Child's Brain

A few complicated parts of the brain (prefrontal cortex) are still under development during childhood and adolescence. This side of the brain is responsible for higher-order and analytical thinking and is not developed until a person reaches the mid-twenties. Conversely, the "Downstairs Brain" (one part of which is the Amygdala) is responsible for rapid processing. This side of the brain is more primitive and lets us act before we think in hazardous situations, which require a faster response.

**1) "Connect and Redirect: Surfing Emotional Waves"** If your child is upset, it's important to connect first using both your right brains to make an emotional connection and let them know you're upset, even if your child doesn't fully understand the 'why' behind it. Then, once your child has more control and is more receptive, you can bring the left brain into this discussion to talk about any lessons, subjects, and discipline that need to be discussed.

**2) "Call It to Tame It: Telling Stories to Calm Large Emotions":** It can be good to talk about experiences. Experience telling and retelling can help calm down big right-brain feelings and emotions because the left brain can help and assist in making sense of the experiences and helping make your child feel more in control.

**3) "Engage, Don't Enrage: Talk to the Upstairs Brain":** In cases where emotions are high, allowing your child to reach the parts of their "Upstairs Brain" that are available to them. Rather than activating the more simplistic "Downstairs Brain" will help engage your child in the process of finding solutions. Be curious by asking questions that provide options/alternatives and use this as an opportunity to exercise negotiating skills.

**4) "Use It or Lose It: Upstairs Brain":** helping your child grow their "Upstairs Brain" while under construction will help build neural pathways, and the process of reaching those pathways helps to build stronger connections in the future time and time again. Creating a game, "What'd you do?" It can be a great practice to let your child discuss and think about a range of approaches to different issues. While it may be appealing for us to share our own ideas/thought, try not to rescue children from difficult decisions, as it does not provide the same experience as when exercising their "Brain Upstairs."

**5) "Move It or Lose It: Movement in the Body to Avoid Losing the Mind:** "One of the best things we can do when a child has lost contact with its" Upstairs Brain "is to help them recover their equilibrium by moving their body. Studies have shown that our emotional state (i.e., our mood) can be improved by exercise (e.g., going for a walk or running) or relaxation (e.g., deep breathing, yoga) by our physical state.

**6) "Use the Remote of Mind: Replaying Memories:** Children never have the opportunity to be in charge of much of what is going on in their lives, and so when they have the opportunity to do so, it can be a great learning experience for them. Children can often be reluctant to talk about painful events/memories. Using a figurative remote that allows them to' stop," rewind,' and' fast-forward' sections of the story will help them feel in control of what they want to say then and encourage them to work up to the more challenging information to speak about.

**7) "Remember: Make Recollection a Part of the Daily Life of Your Family":** Another essential way to help exercise the brain of your child is to help them use the power of remembering. Thinking of significant past events helps to reconcile memories that are subconscious and clear. The simple act of giving children a chance to tell their stories helps them to understand their past and present experiences better.

**8) "Let the Clouds of Feelings Roll by Learning That Feelings Come and Go":** Teaching children that feelings are like clouds that come and go, and letting them roll by helping them understand that these are fleeting states rather than permanent features. It is significant to differentiate between "feel" and "am."

**9) Giving attention to what's going on inside:** making your kids pay attention to the "Sensations, Pictures, Feelings and Thoughts" that exist within them is an excellent way to make them aware of what they experience. This is the first vital piece to help your kids develop "Mindsight," which is the awareness of our minds as well as others' thoughts.

**10) "Exercise' Mindsight': Getting back to the Hub":** the "Wheel of Perception" is a device that can allow us to imagine our mind like a bike wheel complete with an outer rim, spokes, and an inner hub. Our emotions, feelings, visions, memories, perceptions, and body sensations are on the wheel's outer edge, and the center hub is the place where our consciousness resides, this is the location from where we can choose the point on which we want to concentrate (the spokes, see below). Kids, like adults, can find themselves stuck in a particular thought and can help them gain more control over how they feel, showing them that they can shift their attention and focus on another idea. The method of "mindsight" helps kids learn how to relax and focus their attention on where they want it to be.

11) "Improve Family Fun Factor: Making a Point for Enjoying Every Other": many parents/caregivers frequently discover that they invest so much of their time either disciplining their children and going from one activity to another. "Playful Parenting" (for example, being dumb, telling jokes or playing games) is one way you can create healthy relationships with your kids. This encourages children to have positive experiences with their parents/caregivers and also helps to model future relationships and relationships.

12) "Connecting via Conflict: Teaching children to disagree with a' We' in Mind': Conflict is often seen as something to be get rid at all costs, but it is not realistic or necessary. Teaching our children how to use Mindsight's power to handle the dispute in healthy, creative ways can be an excellent learning opportunity to build skills such as taking the perspective of another person, reading non-verbal indications, and making corrections.

## 3.4 Research Study on Nurturing Child's Brain through Mother's Love

Feeding a child early in life may help him or her grow a greater hippocampus, a new study shows the brain region that is important for learning, memory and stress responses. Previous animal research has shown that early maternal support has a positive effect on hippocampal development, brain cell production, and the ability to deal with stress in a young rat. On the other hand, research in human children found a link between early social experiences and the volume of the Amygdala, which helps to regulate the production and memory of emotional reactions. Numerous studies have also found that children born in a nursing setting usually perform better at school and are more socially mature than their peers who have not been nursed. Brain scans have now shown that love for a mother physically influences the hippocampus volume of her brain. Kids of nursing mothers had 10 percent greater hippocampal volumes in the sample than kids whose mothers were not as nursing. We can now confidently say that the psychosocial climate is having a significant impact on the way the human brain grows. Research is a part of ongoing process. This puts a mighty wind behind the sail of the notion that early childcare has a positive effect on their development. Children with rapid onset depression development.

## 3.5 Nurturing Child's Imagination

More than narrating a story or painting a picture, a child who is particularly creative excels. Research studies show that innovative and creative people who work in the sciences and the arts can better perceive what others might think or feel, can see problems from different points of view, and have superior self-control (probably because they can formulate multiple results to a problem). The Academy of Pediatrics, situated in America, now suggests that doctors "prescribe" a certain amount of solo play to spur inventive thinking every day. All the kids can and should learn to tap their creativity. Early breastfeeding, the creative side of your child spills into other areas of your life. A kid who is motivated to think out of the box will be able to search for new and innovative problems solutions. Flexible and creative thinking has become critical to success in school, at work, and in life in our dynamic, fast-paced world. Toddlerhood, as it happens, is a perfect time to focus on imagination because, by definition, it is the most creative phase of a child's life. Two-year-Old only have a poor idea of what's real and fictional. Imagining out of the box is easy because the box's limitations have not yet been met. Nothing seems unlikely for them. A 4-year-old who wants a high counter cookie will likely get out a chair to stand on–a strategy she knows is successful. In comparison, a toddler could pile up her stuffed animals to climb on or try to jump up and down to the counter. She has to invent her ideas because she can't yet understand what works and what doesn't.

## Guidelines for Nurturing Child's Creativity

- **Encourage aggressive pursuits, not passive ones.**

Speak of creativity as a muscle: it will atrophy if it is not exercised. Kids involved in passive behaviors, such as watching TV, take pictures and ideas from other people rather than coming up with their own, says Jane M. Healy, Ph.D., an educational psychologist and author of Failure to Link (Simon & Schuster, 1998). Ordinary experiences like reading aloud or walking outside do much more than television to grow the creative side of a brain, she says. Commit the 2-year-old to the conversation as often as possible. Ask questions that inspire him to share his ideas and thoughts. Tell him stories and let him deliver the ending–or better yet, a range of finishes.

- **Provide plenty of safe deliveries.**

Toddlers love exploring new ways to use stuff, so search for non-toxic finger-paints, markers, and clays and play dough that is harmless when consumed. Dress-up clothes and hats should be comfortable to get on and off, free of anything that might trap or choke a child. No hard edges or thin, detachable pieces should be present in the musical instruments.

- **Let them make choices for your kids.**

Each time it's convenient (and safe), let your child think for himself. Wonder if she wants to drink from the green cup or the blue cup, for example, or if he likes to wear the striped pants or the plaid ones. Although such options may seem trivial to an adult, they will be considered thrilling by a child who is starting to acquire self-control over her life.

- **Tolerate uncertainty.**

If your child is engaging in creative play, resign yourself to chaos and resist such phrases as "That's too messy" or "That's not going there. Normally she is very reluctant to do anything that isn't completely organized." Participate in creative projects.

Research has shown that children whose parents are interested in imaginative play to develop more extensive vocabulary and more versatile thinking skills. So, sit down with your kid and paint his palm. Or get him to play dress-up. "If you're interested, he'll be interested too.

- **Know precisely what to expect.**

To think a kid would draw a recognizable picture of a house or tell a story with a comprehensible start, middle and end are unrealistic. What you can expect. Don't pressure your baby into making things that look like the real equivalent or sound like that. Praise everything, he makes, even if to you it seems like a page full of scriptable. You can also display the artwork of your child in the fridge or above your desk.

- **Don't push them.**

Never demand that a child get involved in creative ventures unless he's interested. And realize that his attention can dwindle rapidly, even if he is. Above all, you want your child to know that it's a joy to savor the creative process and not a burden to endure.

# Chapter 4: Changes in Brain

Neuroplasticity, also term as brain plasticity, neuroplasticity, or neural plasticity, is the brain's ability to change regularly throughout an individual's life. For instance, brain activity associated with a given task can be a move to a different location, the proportion of gray matter can change, and synapses can strengthen or weaken over time. Neuroplasticity is aimed at improving neural networks during phylogenesis, ontogeny, and physiological development, as well as after a brain injury. Studies in the latter half of the 20th century have shown that even after adulthood, many parts of the brain may be changed (or are "plastic." The developing brain does, however, show a higher degree of plasticity than the adult brain. This process is called "brain plasticity"— as we experience the world, develop behaviors, and learn new knowledge, our minds alter, new connections grow, and damaged one's repair. Our experiences and expertise keep our brains functioning, developing, and learning as we age. You may experience significant changes, but not all of them are a sign of concern. We always lose our keys and forget the names of the people. We do it through our lives. It's not until we're older than we get worried about these common mishaps. It is also significant to acquire knowledge that there are several other reasons why memory lapses occur, such as taking certain medicines, lack of sleep, and excessive alcohol.

Neuroplasticity can be observed on various scales, ranging from microscopic changes in individual neurons to larger-scale changes such as cortical regeneration in response to injury.

Behavior, environmental stimuli, thought, and emotions can also induce neuroplastic transform by the help of activity-dependent plasticity, which has significant implications for healthy development, learning, memory, and bra recovery. Synaptic plasticity directs to alterations in the connections between neurons at the single-cell level. In contrast, non-synaptic flexibility relates to changes in their intrinsic excitability.

## 4.1 Research and Discovery of Neuroplasticity

In 1923, Karl Lashley, scientist, conducted experiments on rhesus monkeys showing changes in neuronal pathways, which he concluded were plasticity proof. Neuroscientists have not generally accepted the idea of neuroplasticity, despite this, and other work that indicated plasticity.

In 1945, another scientist Justo Gonzalo concluded from his research on brain dynamics that, opposite to the movement of the projection areas, the "central" cortical mass (more or less equidistant from the visual, tactile and auditory projection areas) would be a rather unspecified or multisensory "maneuvering mass" with the ability to increase neural excitability and reorganize activity through plasticity. Another scientist provided the first scientific evidence of anatomical brain plasticity, publishing her work in 1964.

Other relevant proof was produced in the 1960s and after that, especially from scientists including Paul Bach-y-Rita, Michael Merzenich, along with Jon Kaas and many others. In the 1960s, Paul Bach-y-Rita invented a device that was tested on a small number of people and involved a person sitting in a chair with fixed nubs that were made to vibrate in ways that translated images received in the camera, allowing for a form of vision through sensory substitution.

Eleanor Maguire reported improvements in the hippocampal structure associated with gaining local taxi drivers' knowledge of London's style.

In London Taxi Drivers, a redistribution of gray matter was reported as compared to controls. Not only interested scientists were involved in this research on hippocampal plasticity but also engaged the public and media around the world.

Michael Merzenich is a neuroscientist who pioneered neuroplasticity for more than three decades. He made some of the "most ambitious claims for the field–that brain exercises can be as useful as drugs for treating sickness as chronic as schizophrenia. That plasticity exists from the cradle to the grave, and that radical improvement in cognitive functioning–how we can learn, think, perceive, and remember even in the elderly. Neuroplasticity may occur beyond the critical period. However, Merzenich argued. His first experience with adult plasticity came when he worked with Clinton Woosley is a postdoctoral study. The experiment was based on an investigation of what has happened in the brain while cutting and then regenerating one peripheral nerve. Before and after trimming a peripheral nerve and stitching the ends together, the two scientists micromapped the hand maps of monkey brains. The hand map in the mind which they expected to be jumbled afterward was almost normal. That was a significant development. Merzenich argued that "If the brain map was able to normalize its structure in response to an abnormal input, the prevailing view that we were born with a hardwired mechanism must be incorrect.

**Types of Neuroplasticity**

As described above by Shaw and McEachern, in the study of neuroplasticity, there is no all-inclusive theory that overshoots different frameworks and systems.

Researchers, however, often describe neuroplasticity as "the ability to make adaptive changes related to the nervous system's structure and function.

Two types of neuroplasticity are frequently discussed accordingly: structural neuroplasticity and functional neuroplasticity.

**Structural Neuroplasticity**

Structural plasticity is often comprehended as the capacity of the brain to alter its neuronal connections. Depending on this form of neuroplasticity, new neurons are continually generated and inserted into the central nervous system over the entire life cycle. Scientists now use multiple cross-sectional imaging techniques (i.e., magnetic resonance imaging (MRI), computerized tomography (CT)) to study human brain structural changes. This type of neuroplasticity also studies the effects of various internal or external stimuli on the anatomical reorganization of the brain. The shifts in the proportion of grey matter or the synaptic intensity in mind are known as manifestations of central neuroplasticity. In current academic, structural neuroplasticity is being investigated more in the field of neuroscience.

**Functional neuroplasticity**

Functional plasticity (also called synaptic plasticity) refers to the capacity of the brain to modify and change the neuronal communication. The changes often occur because of, but not limited to, neuron dysfunction or damage; functions from one part of the brain move to another part of the brain based on the need for recovery of behavioral or physiological processes. (LTP) Long-term potentiation and long-term depression (LTD) are known as examples of memory-related synaptic plasticity.

## 4.2 How Brain Changes with Age

As with the rest of your body, with each year, your brain changes. The minds have evolved from the time we are children, studying, making memories, and more. We become wiser and stronger.

We receive the knowledge that only comes with the experience of life. Of course, the less desirable effects of the time mark can also be felt. You should recognize them: an ever-lost set of keys, a to-do that never seems to remain top of mind, a name on your tongue's tip. When we reach our late 20s, the aging process of the brain begins, and we begin to lose neurons — the cells that make up the brain and nervous system. Our minds had practically started to shrink by our sixties. Though these changes in the brain may sound a bit frightening, the process is normal, and it happens to all. Learn how the brain evolves as you age to get better grip on what's going on in this magical part of your body. Then, have a glance at some of the things you can do to help preserve brain health. Although some change is inevitable, a healthy lifestyle will ward some off. Here's how you can participate in playing an active role in slowing down adverse effects and striving towards better, more extended stays.

You're born with necessary survival skills, reflexes, and most of the 100 billion neurons you're going to have for the lifetime. During these early years, the brain grows remarkably rapidly: Neurons grow bigger, work more efficiently, and, as a result of environmental inputs and stimuli, make trillions of connections that fine-tune everything from hearing to vision. The brain is around 80 percent of its adult size by the age of two. About 85 percent of brain development, including intellect, personality, and motor and social skills, has occurred by now. The brain of an infant has twice that number of synapses as the brain of an adult. In a process called pruning, neural links that are most often used and strengthened — those that are used for language — are reinforced, while those that are not used so much fizzle and die. The character has set out like plaster in most of us, by the age of thirty, and will never soften again. The aim is to continually create new pathways and connections to break apart neuronal structures that are trapped in the brain.

Simply put, there is a lot of flexibility and plasticity when the brain is young and not yet fully formed, which explains why children learn so quickly. It concluded that we, as human beings, grow neural pathways, and the more over the years and years we use these neural pathways, they become much trapped and deeply embedded, going into deeper portions of the brain. As we reach the age of 25, we have just so many developed pathways on which our brain depends. It's hard to break free from them. One explanation is that our mind is inherently lazy and will always choose the most energy-efficient path if we allow it. If you want to keep your brain productive and healthy, you'll need to zero in on areas of your mind that you're using less often. And this new exercise has to be so severe that after you complete the job, you will feel mentally and physically tired because you are pushing your brain to work in the ways it is uncommon. Only in this manner can you grow new neurons powerful enough to interact with existing neurons, creating new pathways.

**Depression Causes Brain to age faster – A Research Study**

New research from Yale University suggests that stress can physically change the brain of a person, hurrying an aging effect that could make them more susceptible to old age-related diseases. In this past, scientists have found manner of evidence to show depression affects the brain and other parts of the body.

The disorder has been associated with, among other things, an increased risk of headaches, muscle pains, and sleep problems. And it can develop a negative feedback loop: a study published in the Journal of Clinical Psychology in 2004 found that "the worse the painful physical symptoms, the more severe the depression is." With that in mind, Irina Esterlis, a researcher at the Yale School of Medicine, placed out to learn more specifically about how depression affects the brain.

At the American Association for the Advancement of Science Conference in Washington DC, she discussed her findings on Feb. 14. Her research was based on a new kind of brain-imaging technology that gives doctors better insight into what's going on inside the brains of people. Usually, she works from a Yale laboratory where she experiments with sophisticated positron emission tomography (PET) scanners that can identify biochemical changes in body tissues. In this case, Esterlis analyzed the brains of 20 people—10 diagnosed with clinical depression and ten considered stable after completing a rigorous psychiatric evaluation — and found that those with more severe depression symptoms had lower synaptic density in the brains. Synaptic density is essential since synapses are mostly tiny bridges that rely on nerve cells to pass their impulses from cell to cell. Neurological disorders have been associated with a loss of synapses, and it is shared in people aged 74 to 90. All this to conclude, Esterlis' research suggests that that aging by-product was apparent in people with depression. To be sure, it's a small study, but the outcome was convincing enough to potentially prompt new research into what's happening to the brain when a person is anxious and depressed. Researchers at the University of Toronto are working on a drug that seems capable of preventing memory loss associated with depression and aging. According to the Financial Times (paywall), the scientists behind that research have introduced themselves at the conference in DC. The work is still in its early stages— only being conducted on mice— but it could wind up solving the very question Esterlis is uncovering in work.

**Improved Functioning of Brain with Aging**

We are watching younger colleague's quickly master new computer systems or pull all-nights out of place with nary a hair and — quite naturally— we're concerned.

Thankfully, modern brain science research suggests that maybe we should be less fretting. Neuroscientists have begun to home in on the changes in the brain in the middle age over the past few years, and what they have discovered is promising. Long-term studies results show that — contrary to myths — we are growing smarter in key middle-age areas that now range from our mid-40s to our mid-60s, with longer life spans. The brains function better than they did in the 20s, in fields as diverse as language and inductive reasoning. As we get older, we get the "gist" of claims more quickly. It even strengthens our assessment of others. Also, we literally "know" whether to trust someone — or some concept. We're all getting better at knowing what to ignore and when to hold our tongues. Not long ago, a mid-level executive told his colleague how the way he interacts with younger colleagues he'd recently changed. He keeps his "mouth shut" and listens when he has gathered to address a question. Even though he has the right solution— more often than not— he awaits. He is not thinking. Indeed, although he did not realize it, the executive used the best pieces of his peaceful and more experienced middle-aged brain to help him manage his situation— and achieve better results. Our minds will indeed show a bit of fraying by midlife. The speed of brain processing is slowing down. We often cannot master it as fastly as our younger peers in the face of new knowledge. And there is little question which our short-term memories are suffering from. When you find that you can't think back to the name of that person you know in the elevator or even the movie you saw last week, it's easy to panic. But it turns out that those abilities don't matter that much. Our minds have built a whole host of talents by midlife that is just as well suited to managing the new, dynamic workplace. As we age, we get to see the possible better. Predictably, younger minds are set up to focus on the negative and future issues. Studies show that older brains frequently find solutions faster, in part because they concentrate on what can be achieved. By the time we arrive middle age, millions of patterns have been formed in our brains, and those linked pathways provide invaluable perspective— even when it's subconscious.

## 4.3 What Happens to Brain as we Age

It has been commonly observed that the volume of the brain and its weight decreases with age at a speed of around 5 percent per decade after period 401, with the actual price of drop likely to increase with age, especially over period 70.2. How this occurs is less clear. Shrinking gray matter is often reported to have been caused by neuronal cell death, but it is not entirely clear whether this is solely responsible or even the primary finding. It has been suggested that a decline in neuronal volume rather than number contributes to changes in an aging brain and may be related to sex with different areas most affected by men and women.

Additionally, the dendritic arbor, spines, and synapses can alter. Therefore, dendritic sprouting can occur, maintaining a similar number of synapses5 and compensating for any cell death. Four conversely, a decrease in dendritic synapses or loss of synaptic plasticity has also been described. Functional organizational change can occur and compensate similarly to that found in patients after recovery from moderate traumatic brain injury. However, latte research has been conducted. We also need to think about the role of white matter in the aging brain. White matter can decline with age, myelin sheath may deteriorate even in healthy aging after about 40 years of age, and it has been reported that the late myelinating regions of the frontal lobes are most influenced by white matter lesions (WML). However, not all studies support this view. Leukoaraiosis / WML increases with age and may suggest ischemia in subclinical cases. They'll be covered in the more fabulous description below.

Brain alteration does not occur to an identical degree in all brain regions. A longitudinal study supports the fact that these brain changes are not consistent, using two MRI scans separated by about one to two years, and a cross-sectional research examination. The latter included only those research that contrasted younger (under 30 years of age) and older (over 60) groups to compare broader age ranges and in comparison to much of the other work in this area. The study looked at range and found the most affected was the prefrontal cortex. With the survey covering over seven tests, the striatum came in second. The temporal lobe, cerebellar vermis, cerebellar hemispheres, and hippocampus also decrease volume with between 8 and 18 studies and also showed a reduction in prefrontal white matter (five reviews). The occipital cortex was the last one to be affected (five studies). The result that the prefrontal cortex is most affected, and the occipital least, matches well with the cognitive changes seen during aging. However, some studies do indicate that aging has the most significant effect in the hippocampus. Men and women may also vary as opposed to the hippocampus and parietal lobes in women with frontal and temporal lobes most impact on men. Finally, the rate of brain volume reduction may increase, especially over 70 years of age, although the number studied is minimal. Due to the individual differences in brain growth and aging mapping structure to function and change due to aging is a complicated task. Still, there are studies showing connections between volume and neuropsychological function. A study examining the amount of cortical volume and white matter hyperintensity in 140 people between the ages of 50 and 81 pre-screened for dementia and depression found an association between increased ages, decreased prefrontal cortical volume, increased subcortical white matter lesions, and increased perseverance (decreased executive function).

## Cognitive Change

The most frequently observed cognitive change associated with aging is memory. Memory function can be commonly split into four parts, episodic memory, semantic memory, procedural memory, and working memory. In terms of aging, the first two of these are most relevant. Episodic memory is described as type of memory where information is stored with' mental tags,' where, when, and how it was collected." An example of episodic memory would be a retention of your first school day, the critical meeting you attended last week, or the lesson you learned that Paris is France's capital. The performance of episodic memory is thought to decline from middle age on. This is specifically true in the case of recall during healthy aging and less so for identification. It is also a symptom of memory loss found in Alzheimer's disease (AD). Semantic memory is defined, for example, as "memory for meanings," knowing that Paris is France's capital, that 10 millimeters make up one centimeter, or that Mozart composed the Magic Flute. Semantic memory gradually increases from middle age to young, older adults but then declines in the very elderly. It is not yet understood why these alterations happen, and it has been hypothesized that the very elderly have fewer resources to draw on and that their performance may be affected by slower reaction times. Lower attention levels, slower processing speeds, detrimental sensory and perceptual functions, or potentially less ability to use strategies in specific tasks. Studies have been conducted using neuropsychological testing and neuroimaging to explore different types of memory in aging.

Nevertheless, it must be pointed out that some of these features, such as episodic memory encoding and semantic memory retrieval, are sometimes methodologically difficult to separate. Notwithstanding, these experiments of aging and neuroimaging are starting to investigate success on memory tasks.

A review article focused on this area illustrated improvements in the activation of regional brains. Older brains tend to show more symmetrical activation, either because they have raised activation in a less activated hemisphere than in younger adults, or because they have reduced activation in the most activated areas of younger adults. It has been shown in memory tasks and for visual perception. The observed changes inactivation in the prefrontal left and right cortex are in line with alterations in the performance of the memory, particularly episodic memory, as this is thought to be centered in this region. It has also been proposed that the actual brain stimulation level, as shown in neuroimaging, may be more directly related to the memory performance levels. A research analysis using electroencephalograms to analyze event-related potentials in response to stimuli also provides some evidence for the improved similarity of age-related brain activation. The increased symmetric hemispheric activation in older adults is a reliable finding and has been referred to as HAROLD or reduction in hemispheric asymmetry. It is not understood whether this shift is the attention of the response seen in younger participants, an inability to recruit specific areas, or an effort to compensate for the aging process. Nevertheless, this increase in activation occurring in the frontal lobes matches with improvements in memory performance and the possible changes in the white matter listed above, but other factors such as changes in neurocranium.

**Mechanism Changes**

The most often addressed neurotransmitters as regards aging are dopamine and serotonin.

Dopamine levels are decreasing by about 10 percent per decade from early adulthood and have been associated with cognitive and motor function declines. It may be that the dopaminergic pathways between the frontal cortex and the striatum decrease with increasing age, or that dopamine levels themselves decrease, synapses/receptors decrease, or that binding receptor decrease. Neurotrophic factor levels derived from serotonin and brain often drop with increasing age and may be involved in controlling synaptic plasticity and neurogenesis in the adult brain. A neurotransmitter-related product, monoamine oxidase, increases with age and can release free radicals from reactions that surpass the endogenous antioxidant reserves. Other factors involved in the aging brain include calcium dysregulation, mitochondrial dysfunction, and reactive oxygen species production. The hormonal effect is another factor to consider about the developing brain and its cognitive performance. It is known that sex hormones can influence cognitive processes in adulthood, and changes in sex hormones occur during aging, particularly in menopause women. Females also have a higher incidence of AD, even when given more extended life expectancy. AD is characterized by memory loss, and suggestions have been made that estrogen therapy can increase dopaminergic reactivity and play a protective part in AD. It should be recalled, however, that recent use of HRT has been shown to pose cancer risks. Growth hormone levels often decline with age and may be correlated with cognitive performance even though the evidence is far from conclusive. The aging brain may also suffer from decreased glucose metabolism or diminished glucose or oxygen intake, as cerebrovascular effectiveness declines. In contrast, glucose loss may be partially due to atrophy rather than any improvement in the metabolism of glucose. Change in the vasculature is significant, and ischemia-related white matter lesions and stroke are other common findings in older brains.

## Vascular Factors

For rising age, WML, strokes, and dementia increase. WML shows heritability levels are reasonable in the elderly, even when asymptomatic and are not the innocuous finding they were once considered to be.

For a summary, see Hsu-Ko.42 WML or hyperintensities are related to increased cardiovascular risk and decreased cerebral blood flow, cerebral reactivity, and vascular density. However, it is uncertain whether the WML causes loss of vessels or vice versa.

When using magnetization shift magnetic resonance imaging, they may also be correlated with further tissue shifts in visible grey matter.

WML is found more in frontal rather than posterior brain regions in line with the cognitive and morphological findings discussed above) and it has been shown that WML is related to poor cognition. Other damages associated with aging and blood pressure and vascular factors include strokes and small vessel disease. Moderate to high outpatient blood pressure 24 hours was associated with increased brain atrophy, as the amplitude of systolic blood pressure increased.

In Japanese subjects, elevated systolic blood pressure was correlated with loss of grey matter volume in a cross-sectional analysis, and an increased 10-year risk of the first stroke was associated with declines in cognitive function in the Framingham offspring cohort. The authors recommend that this may be attributable to cerebrovascular-related injuries, progressive atrophy, white matter disorders, or asymptomatic infarction.

The fact that cerebral vasculature may be associated with cognitive function is not surprising, as microvasculature's ability to respond to metabolic demand declines with increasing age, and functional adult neurogenesis may also be correlated with good metabolic demand. See Lie et al. for reviews, and Riddle et al. Besides this, many links have been made between dementia, even AD, and risk factors for vascular disease. Increasing evidence points to vascular factors contributing not only to aging cognitive issues but also to the two most common dementias seen in the people. The happening of dementia rises almost exponentially, with about 20 percent of those aged 80 affected rising to 40 percent of those aged 90.39 The most commonly observed forms of dementia in the elderly are AD, which accounts for about 40 percent –70 percent of dementias, and vascular dementia (VaD) has risen to 15 percent –30 percent. A postmortem study found that 77 percent of VaD cases showed AD pathology60, and high blood pressure was associated with increased AD characteristic neurofibrillary tangles. Several forms of vascular disease have been related to AD, including microvascular degeneration, blood-brain barrier disorders, WML, microinfarction, and cerebral hemorrhage. Significant vessel causes, such as atherosclerosis, have been suggested to increase the risk of AD and may play a role in the amyloid deposition of the cerebral vessel. AD patients show significantly higher levels of cerebrovascular pathology compared to postmortem examination controls, although this did not correlate with cognitive decline severity. The same research finding resulted that small infarcts in AD do not affect the rate of cognitive decline, suggests that vascular factors may unmask or magnify the underlying AD pathology, or lowered the pre-clinical phase of AD, at least in Western populations. At postmortem examination, the characteristic neurofibrillary tangles and plaques found in AD are also evident to some extent in most elderly brains, even those without symptoms, as are white matter lesions. The issue of healthy aging is complicated because studies are showing cognitively intact adults aged and yet an increasing percentage suffer from dementia and the line between mild cognitive ages. Without question, changes in brain vasculature, WML, and intra / extracellular changes are likely to begin in midlife. There are many factors on the aging brain, biology, biological, and environmental influences, all leading to physiological and cognitive changes. Mattson gave it a review.

Risk factors proposed in terms of aging and dementia development include hypertension, diabetes, hyperhomocysteinemia, and high cholesterol, although evidence for all but hypertension is far from conclusive. Safeguarding factors include diet, alcohol, exercise, and intellectual pursuits.

## 4.4 Aging Slows down the Brain

Processing speed means just that to a brain scientist: the pace at which a person can take in a bit of new knowledge, make some conclusion on it and then formulate a response. Studies suggest that the speed of information processing varies with age along an inverted U-shaped curve, such that our learning accelerates from childhood to adolescence, retains a period of relative stability leading to middle age, and then, slowly but steadily decreases in late middle age and onward.

It is usual for most people to see that processing speed slows with age.

Many older adults had noticed they take longer to solve problems or make decisions than they did when they were young. Yet the explanations for this age-related deceleration in the processing of information are not fully understood and can vary from person to person.

Some compelling evidence indicates that such a deterioration represents wear and tear of white brain matter, which consists of all the wires or axons that link one part of the brain to another. Slowed transmission of information along axons can hinder processing speed. But what initially causes the axonal contact to slow down? Diabetes, smoking, high blood pressure, or other so-called vascular risk factors in some people can wear away at the blood vessels feeding the white matter of the brain, starving axons of much-needed oxygen and glucose. Many individuals may have a genetic predisposition to decay of white matter related to age, a theory that is poorly understood but has been extensively studied. Slowed processing rate could be the first indicator of neurodegenerative disease in other people, such as Alzheimer's disease. Head trauma may play a role, including concussions. These are just a few of the many ideas out there — other factors certainly still to be discovered. Most specifically, slow processing of information affects almost every aging person to some extent, and the distinction between natural and abnormal becomes blurred. By paying close attention to vascular risk factors, participating in daily aerobic exercise, eating well, and continuing to challenge oneself mentally, a person may maintain or even increase the speed of information processing.

Think achy joints are the main reason we're slowing down as we age? But blame the brain: The portion responsible for movement will start a slow downhill slide at age 40. How easily you can throw a ball, or sprint or turn a steering wheel depends on how quickly brain cells fire off muscle commands. Fast firing is dependent on good insulation for cabling your brain. Now new research suggests that even stable people in middle age begin to lose some of that insulation in a section of the brain's motor-control — at the same time as their speed slows slowly. This helps explain why it's hard after 40, to be a world-class athlete.

**Research Study**

Stuff starts going south at age 24, according to researchers at Simon Fraser University in Canada. Since researching 3,305 volunteers aged 16 years to 44 years, they came to that conclusion. The participants played a real-time game that approximated real-world situations of everyday life that test our cognitive abilities, from attention to juggling multiple tasks to changing our emphasis from immediate to long-term problems. The game captured moves from the players, and researchers were analyzing hours of data from it. The pace with which the volunteers made decisions, and moved between tasks, declined with age as planned. Several studies have recorded an increasing loss of cognitive competencies over time. But in this report, published in the PLOS One journal, the drop was first observed among 24-year-olds, although tiny. Cognitive speed dropped by about 15 percent every 15 years after age 24. And the results could not be explained by the fact that, over time, the players were getting better at navigating the game; the age-related decline remained, even among those with more skill playing the play. This doesn't mean everything is downhill until your mid-20s. When processing speed slows, the brain compensates for some of the loss in a variety of ways. For instance, by relying on experience to foresee and predict future activities more accurately, as well as by using mental shortcuts such as removing foreign information and stopping incoming information into only core nuggets of relevant material. And while we might get slower, we might get smarter, too.

## 4.5 Effects of Aging Brain on Thinking

The brain controls many facets of thinking— remembering, planning, arranging, decision-making, and more. Such cognitive skills influence how well we do our daily tasks and whether we can live independently.

Aging can bring about positive cognitive improvements, too. Those from a lifetime of experiences often have more knowledge and insight. As a person grows older, changes are taking place in all parts of the body, including the brain. Some parts of the brain shrink, especially those that are necessary for learning and other complex mental activities. Communication between the neurons (nerve cells) may be reduced in specific brain regions. Blood flow can decrease in the brain, too. Inflammation may increase, which occurs when the body responds to an injury or disease.

Such brain changes can impair mental function, even in stable older persons. For example, some older adults find that complex memory or learning tests do not do as well as younger people. And they can do as well, given enough time. There is increasing evidence that, as people age, the brain remains "plastic" — capable of adapting to new challenges and tasks.

It is not understood why some people think well while others do not. One possible reason is the "cognitive reserve," the ability of the brain to function well even when a part of it is disrupted. Those with more experience tend to have a higher amount of memory than others. Many changes in the brain, such as those linked to Alzheimer's disease, are not a standard part of aging.

It's irritating, but it's sadly true: most parts of the bodywork less well as one gets older. This is the fact of the brain, which is part of why having a "tip of the tongue" moment becomes more regular as one gets older.

These age-related changes are called "cognitive aging," in how the brain regulates memory, thought, and other mental processes. Understanding how aging affects cognition is crucial. It can help you to understand what to expect when it comes to aging yourself.

It can also help families better understand the alterations they observe in an older person, and whether or not those changes are out of the ordinary. As you will see, over time, most mental processes get less agile. Just as your 75-year-old self cannot run as fast as your 30-year-old self, so, for the most part, your 75-year-old brain will not think as quickly either. To many people, this can be disappointing news. What does it mean they might feel hesitant to know more about this? But they're not just bad news. Sure, things tend to work a little slower and less well, but by relying on their experience, older adults can often compensate. When I clarify later in the article, cognitive aging often helps older adults become more positive and emotionally resilient. You'll be better provided to comprehend the older adults in your life by better understanding cognitive aging, whether it's yourself or an older loved one.

People often think about memory when they talk about learning or "brain function," but there's a lot more to think about and the functioning of the brain. Here are six key ways in which aging affects cognition.

**Processing Speed**

It refers to how easily information can be interpreted and then generated by the brain, such as making a gesture or delivering a response. Processing velocity affects just about every brain function. Processing speed is not a specific mental task in itself. It's about how easily you can handle a mental job. Rate of processing declines with age, with one expert defining it as an almost linear decline. The fall starts in early adulthood, so as long as people are in their 70's or 80's, processing speed is significantly lower compared to one's 20's age.

**Memory**

This is a broad category that covers the ability to recall information. Main subtypes include:

Working memory It refers to the ability to keep information in mind briefly and mentally manipulate it, including remembering a new phone number and then dialing it.

- Working memory includes a variety of mental functions, including problem-solving, decision-making, and language processing.
- Long-term semantic memory, it applies to the factual information you gain over time, such as the name of the state capital.
- Episodic memory. This applies to one's mind for specific observed events that have occurred at a given time or place.
- Prospective memory. This refers to the ability to remember going forward to do things.
- Procedural memory. This is also called capacity learning. This applies to study and reminding of how to do certain things.
- Building up usually requires time and practice.

Memory is also a complicated topic, many other subtypes can be described, and researchers are also still researching how to categorize and explain the many different ways that people remember knowledge or how to do stuff. Technically, generating a memory (which is sometimes called encoding) and recalling it is also a different task for the brain. So, a person may have issues in remembering something either because they were having trouble encoding it in the first place, or because they are having trouble getting it back promptly. Some memory aspects decline with age, but not all: memory types that reject: working memory episodic memory (especially for more recent events). Prospective memory types that stay stable Procedural memory Semantic long-term memory (may decline after the 7th decade).

**Attention**

Attention is the ability to focus and concentrate on something important to process-related information. Main subtypes include:

- Selective attention. This is the ability to focus on something particular despite the presence of other distracting knowledge or stimuli that are "irrelevant." Examples: finding the relevant information on a cluttered website while being in a busy environment, following a conversation.

- Divided focus, Also known as "multi-tasking," that is the ability to manage multiple tasks or information sources simultaneously. Examples: while listening to music, reading a recipe, driving while talking to someone.

- Sustained concentration. This is the ability to stay focused on something for an extended period.

With aging, some aspects of attention get worse. Specifically: With aging, selective attention gets worse. Foraging, the split focus gets worse. The sustained concern with aging doesn't seem to get worse.

**Executive Functioning**

It applies to the mental skills needed for planning, organizing, problem-solving, abstract thinking, mental flexibility, and effective behavioral behaviors. Executive function helps people to do things like: solve new problems. Organize information and schedule tasks. Think abstractly Using rationale (especially when it comes to explaining with unfamiliar material), adapt to new situations, behave in socially appropriate ways, make complex decisions how it changes with aging: Executive function generally decreases with age, especially after period 70.

## Emotional Processing

This refers to how one expresses and regulates emotions, particularly that contrary. Factors include: How quickly one gets out of a negative emotional state, how physically or emotionally sensitive one is to interpersonal stressors, behavioral techniques to reduce negative stimuli, such as paying little attention to the How it improves with aging. Older adults undergo many changes that generally make them more positive and hopeful. These include: paying less attention to negatively simulating conditions or removing them. Paying more attention to anything good. Remembering positive things more.

# Chapter 5: Parenting Role in Nurturing Child's Brain

The development of children's cognitive and social skills needed for later school success can best be facilitated by a parenting style known as sensitive parenting. Responsiveness is an aspect of positive parenting that is defined through various theories and research contexts (e.g., attachment, sociocultural) as playing an essential role in providing children with a strong foundation for successful growth.

The effective-emotional aspects of a sensitive style are parenting that offers healthy affection and high levels of comfort, and is responsive in ways that are contingently linked to the signals of a young child ("contingent responsiveness").

Such factors, combined with activities that relate cognitively to the needs of the child, including providing precious verbal feedback and sustaining and enhancing the interests of the child, provide the continuum of support needed for multiple aspects of the learning of the child.

Acceptance of the child's attention with prompt and flexible responses to what the child communicates facilitates learning, in part, by encouraging the creation of the child's strategies for coping with stress and excitement in its environment. Through repeated positive experiences, the child and the parent build a confidence and connection that, in effect, helps the child to internalize this trust and then generalize their learning into new experiences.

Such proactive support facilitates the ongoing involvement of the child with his or her parent in learning activities.

Therefore, these affective-emotional behaviors reflect the parent's concern and approval, promoting self-regulation and co-operation, which are critically essential behaviors for active learning. From a socio-cultural point of view, cognitive sensitive activities (e.g. holding interests versus redirecting interests, rich verbal input) are thought to promote higher learning levels because they provide a foundation or scaffold for the immature skills of the young child, such as improving focus and cognitive abilities. In this context, sensitive actions encourage mutual participation and reciprocity within parent-child interaction, and help a child learn to play a more involved and eventually independent part in the learning process. Responsive encouragement for the child to actively engage in problem solving is often referred to as parental scaffolding, and is also believed to be crucial to promoting the development of children's self-regulation and executive function skills, behaviors that eventually allow the child to assume responsibility for their wellbeing.

## 5.1 Effect of Parenting on Development of Child's Brain

Responsive parenting is one of the most often discussed elements of parenting as we try to know the role that the environment plays in developing children.

Parenting strategies around the world share three main goals, according to the American Psychological Association: ensuring the health and safety of children, preparing children for life as productive adults, and communicating cultural values. Those targets are optimistic. Being a good parent is no small feat and depends on several environmental and biological factors on how children become capable, happy, productive adults.

There are various factors on child outcomes, but a wealth of literature suggests that parenting is an essential part of the equation. The degree to which parenting strategies influence behavioral development in children is a complex issue. While we may not be able to answer it with confidence, we can be sure that parents are essential factors in the behavioral outcomes of their children. Research shows that it can encourage appropriate developmental trajectories for children at high risk, such as those from low-income families and those with very premature births.

Research has found strong linkages between parenting and change of child behavior. For example, parenting practices of a mother, including the degree to which she shows affection towards and maintains behavioral and psychological influence over her child when that child is five years of age, is related to later internalizing and outsourcing behaviors of the child. Internalizing behavioral problems, or emotional ones, also relate to anxiety and depression. Externalizing, or destructive, behavioral problems are commonly associated with attention deficit hyperactivity disorder and conduct issues. These are just a few typical behavioral issues which are partially influenced by specific parenting styles. Unresponsive parenting, by contrast, can jeopardize the development of children, particularly those at higher risk for developmental problems.

Recent evidence suggesting correlations between high levels of early responsive parenting and more significant hippocampal volumes for typically developing preschool-aged children highlights the critical importance of responsive parenting. Increased capacity in this brain region is associated with several psychosocial variables

(e.g., stress reactivity) progressing more optimally.

Links between early responsive parenting and increased volume in the hippocampal region also indicate that the first developmental period is an essential time for promoting responsive parenting practices, especially in high-risk families, to improve the relationship between parent and child. Given the potential value of proactive parenting, our awareness of how to promote successful parenting activities could be further enhanced by more specific knowledge of the types of behaviors most necessary to support specific areas of child learning.

The learning of problem-solving, vocabulary, and social-emotional skills by young children is encouraged by experiences with their parents. There is some evidence that in this parenting style, the mechanism by which responsively promotes the development of a child can rely on consistency through development. Since the child and the parent are part of a broader social context, many factors may support or impinge on the consistent use of responsive behaviors by a parent. Personal factors that may undermine the sensitivity of a parent include stress, the view of the parent's own experience of child-rearing as unfavorable, or beliefs and attitudes that distract from a parent's sense of importance in the life of his or her or her child. Other variables, however, such as higher levels of social support from friends and family, can mitigate some of these negative social-personal factors as well as predict which parents move with intervention from a non-responsive to a responsive style. This is a promising finding since parenting strategies can be designed to provide mothers from high-risk social backgrounds with a level of social support needed to develop sensitive parenting styles.

Responsive parenting is an essential process for supporting the learning of young children according to many descriptive studies and fewer experimental studies.

A causal role of responsive parenting is now recognized, as more significant improvements in parental behaviors associated with responsive style were responsible for the impact of multiple parenting interventions on more significant gains in learning for young children. Recent evidence for typically developing children showing linkages between early high levels of responsive parenting and increased volume in brain regions responsible for stress regulation also suggests the critical importance of rapid development of this parenting practice. Because both routine and high-risk children enjoyed responsiveness that offered affective-emotional and cognitively responsive support, the efficacy of responsiveness is best understood when identified as a specific construct. Recent evidence shows that certain reactive behaviors can provide different kinds of support for the learning of children, and this support may vary depending on the developmental needs of a child. Many new research directions need to be explored, and issues that need further review are discussed in recent studies.

The attempt to research the effect of parenting strategies on child outcomes is complicated because an incredibly wide range of parenting activities and an equally wide array of child behavioral outcomes occur.

The causal relationship between parenting practices and consequences of child behavior is similarly opaque, depending on the timing and measurement of the actions at issue. For example, in a study of adolescents' understanding of the psychological control of their parents,

or the degree to which parents attempt to control the emotions and beliefs of their children,

and the self-reported internalizing and violent behaviors of adolescents, researchers and scientists discovered behavior of a child as a powerful predictor of changes in parental psychological control than parental behavior as a predictor of changes. Because this connection is multi-directional, it becomes even more challenging to research the effect of parenting strategies on child behavioral outcomes.

## 5.2 Parenting Styles

A common way of dealing with these complexities is to organize parenting behaviors into four distinct parenting styles: authoritarian, permissive, implicated, and authoritative). These four parenting ways are based on two parental dimensions: parental warmth related to the child's parental affection and acceptance, and parental control related to the active role parents play in promoting compliance with rules and social conventions. Extensive research has been done on the implications of parenting styles on children's behavioral outcomes.

**Authoritarian Parenting Style**

The strict parent blends low warmth with high control levels and employs a rigid parenting style marked by minimal interaction with the infant, high expectations, restricted tolerance, constant use of punishment, and one-way parent-to-child contact. Authoritarian parenting was linked to child outcomes such as hostility, delinquency, rebelliousness, and anti-social aggression. Research has also found that early experience of an infant with excessive parental control appears to correlate with anxiety development. This fear is likely due to a lack of opportunity to develop autonomy through autonomous environmental exploration. It has also been recommended that the low warmth characteristic of authoritarian parenting may be associated with childhood depression.

## Permissive Parenting Style

The permissive parent shows high warmth levels and low control levels. He or she behaves more like a friend than a parent, using a loose form of discipline with few guidelines, little to no standards, and little supervision or direction. Parents with this style tend to be very affectionate and caring, but also allow their children to solve problems without the intervention of the parents. Significant predictors of child behavior problems reported by both parents and teachers were in a permissive parenting survey, lack of participation, lack of follow-up, and lack of confidence in parenting. Because permissive parents tend to be non-demanding, control of the actions of children, and define limits in children's environments becomes much more difficult. Research has found correlations between the excessive parental indulgence often seen in permissive parenting activities and the reduced social skills and academic achievement of children. Permissive parenting has been associated with bossy, dependent, impulsive behavior in children with low self-control and achievement rates, and a failure to learn resilience and emotional control.

## Uninvolved Parenting Style

The uninvolved parent combines low warmth and low control levels and uses no particular style of discipline. Sometimes, he or she shows no interest in being a mom. Communication is limited. Nursing is low, and, in general, the child has excessive freedom. Since the uninvolved parent is neither demanding nor attentive, and since the young children are highly dependent on parental structure and care, uninvolved parenting has been associated with behavioral problems and depression in children.

Furthermore, teenagers who are subject to uninvolved parental activities also experience high rates of alienation and appear to exhibit more externalizing attitudes, aggressive behaviors, criminal behaviors, aggression, and attention problems. The consequences of unchanged parenting may also extend through puberty and into adulthood. Researchers found in a study of first Year College students that individuals who reported being raised by uninvolved parents showed more internalizing and outsourcing issues in reaction to negative emotions such as homesickness. However, these students were significantly less successful in dealing with problems than individuals who described growing up in a loving home environment.

**Authoritative Parenting Style**

The dominant parent displays both high warmth levels and high control levels. People in this group are compassionate and caring, set high standards, clearly explain discipline guidelines, and communicate with their children in frequent communication.

Authoritative parenting has been linked to increased child competence, great maturity, assertiveness, and self-control. Authoritarian parents who use child-centered parenting methods and use verbal reasoning and explanations tend to raise children with high levels of moral reasoning, moral awareness markers, and prosaically behavior.

Evidence has shown that authoritarian parenting can be the most effective type, but in terms of parental energy and time, it also appears to be the most demanding. Parents living under adverse circumstances, such as deprivation, may be less likely to exhibit authoritarian parenting strategies and more likely to use less successful parenting practices.

Research suggests that parents with a higher socioeconomic status household are more likely to adopt egalitarian and child-centered parenting methods, as compared to the hierarchical and parent-centered style that characterizes homes with lower socioeconomic status. This would guide to an increased likelihood of raising children who show problems of internalizing and outsourcing behavior, which, in effect, is likely to place more burden on the family. The circular pattern has enormous implications for the future because it leads to structural inequity of deprivation for families.

**Implications of Positive Parenting Style**

Parents have to find a parenting style that works best for them and their kids. Authoritative and redirection have a positive effect on a child's cognitive development.

Hence the child has higher self-esteem and academic success. Authoritarian, forgiving. And uninvolved tend to affect the cognitive development of a child negatively.

Therefore, the child has lower self-esteem and less academic achievement. Parenting is successful when the parent is warm and caring, yet challenging, on the cognitive development of the child.

Parents should allow for independence and discovery, but they should set limits.

Observing their actions is critical for parents because it affects the cognitive development of a child. Whatever parenting methods are used, parents should aspire to use some sound principles to allow the child to develop independence, self-esteem, and maturity.

There are many policy implications for the value of sensitive parenting for the welfare of young children.

Policy and practice decision-makers need to pay particular attention to parents who are most at risk, to optimize performance, they need to find ways to promote improvement in parent behavior, taking into account factors such as parent values, social support, and mental health status. The synthesis of relevant research will direct new investment in parent services as well as the creation of proactive parenting research initiatives. Developmental science is often not well incorporated into the implementation of policies or programmers. Considering the critical role early experience plays in brain development, policymakers have an interest in ensuring that the atmosphere for young children (e.g., home, child care) is of sufficient quality to promote positive outcomes. As new investments are made in publicly funded child and family care, the focus on transparency is often higher. This should help to encourage more significant consideration of evidence-based research that can better guarantee the feasibility of the program.

## 5.3 Effects of Negative Parenting Style on Child's Brain

While parenting is not always sunshine and roses, concentrating too much on the thunderclouds could put your child in an inferior position. Parents have a strong influence on the actions of their children. Kids are like sponges — they model everything that a parent does and integrate into their own lives what they see. It's crucial that parents set their children the right examples. Negative examples may affect the growth of a child and may lead to bad behavior. Negative tactics of parenting, such as lecturing, moaning, threatening, and yes, even nagging, will seriously affect the actions and activities of your child later on in life. What does happen at home affect the long-term mental health and development of children? But it's not just the parent-child relationship, which is essential. The way parents get along also plays a significant role in the wellbeing of a child, which can affect everything from mental health to academic success and future relationships. Bad parenting is defined as a sequence of actions that can affect the personality and psychology of the child severely. Bad parenting is not confined to a single act; it is a collection of these acts that usually contribute to the child's harmful effect. Most poor parenting may not be deliberate, but this does not reduce the negative impact it has on the infant. Some parents are unaware of the consequences of these acts, and some may not even know. Poor parenting could be caused by not knowing enough to be a better parent or by a general lack of apathy to learn the right way. There exists no relationship that is entirely free of conflict and dispute, and indeed, all the children see their parents argue at some point. Parents relate calmly and positively to each other during a disagreement, solve the problem, and show the children through their subsequent interactions that the conflict has been resolved. The children may not be affected by conflict (few of the research suggests that they may even understand skills related to the resolution of disputes that they can apply to their relationships along the way). (The impact of observing domestic violence on children is not discussed in detail in this book, but it has also, of course, been shown to be very harmful). And conflict is damaging whether parents are married or even living together. The UK and international research conducted over several decades through home observations, long-term follow-up work, and experimental studies suggest that children exposed to conflict may have higher heart rates and reactions to stress hormones from as young as six months. As a result of living with extreme or prolonged inter-parental battle, babies, children, and adolescents may show signs of disturbed early brain development, sleep disturbance, anxiety, depression, conduct disorder, and other pressing issues.

From a very early age — some researchers say as young as six months — children show anxiety when their parents fight. Their reactions may include anger, fear, sadness, and anxiety, and there is an excessive possibility of experiencing a wide variety of problems related to health, disturbed sleep, and trouble concentrating and succeeding in school. They may "externalize" their distress in the form of "aggression, hostility, anti-social and non-compliant behavior, delinquency, and vandalism," or "internalize" it in the way of "depression, anxiety, withdrawal, and dysphoria." Moreover, "children in high-conflict homes are more likely to have poor interpersonal skills, problem-solving skills, and social skills."

## Research Study on Negative behavior of Mothers towards Children

Researchers at the University of Minnesota researched more than 260 mothers and their kids from birth to first grade. Based on both findings and parent accounts, they assessed the complicated disposition of children as well as how they were looked after between the first week of their birth and the sixth month of life. When the kids were two and a half and three years old, the researchers looked at mothers with their kids doing tasks that challenged the kids and required parental assistance. Researchers defined negative parenting occurs when parents expressed their children's negative emotions, handled them roughly, and the like.

The researchers also found that it was an escalating or progressive conflict that predicted later conducting problems between moms and their infants–that is, a conflict that worsened over time.

And in a cyclical pattern, when moms were negatively parenting their infants, that resulted in their children showing high levels of anger as infants, which in turn caused more hostility from the moms. Besides, moms who had negative parenting of their infants may also have had angrier children because these moms were more hostile towards their infants. Negative parenting in infancy seemed to set the stage for both moms and their children to be more hostile and angrier in their childhood, bringing out the worst in each other. The results of our research go beyond descriptive findings to clarify the fundamental mechanism of connecting how mothers raise and look after their children in their childhood and children's issues in early primary education. Researchers suppose that the outcomes of the study can help in developing appropriate interventions for targeting negative parenting — starting as early as three months— to help prevent problems in children later on.

# Chapter 6: Ways to Improve Baby's Brain Development

The way a child thinks acquires information and communicates with its surrounding environment is characterized by cognitive development. Different cognitive abilities are gained as a child reaches certain developmental milestones, but practices that encourage active learning will support a child of any knowledge. As a parent, by integrating basic tasks into your daily routine, you can facilitate your child's cognitive development in the areas of memory, focus, attention, and perception. The brain of an infant needs a stimulating environment where it can develop. Children fulfill their curiosities by their day-to-day tasks and explorations. Children have the most compelling interest in learning about the world. Families need to create a healthy, stimulating environment that allows children to develop their cognitive abilities. Since most kids learn through play, parents can use various games and toys to target particular mental recourses. Ultimately, that will provide your children with a fun experience and, at the same time, develop their cognitive domains. New parents want to make the best start in life for their infant, and a large part of encouraging early baby brain growth stimulates the brain of your baby. It may appear like an intimidating task, but it doesn't have to be challenging to improve your small mind.

## 6.1 Developing Cognitive Skills in Children

**Provide a loving environment**

Providing a nurturing environment is an essential factor in your children's cognitive development.

A concentrative atmosphere with both physical and verbal expressions of love will create the ideal atmosphere for developing the emotional skills of your child and for building a strong bond between you and your child. This boosts their self-confidence and allows them to focus their attention on other developmental aspects, as they don't have to waste time seeking approval and love. Children also get to know how to express affection through kisses, hugs, massages, and general touch and use body language as a means of communication successfully.

**Exercise the Body**

Exercise is essential to the development of the brain, and hence cognitive thinking. Children oxygenate the brain faster through use and physical activity, and that helps it develop. In turn, they create stronger synaptic connections through the growth of their motor skills, which help to respond to muscle nerve in a faster brain. Going outside allows for the absorption of fresh air and offers a healthy physical growth environment. Swimming, however, is the best exercise of all, as it includes all muscle groups.

**A Good Sleep**

Sleep helps the brain to refresh and process all of the information learned every day. A child needs 8 to 10 hours of good, high-quality sleep to recover and energize itself. Parents should make use of the time right before bedtime to reflect on the day's actual events and specific ways of demonstrating passion. This will develop a sense of well-being, resulting in optimistic visions that will ignite creativity and imagination.

**Healthy Food for Fast Cognitive Functioning**

Healthy brain growth demands a healthy diet. Parents should provide a varied and nutritious diet for their children that includes fresh produce, meat, and dairy products.

Protein-rich foods are essential to brain growth by helping the brain to absorb more mass. Omega-3 fats (usually come up with fish, nuts, and eggs) also help in concentration, acquisition of knowledge, and logical thinking. Therefore, adding them into your child's diet will aid in their cognitive development.

**Learning through Fun**

By play, children learn most about the world around them. In some areas of cognitive development, almost all behaviors can benefit. Parents can provide different toys for their children and teach different games for children to target specific cognitive development. This can include the event of any type of skills: from language, concentration, creativity, logical and abstract thinking, to physical abilities such as hand-eye coordination, individual awareness, and motor functions.

**Singing them a Song**

Let's be honest: while you're in the front seat focusing on the road, there's not too much you can do with your baby, and your baby stares at the upholstery on the back of the rear seat. But singing is a hands-free activity, and it will significantly boost the development of his baby's brain. When parents sing to babies, they often sing with a lot of intonation, which is of interest to the baby. "Songs can familiarize with new words and repetitive patterns which are essential to the development of language. Singing often teaches babies about rhyming, which is vital for later reading success.

**Take Child to Grocery Shopping**

You may be tempted to keep your baby occupied with a phone or tablet when you have your baby in the cart. "Describe the places, the odors, the shapes.

Let the baby hold a kiwi and show him how different it feels from an orange." You can also call out colors and count fruit and vegetables as you place them in a jar. And your babe will love a "Where did it go!" game. You plop items in the cart behind him (and you're going to love that he's learning object permanence).

### Taking to Walk

There's so much your baby needs to see when you're out for a stroll, says Shaw. Point things like the stars, trees, and birds and call them, and improve the growth of the baby's brain by using words to describe the rhythm of different terrain you're walking over: "This path is bumpy" and "The road is smooth." If your walker moves so that your baby faces you, she'll be able to watch your mouth while you're forming sentences, which will help her learn to speak.

### Mealtime In a high chair

Babies play a universal game; let me drop this food (or spoon, or cup, or toy) on the floor and see what's going on! But it is not just fun— it's another opportunity to learn the permanence of things. She is also working on her hold as she picks up foods with small fingers, an essential skill in fine motors. Mealtime can also be used to teach your baby new concepts, such as different textures, and to describe the difference between hot and cold.

### Bedtime

Most parents include a bedtime story as part of the end-of-day routine that's a great way to boost the growth of the baby brain.

"Make time to read or just look at pictures in a book, right from birth.

"You don't have to read a story from start to finish." The bedtime routine is also a wonderful time of bonding. "We know that the way they learn is when babies and children have a secure attachment. Then they fall asleep, and the brain becomes refreshed for another day of development and discovery.

## 6.2 Improving Cognitive skills through Games

Cognitive development means the way kids think, learn, and find out things. It is the creation of awareness, skills, and strategies that help children think about the world around them and appreciate it. Fostering the cognitive development of your child as soon as he/she is born provides the basis for both school and later life success. Here are suggestions for promoting cognitive development through various activities.

Memory games help to build short- and long-term memory. Besides that, they have practical implications since they can enhance all three forms of learning (visual, auditory, and kinesthetic). Challenges of verbal and picture recall, puzzles, and pantomimes all help improve memory skills.

Word and number games like Sudoku games and crossword puzzles help improve the logical thinking, pattern recognition, and language skills of your child.

Simple games also provide a way for child to expand his or her vocabulary and adjust to a symbolic way of thinking. Sudoku and crosswords also have health benefits, because they minimize the likelihood of dementia and Alzheimer's. Reading is another activity which makes cognitive development better.

Kids can improve their imagination and visualization skills through stories. In fact, the reading process itself lets them learn vocabulary and develop their linguistic competencies.

Parents must provide age-appropriate books to their children. Their first collection of books should have plenty of colors and illustrations to attract attention and spark interest so that your child will want to pick up books themselves later on. Reading books also features top watching films, as they are more engaging and require more mental recourse.

Performance is another way to help children develop cognitive competencies. Music listening is a great stress reduction tool, and it provides a healthy and toxic-free atmosphere where the brain can grow properly. Playing musical instruments is a way of developing coordination and creativity, which stimulates emotion. The drums, keyboards, and piano are the most engaging instruments for children because they produce both hemispheres of the brain in an identical comparison, through coordinated use.

Today's technological advances have provided children with several ways to develop their cognitive abilities, primarily through child-friendly computer games. Online math and word games are interactive learning sources allowing parents also to participate. And, as most of them are time-based, they develop rapid thinking, quick memory retrieval, and improved decision-making and speed of reaction.

## 6.3 Cognitive Nurturing in Early Childhood

Parents should facilitate practices that will enhance the mental development of young children. Pre-operative children (age 2 to 7 years) learn efficiently, so direct play and interaction are the best vehicles to teach them concepts. There are a lot of fun practical skills that children can learn to improve their focus, memory, abstract thinking, and ability to make decisions. Age-appropriate puzzles are fun challenges that promote skills in problem-solving and critical thinking. Easy board games can also develop problem-solving skills and teach young kids how to follow a set of instructions.

Additionally, games and puzzles can help teach categorization (e.g., sorting by type, shape, or color), concentration, and memory skills into groups. The rules and aims of the games they play can become more complicated and exciting as children grow. Classic games such as checkers are useful to introduce right now. There are plenty of fun puzzles and board games to buy in the store, but families can easily make their own too. Extra photos or large magazine pictures, for example, can be covered with bright plastic contact paper, and then cut into big inconsistent, irregular shapes to create puzzles.

Young children continue to take advantage from make-believe play throughout the pre-operative period. Children learn to stretch out their imagination and creative thinking skills by creating their imaginary setting and placing themselves within it. Most kids spontaneously play "pretend" games in which they act as something other than themselves, a dinosaur or a princess. Though parents may not find such games meaningful, children will still generally benefit from playing them. By merely jumping into the game as best they can, parents will promote such make-believe games. Most children will be gleefully playing along with mom or dad. Many kids, however, have an internalized collection of instructions or values that surround their make-believe scene and will immediately correct any adult who doesn't abide by those arcane rules that seem so clear to them. As long as kids don't hit or scream to make a point, parents should just play along and adjust as best they can to the creative thinking train of their child.

When children are themselves out of ideas, parents can take a turn creating the setting to make-believe and encourage the little ones to play along.

The make-believing play of parents can be as dumb and off-the-wall as the result of their kids, or it can be more organized to provide lessons on specific topics. Maintaining and loving scenes (such as taking care of a baby or playing house) or rough and tumble, immersive scenes (such as playing good guys versus bad guys or pretending to be a wild animal) can include themes for adult-driven make-believe play. Parents should promote a variety of different playing types (even if they aren't always excited about playing all kinds themselves). As long as play themes aren't hurtful or violent, they're probably okay.

May be improved by using props or masks to make-believe "pretend" games. Parents should buy all sorts of dress-up clothes and plastic toys that mimic adult items (such as kitchens, vehicles, lightsabers, etc.). Make-believe props needn't be expensive, though. An old Mom's shirt plus pieces of ribbon that serves as a gown for the ball. Hats from the old trunk of clothing that Grandma has can work well as accessories. The kitchen table with a table cloth spread over the top can also become a cave, while a couple of empty toilet paper rolls taped together and decorated can become the wand of a magician. Creating the rod or other props may turn into a craft project.

Because kids of this age learn so much through making-believe play, it's no surprise that many young kids like to pretend they do whatever activities they see their parents do around the house.

Families can exploit the natural interest of children in adult activities by enlisting them to help with household chores. Although chore operation can seem monotonous to adults,

it can serve as educational opportunities for children. For example, younger kids can sort laundry into various piles based on the type of color and clothing (e.g., pants vs. shirts).

Older preschoolers can help to make meals or snacks, an activity that can teach them how to make healthy food choices, safety in the kitchen, and the art of making tasty foods. Young children of school age can be given routine tasks to complete and take pride in, such as setting the dining table, making their beds, or putting away their clothes. The creation of recipes can be a fun activity for all ages. When children are helping with chores and household tasks, it is essential to remember that the description of "help" may require to be made quite flexible, especially when very young children are "helping." Some of what kids think help will be detrimental from the adult perspective. Parents should remain calm and encouraging to help children, wherever possible, rather than toughly correct them for failing to meet adult standards. Waiting until the child is distracted or otherwise occupied is best before taking over and correcting any mistakes that children may have made. The point of letting children to help with household chores and events is to encourage family bonding, and to boost learning opportunities and self-esteem for children, not to perfect the household cleaning program.

# Chapter 7: Impact of External Surrounding on Brain Development

Several research studies have shown in recent years that early-life experiences can influence brain development in children. Two recently published studies have further clarified early-life influences on brain growth and behavior. Joan Luby and colleagues reported in an article published in the Proceedings of the National Academy of Sciences USA (PNAS) that increased parental support during pre-school years is associated with faster growth of the brain's hippocampal region as quantifying by neuroimaging. Those children with great motherly support had a double increase in this region's growth rate as compared with children with lower maternal support levels. The research team also showed that higher growth rates in hippocampal areas were interlinked with better emotional growth.

In a different study published in Biological Psychiatry, Scott Mackey and colleagues studied the correlation between childhood adversity, impulsivity, brain growth patterns, and antisocial behavioral development. They found that higher impulsivity levels were associated with lower growth in specific neocortex regions, and increased growth in specific subcortical brain regions.

Childhood adversity influenced the growth patterns in brain regions thought to contribute to impulsivity, and these growth patterns were associated with antisocial behavior development.

These two studies strongly recommend that environmental influences on young children have direct effects on brain maturation patterns, which, in turn, are linked to specific behavior patterns.

Others will increasingly employ the approaches used by these investigators to determine the roles of psychosocial influences in children and adolescents on regional brain development. Such data will enhance our understanding of neurodevelopment relationships, the environment, brain structures, and specific behaviors, including psychiatric diseases. Elucidating structural changes associated with environmental challenges and improved methods for quantifying ecological variables can also provide measurable markers that would help to determine the effectiveness of early interventions. For example, would the degree of hippocampal growth have associated with better emotional development in adolescents and young adults in response to therapies aimed at improving parental support? Would the degree of normalization of cortical and subcortical growth patterns through specific therapies targeting impulsive behaviors minimize the development of antisocial behaviors? Neuroimaging methods provide more sophisticated tools critical to advancing our understanding of normal and abnormal brain development ever. Therefore, these approaches may be useful in predicting risks for the development of different psychological conditions and in assessing the effect of psychiatric illness prevention interventions on children at high risk.

## 7.1 Early Childhood Experiences Effect Brain for Long Term

For a lifetime, what happens in early childhood can be significant. To manage the future of our society successfully, we need to recognize and address problems before they get worse.

Work on stress biology in early childhood demonstrates how severe trauma, such as extreme poverty, violence, or neglect, can disrupt the production of brain architecture and permanently high-alert the body's stress response system. Science also suggests that providing stable, responsive, nurturing relationships in the earliest years of life can prevent or even reverse the harmful effects of early-life stress, with lifelong learning, behavior, and health benefits. It is long known that experiences of early childhood can have a profound impact on later chances and life opportunities. Now, a collection of new studies recommend that those experiences can affect the brain's size and function. Children are born ready to learn, and over many years, they have many skills to learn. As their first teachers, they rely on parents, family members, and other cares to build the right talent to become independent and lead healthy and prosperous lives. The way the brain develops is strongly affected by the interactions the child has with other people and the world. Nursing the mind is critical for the growth of the brain. In a safe environment where they are protected from neglect and extreme or chronic stress, the children grow and learn best. External with plenty to play and explore. Through talking to, playing with, and caring for their infant, parents and other cares will encourage healthy brain development. Children learn best when parents speak and play turns, and build on the skills and interests of their children. Nursing a child by knowing their needs and sensitively reacting to them helps protect the brains of children against stress. Speaking with kids and exposing them to books, stories, and songs help to strengthen the language and communication of children, which puts them on a path to learning and success in school. Stress and stress exposure can have long-term detrimental effects on the brain of the infant while speaking, reading, and playing can promote brain growth. It is a critical public health priority to make sure that parents, caregivers, and early childhood care providers have the tools and expertise to provide healthy, secure, caring, and stimulating care. If children are at risk, monitoring the development of children and ensuring they meet developmental milestones will help ensure early detection of any issues, and children may obtain the support they may need.

The brain undergoes it most fastly growth from the fetal era through the first years of life, and early experiences decide whether its construction is robust or fragile. The circuitry of the brain is most open to the influence of external expertise, for better or for worse, during the early sensitive periods of development. Healthy emotional and cognitive development during these

vulnerable times is influenced by receptive, dependable contact with adults, whereas persistent or extreme adversity can disrupt healthy brain development.

For example, children who were placed in orphanages shortly after birth with conditions of severe neglect show dramatically reduced brain activity compared with children who have never been institutionalized.

Understanding how to deal with challenges is a vital part of having healthy children.

Our bodies cause several physiological responses when we're threatened, including changes in heart rate, blood pressure, and stress hormones like cortisol.

When a young child is supported by nurturing relationships with adults, he learns to cope with daily challenges and returns to normal with his stress response system. Scientists refer to that as positive stress.

Tolerable stress occurs when more severe difficulties, such as a loved one's loss, a natural disaster, or an alarming injury, are buffered by caring adults who help the child adapt, mitigating the potentially harmful effects of abnormal stress hormone levels. Without adult intervention, stress is toxic when massive, regular, or sustained adverse experiences such as extreme poverty or persistent violence are encountered, as excessive cortisol interferes with the production of brain circuits. Toxic stress encountered early in life and familiar precipitants of toxic stress— such as poverty, abuse or neglect, abuse of parental substances or mental illness, and exposure to violence — can affect a person's physical and psychological health cumulatively. The more painful and damaging childhood experiences, the higher and more significant the likelihood of developmental delays, and other issues. Adults with more negative early childhood experiences are also more likely to experience health issues, including obesity, depression, heart disease, and diabetes.

## 7.2 Environmental Impact on Child's Brain Development

Human beings have had to be sensitive to their surroundings since the earliest times to survive, which means we have an innate awareness of our surroundings and are looking for environments with certain qualities. First of all, humans have a deep need for safety and security and look in their surroundings for those attributes. We're also looking for physical comforts, like a proper temperature environment.

Furthermore, we're searching for a mentally comfortable environment: for example, familiar surroundings, while providing the right amount of stimulus.

Nature, as compared to nurture, is a topic of the great debate that has been undergoing on for many years, with people on both sides of the trouble agreeing that both genetics and environment play a significant role in a person's growth.

There is no question that both sides of these points are valid, especially when it comes to brain development and learning in children. While genetics are factor when it comes to the pruning of brain and the reorganization of the brain structure, the setting in which a child is exposed during the early years when brain development is at its peak has an immense influence on the development of his brain. To further understand this, below is a look at various environmental factors and how they might impact a child's brain growth.

**Stimulants**

Stimulants are one of the significant environmental factors affecting the development of a child's brain and his / her ability to learn and understand. During the early years of childhood, when brain growth and development are at their height, the mind of a child should be continuously stimulated using audio and visual stimulants to activate synaptic changes and reconstruction of neural pathways that characterize brain growth. The audio and visual stimulants that are the source of these alterations are found in the environment of the child and include music, sound patterns, speech, pictures, decorations, displays, etc. These audio and visual stimulants have a significant impact on the development of their brain. Depriving an infant of sight, for example, can cause the neural pathways involved insight to develop improperly, leading to problems like congenital cataracts. While on the other hand, a child who is disclosed to various visual stimulants can create a sharp perception of the environment, which helps him/her to interact with the environment easily and to recognize and identify different objects quickly. In the case of auditory stimulants, the situation is also similar where an infant can learn to speak and understand speech more rapidly if they are regularly spoken to and exposed to other sounds.

### Drugs, contaminants, and diseases

Another significant environmental determinant that can have a substantial impact on a child's brain development is drugs, viruses, and toxins. Children who are open to (even before birth) to substances such as alcohol, nicotine (tobacco), and medications such as heroin and cocaine are at very high risk of slow brain development, leading to problems such as speech impairment, reduced mental abilities, poor language skills, low intelligence, and learning issues. Children who are open to numerous toxins such as lead, mercury, manganese, toxic solvents and other toxins found in their environment also face a high risk of developing cognitive problems such as poor memory formation, mental retardation, speech problems, hyperactivity, reduced IQ and poor motor skills. The case is also the same for children exposed to disease as different viruses and bacteria can have an important impact on the development of the brain by either hindering or lowering the rate of growth, thus affecting the ability of a child to learn and understand.

### Abuse and neglect

Abuse and neglect are part of a child's emotional environment and have been shown to have a very significant negative impact on the child's brain development and learning skills. According to several studies, due to the constant state of fear and insecurity in which these children live, physical abuse, emotional abuse, and neglect of children during their early childhood years has a devastating impact on their brain development. As a result, they are at a high risk of having mental, behavioral, social, physical, and academic issues during their childhood and even adulthood years.

### Love and emotional attachment

Love and emotional support from the other part of the loving environment to which a child may be exposed, and it also has a significant impact on the development of his or her brain. As seen from the abuse and neglect factor, the mind of a child is heavily influenced by the early-age emotional environment to which they are exposed. Unlike abuse and neglect, however, love and emotional support offer a positive influence by providing the children confidence and security and allowing them to develop a positive, loving environment. As a result, the brain develops quickly, healthily, flexibly, and in a variety of ways, and the child can obtain optimal cognitive functions. A loved child also acquires self-confidence, high self-esteem, and excellent social skills, and is thus capable of forming meaningful life relationships.

## 7.3 Brain Development Affected By Poverty

The stress of living in poverty affects the brains of children in ways similar to the effects of abuse. Many neglected children show high levels of stress, but there are an increase and decrease, said of the professor of psychology at the University of Wisconsin-Madison named Seth Polla. Poverty children may not reach those high levels of stress, but there is constant stress that never comes down. Pollak spoke about poverty neurobiology as part of the Sulzberger Distinguished Lecture Series presented by the Duke Center for Child and Family Policy. He and his colleagues looked at 823 brain scans of 431 children between the ages of 4 and 17 and lived in urban and rural areas. They found poverty affecting brain growth, and they can see the difference as early as infancy.

Children living in poverty have shown a different developmental trajectory as soon as age 2, recommending that the longer the child is open to an impoverished environment, the more significant the difference in brain development.

Also, the brain images of children living in poverty showed unusually high levels of cortisol— similar to those of children who were abused. That leads Pollak to believe the common denominator could be the stressful circumstances. The human brain is very adaptive, and human species are resilient. Poor children have a low level of approach to medical care, more exposure to toxins, more violence, and less inequality in income. If kids were only dealing with one thing, such as inadequate medical care, we would not see an effect. It's more than anyone can deal with having to deal with all of those factors. It is stressful, which ultimately inhibits developmental progress. Pollak said that the differences in brain growth and development could also impair educational achievement and executive function. A delay in the growth of the brain area that regulates problem-solving, attention, and judgment accounted for an achievement gap of 16 percent for high school students living below the federal poverty line. Similarly, a delay in the growth of the brain area, monitoring memory, emotion, and language accounted for a difference in the academic achievement of 21 percent. Consuming neuroscience to know that poverty is a relatively new method of research, and Pollak believes that this type of analysis can provide clues to targeting and refine youth interventions. No one likes child poverty-related outcomes. This scientific research indicates that poverty is not only a question of social policy but also of biomedicine.

## 7.4 Development Affected by Technology

Since media expansion to newer platforms, including cellphones and tablets, improved portability and connectivity has expanded the use of technology–not only for business professionals but for children. While television time is still the critical channel for children, clocking in at more than four hours per day on average.

According to a recent research study by the American Academy of Pediatrics, almost a third of the time is spent on a monitor, laptop, cell phone, and not in front of the television. What is also interesting is that mobile phones and tablets cannot be borrowed from a relative, considering that cell phone ownership among 12-to 17-year-olds has increased over the past decade, rising to an estimated 75 percent in 2004 to 45 percent of teenagers with their cell phones. Apart from watching television shows, preteens and adolescents most often use text to access social media. The question isn't whether children are increasingly exposed to technology–that's obvious–but what that exposure to technology means for childhood development. Many schools doll out smartphones for classroom events, while others are dolling out a fully technology-free environment. Although there have been influential voices in childhood development both for and against technology, it is essential to note that the impact of technology on childhood development may be more complicated than merely a "positive" or a "poor" phenomenon. Instead, we can collectively enhance the positive and work to reduce the negative by better understanding the overall effect.

## Effects of Technology on Child Development

### Harms Attention Spans

Perhaps the most frequently raised concern regarding children and technology is the impact on the span of attention. Research is backing this concern. In Psychology Today,

Jim Taylor, Ph.D., wrote that increased technology use could change the way children's brains are wired. Why? For what? Because unlike the mind of an adult, the spirit of a child still develops, and as a result, is malleable.

. When children are exposed to high-rates of technology, their brains may adopt an internet approach to thinking–quickly scanning and processing multiple information sources.

Brain development is particularly vulnerable to this, and where previous generations may have spent much more time reading, imagining, or participating in activities requiring focus attention. Brains in children open to the high intensity of technology may adapt to frequent visual stimulation, rapid change, and little need for imagination.

### Reduces Self-Soothing and Self-Regulation

Anyone who has raised an infant would recognize the beauty of distraction in soothing an infant in a tantrum. But parents today are always given an enticing entertainment: technology. And while a screaming preschooler may be soothing in the immediate handing over of a cellphone or laptop, the American Academy of Pediatrics notes that the intrusion of mobile devices may negatively affect the ability for children to learn how to soothe themselves and control in those moments.

### Increases Aggression

Multiple studies, including one conducted by the Seattle Children's Research Institute and the Youth and Adolescence Journal, found a correlation between simulated violence, often found in popular video games, and increased aggression. Exposure to violence has been found to make kids and teenagers more likely to argue with peers or teachers, and less empathic and impacted by actual violence.

### Physical Activity Stagnates

The time that is spent on technology means time spent sitting. Even with portable devices, the operation itself demands that users remain mostly still. Given the vast amount of time that children are reportedly spending with technology now, this also means that this sedentary activity has now primarily replaced active indoor or outdoor playtime. In extreme cases, when engaged in a video game or other media, children or teenagers may even forgo other fundamental activities, likely eating or sleeping.

## Hurts School Performance

Short periods of concentration can also affect how children take participate in the classroom. One experienced English teacher talked to the New York Times that because of cellphones and social media, students deprive of the attention span to read assignments alone. By watching YouTube, Facebook, Snapchat, texting, and e-mailing a bunch of abbreviations, you can't become a good writer. Technology habits the brains to continuously move between tasks, which may result in reduced spans of attention. Michael Rich, executive director of the Center for Media and Child Health in Boston, says that children's brains are rewarded for jumping to the next task rather than staying on the job, leading to "a generation of children in front of screens whose brains will be wired differently." Anecdotally, some teens admit that they prefer the immediate gratification provided by a quick video. Other scientific research recommends the availability of a computer can simply serve as a diversion, even if intended for educational purposes. In reality, Jacob L. Vigdor, an economics professor and researcher at Duke University, found that children most often used home computers for amusement rather than learning when left to themselves. Adult oversight is critical.

## Limits Interpersonal interactions

Leaning to distract children on a mobile device can reduce their interpersonal interactions.

Whether it's a need to reconcile with a friend or sibling, have fun on a long trip, or settle down at night,

if children are always armed with technology, they're never going to navigate an interconnection with a friend, parent or sibling that may be critical to solving the problem in the long run.

Technology may act as a distraction from problematic issues for older children and teens: not fitting in at school, parents fighting at home, etc. But rather than learning to navigate these issues, children and teens may find that technology can give shelter illusion–without arming them with the interpersonal skills needed to navigate uncomfortable adult life situations.

## Effects of Emotional Development

Even in the hands of only parents and careers, technology can have an impact on the development of childhood. Observation is the primary way children learn by listening to language learning, observing conversations, interpreting facial expressions, and watching how others handle emotional situations. Rampant screen time intentionally fades away, time connected with children that is critical to emotional development. A large dependency on technology to communicate hinders their people's skills for older children and teens and may even establish a sense of indifference from the feelings of others, according to the head of UCLA's memory and aging research Centre named Dr. Gary Small. The impact can be felt for young children as screen time replaces time previously devoted to playing, peer interaction, and exploration, which are thought to foster empathy, problem-solving skills, curiosity, intelligence, and listening skills, says Harvard-affiliated clinical psychologist Catherine Steiner-Adair. Boston University researchers also argue that the use of the mobile phone may prevent children from developing empathy, social skills, and problem-solving skills.

## Visual-Spatial Helps

In fact, according to Science Daily, video games have been proven to help improve peripheral visual skills. More generally, with the use of technology, the general visual-motor skills (tracking objects or visually looking for something) can develop.

## Helps Multi-Task

When appropriately implemented (as compared, for example, to driving and texting), a well-honed multi-task capacity brought about by the use of technology equips children with the abilities required for modern adult life, according to Psych Central.

**Aids Learning**

Internet users more frequently flex their brain decision-making and problem-solving functions and are more likely to handle quick cyber searches well. And, technology can present the next wave of vocational training for students who might not thrive on traditional academic subjects. The New York Times, for example, tells the story of Woodside High's audio class, filled with at-risk students engaged, engaged, involved, and learning. Not only is the technology-driven level inspiring students to show up, it provides job learning, and offers an opportunity to trigger interest in other topics. Besides, technology can support education in more traditional ways, including games to improve vocabulary, or through electronic books. Like with almost everything in existence, when implemented in moderation, technology is not a concern. Nonetheless, the numbers suggest that most have not yet reached the right healthy balance, as published rates are well above the standards of the American Academy of Pediatrics for electronic media. Given that the AAP recommends no access before age 2, and a limited 1-2 hours per day with entertainment media, it's secure to say that most kids surpass the limits suggested. We require to pursue a technology balance for our children, capitalize on the benefits, and mitigate the adverse effects of technology in the development of childhood.

## 7.5 Play deprivation can damage the childhood development of the brain

Individuals have similarities with extreme play-deprivation–especially young children who find themselves unable to play because, for example, they are caught up in conflicts, severe poverty, or abusive home environments. When these children do not play regularly, they may have real difficulty engaging with and healing from their encounters with the human community. That is because it is a sophisticated social and emotional learning experience that belongs to your social group, catalyzed by play. When they reach elementary school, children who are severely play-deprived may not have learned the complicated languages of the game that harmoniously combine the cognitive, emotional, physical, and social elements that are all necessary for personal skill in playing. Slowly occurs the social and emotional learning that allows for safe play among children.

A child who has not experienced good game early may overdo the process of playing, or may simply not know what is going on. These kids may get isolated or bullied, or they may become bullies. In later adult attitudes, the lingering effects of childhood play deficits echo about becoming a viable part of a community. Studies of rats reinforce the behavioral evidence around play-deprived children.

These experiments demonstrate the anatomical advantages of good play, which activates a wide range of genes in the prefrontal cortex.

This is the brain's executive area, which regulates rat decision-making as well as other social mammals, including humans. At Northwestern University, Jeffrey Burgdorf developed an experiment in which rats, aged between four and fifteen weeks, are engaged in rough and tumble play.

He discovered that between 300 and 1,200 genes had been activated in the prefrontal cortex after they had experienced the intense game. The late Jaak Panksepp, a play neuroscientist and co-author with Lucy Biven of' The Archaeology of the Mind,' proposed that play may trigger as many as 3,000 genes in the cortex. In short, play in the shaping of social brains seems essential. Rats don't work well if they don't play. They cannot make a distinction between friends and foes. They are not matting well, and in their responses to stress, they are less resilient than normal rats. "This work requires a more exceptional analysis. We still don't fully know the processes that release chemicals such as dopamine, endocannabinoids, opiates, and IGF-1 into the brain. Children who are severely play-deprived will tend to engage in automatic and repetitive activities without social involvement. A child who is deprived of play may have more explosive reactions to circumstances in later childhood, rather than a sense of belonging. They are often unoptimistic as adults and are subject to smoldering depression due to a lack of joy in their lives. We seem to be more politically set and confident in their social environments with little uncertainty. That's because playing promotes social and emotional learning and acceptance that ambiguity is part of complex interactions with people.

# Chapter 8: Importance of Nurturing Child's Mind

What a person learns during childhood or does not learn will influence his future abilities. What, then, is it that children need from their parents to become balanced, successful adults? Remember what some have found in recent decades, based on research undertaken. Advances in brain imaging technology enable scientists to study the development of the brain more in-depth than ever before. These studies indicate that early childhood is a crucial time to develop the brain functions that are required to handle information, express emotions normally, and become language proficient. "In the early year's brain connections are wired at an extremely rapid rate, as the brain landscape is formed by moment-to-moment experiences of genetic information and environmental stimuli. Scientists believe that most of those associations are made in the first few years of life, called synapses. According to Dr. T. Berry Brazelton, a child development specialist,

this is when "the potential future wiring of a baby for intelligence, sense of self, confidence, and enthusiasm for learning is set."

During the initial few years, a baby's brain is growing dramatically in size, structure, and function. Synaptic links multiply in an environment that is rich in stimuli and learning experiences, producing a large network of neural pathways within the brain. Such pathways make it possible to think, understand, and reason. It may be that the more reproduction an infant's brain gets, the more nerve cells are turned on, and the more associations between them are made.

This stimulation is interestingly not merely intellectual, acquired through exposure to facts, figures, or language. Scientists have found the need for emotional enhancement, too. Research suggests that infants who are not held and touched and who are not being played or stimulated will develop less of these synaptic ties.

## 8.1 Children Develop Cynicism at Early Stage

Kids might not be as gullible as we would imagine. A new study shows the roots of cynicism are appearing as early as an elementary school in adolescents. Studies found that children are already suspicious of the things people tell them that they are in their self-interest by the time they're in second grade. As adults, we understand that the self-interests of an individual, such as their desire to gain attention or fit in with their peers, may affect what they say and believe about the world, "says a researcher from a psychology graduate student at Yale University, Candice Mills, in a press release. Our research study shows that children may be more naive, innocent, and trusting than adults, but there are also seeds of doubt in an ear. In the report, which appears in the current issue of Psychological Science, researchers examined what age children are beginning to take a cynical view of what people are saying to them. Researchers included twenty children each in kindergarten, second grade, and fourth grade, and told them short stories in which the characters made statements in or against their interests.

They found kids in kindergarten more likely to believe claims of self-interest in character. But by second-grade kids were already more critical and recognized that statements made in someone's self-interest might not be right. We question individuals who make statements in compliance with self-interest while growing their confidence in individuals who make statements against self-interest.

Researchers in the second part of the study asked the children which of three factors could cause somebody to make a false statement: deliberate deceit (lying), unintentional bias, or a simple mistake. Children of younger ages were more likely to think that lying was the best explanation for self-interest claims, whereas, in terms of being a mistake, they clarified incorrect statements against self-interest. Bias, as a possible explanation, was rarely supported by kindergarteners through fourth graders. Nevertheless, sixth-graders acknowledged both bias and lies as possible factors behind false statements made in an individual's self-interest. The authors write in this task that in a way, young children tend to be even more cynical than adults, assuming that people will intentionally mislead others even when they are not. There can be many causes for a cynic or pessimistic outlook, and symptoms of depression or anxiety can appear alongside them. For the latter, it may be a kind of defense mechanism to be cynic about a method or situation, a way to plan for the worst. And that can be both efficient and productive in some cases. From an evolutionary psychological perspective, most likely to succeed were our ancient predecessors, who always planned for the worst. The worst in those days was a predator attack, and the risk was serious damage or death. But the consequences are much less serious for our children today, and so that strategy serves little to no purpose. And start talking to your kids, and try to find out why they are and pessimistic and where they come from.

The first step is to try and understand where that cynicism could come from. There are many feasible causes. You know your child's attitude and behavior than anyone else and are likely in the leading and finest position to influence which of the following profiles most accurately describes his or her situation.

A cynic attitude may sometimes be embedded in the natural inborn temperament of a child.

Many children are easy-going; others are having difficulty adapting to transition. Some are aggressive and dominant, while others tend to be quieter and introvert.

Similarly, some kids have a naturally sunny disposition, while others are inclined to focus on life's wild side. The first group considers the glass half full, and the second half empty. Some studies indicate that those temperamental variations have an active genetic component. This is a consideration that you'll want to carefully consider when trying to get a handle on the attitude and behavior of your family. Hippocratic medicine and medieval psychology's four "touches of humor"–choleric (dominant, passionate, idealistic), confident –while not strictly "scientific" in the modern sense, may provide useful categories for thinking about distinctive personality types Your son may simply have a classic temperament for melancholy. But while character and biology can play an essential role in such a situation, environmental influences can be responsible as well.

To put it another way, children can learn that the people around them are negative. If mum and dad are serious about addressing this issue, they should start by questioning themselves some fair things. Could it be that they have restructured this kind of behavior and attitude towards their children? If you don't see yourself pessimistic now, might either you or your spouse have been discouraged or going through a particularly low point of life when your son was a baby and a mother? If not, could it be that you have made the mistake of reinforcing his anger by giving in and coddling his complaints? Perhaps your child did this in his early and younger age and see the effects only now.

Whether the issue is temperamental or environmental, you can fix it by making some changes to the style and methods of your parenting. Work on removing your child's moaning habit by avoiding him when he is negative. Don't give up on his dull mood.

When he begins to sob and moan about something, don't shower him with praise. When he talks about his day at school, or the birthday party he missed, or some activity he's just been involved in, tell him you're sorry he feels like that and then go about your business. Don't prolong debate. Only going on. While on the other hand, when your son says something encouraging or displays the slightest bit of excitement, you can reinforce the action by smiling, thanking him and letting him know how much you appreciate his upbeat attitude. You could even start rewarding him for positive statements and behavior by putting a star diagram on the fridge door and adding a sticker whenever he says or does something that brightens your day. That said, you should probably consider another possibility. There is a possibility that the negative attitude of your son might be clarified in terms of both factors including physical ones and biological ones. There is a psychiatric situation termed as dysthymia, which is in reality a low-grade depression of a long-term type. It is often characterized by a low level of energy, a lack of interest in life and even a recurrent pessimistic outlook.

## 8.2 Impact of Cynicism on Child's Life

Cynicism is part of a defensive stance we take to guard ourselves. It's typically triggered when children feel hurt or angry at something, and they allow them to fester and skew our outlook instead of addressing those emotions directly.

As child become pessimistic in their lives about one thing, they can slowly start turning everything on. When they become cynical, they often indulge in self-righteous attitudes and form expectations that individuals should behave in a certain way. Many of child's pessimistic emotions come up when they feel vulnerable.

Children are far more likely to react by toughening up and becoming aggressive at times when they feel helpless and are let down. Greater vulnerability to cynicism can be a sure sign they have turned themselves on. When they get into that state of mind, they often see those around them through the same critical filter we see ourselves through.

This "critical inner voice" is often directed at us, telling children that they are not good enough or will not fit in. Yet this inner critic's harsh judgement can be quickly reflected outwards on the people around a cynic child. They may tend to see someone from our closest friend to a distant relative solely because of their failures and fail to have compassion for their own problems and distractions. Since pessimistic and skeptical attitudes build a negative lens through which child view his environment, he tend to miss out on the joys in life when he is in this state.

They engage in a mentality of "us versus them" which pins us against some person or group. Distorting people is simple, and making a caricature of their faults. When we do this, it's worth asking ourselves, "Whose perspective is coming through? Is that how I really feel, or am I overreacting based on old feelings from my past?

" Such comparisons aren't always easy to make, but very often, our negative views mirror those of influential figures from our history. Such negativity can be infectious and can drag those around us down. It will cause us to alienate others, behave in a hostile way or become self-protective and alienated. In the end, being straightforward, unprotected and helpless is always in our own self-interest, rather than being mean or writing off men. The only person we are allowed to control is ourselves. When we become cynical we are the ones that are suffering.

## 8.3 Importance of Nurturing Child's Mind at Early Stage

They're developing brains. Experiences face by people in their early childhood have a profound effect on brain development— influencing learning, well-being, behavior, and, eventually, adult social relationships and earnings. Yet in the way we are trying to care for their bodies, we could do more to care for the young children's brains. Early years investment is one of the most effective and efficient investments a country can make to eradicate extreme poverty, improve shared prosperity, and build the human capital required to diversify and develop economies. The increasingly global digital world places even higher premiums on the capacities that derive from early childhood, such as the ability to reason, constantly learn, communicate effectively, and cooperate with others. Any people who don't early learn these skills and don't develop them through childhood and adolescence are likely to be left behind more. They know millions of young children are not achieving their full potential because of insufficient nutrition, lack of early stimulation, restricted early learning opportunities, and stress exposure.

Scientific findings from a variety of disciplines have demonstrated over the last three decades that the most critical elements of infant, adolescent, and adult health, well-being, and productivity take shape during the early years and especially the first 1000 days.

By the time a baby is born, the brain has all the cells and neurons, and by the age of two, massive numbers of neuronal connections are created that are later cut based on which they are most widely used The ideal environment encourages brain development, whereas a harmful climate inhibits growth in the short term but also in the long run.

Throughout pregnancy, for example, undernutrition, leading to low birth weight, increases the risk of chronic adult illnesses. Extreme poverty-related deprivation may result in reduced treatment by overworked, overwhelmed, and demoralized caregivers. The psychological and neurological growth of young children is compromised by constant trauma, without prospects for rehabilitation or healing.

Children who do not receive the treatment needed to enable their ability to quadruple, are less healthy, develop poorly, learn less, and achieve fewer grades at school, are more likely to have problems related to others with trust, and earn less as adults. As adults, they are expected to draw nearly a third less than their peers' average annual income without interference. It makes betting on their futures more difficult for them and their families, leading to crippling cycles of poverty between generations. Those individual costs aggregate throughout society, restricting the creation of wealth and eroding national earnings. As an outcome of the high level of pressure of weak early childhood growth and development, it is projected that some countries spend less on health than they are predicted to lose in the future. Fundamental learning skills and personal-social skills are learned at a young age, and the following qualifications are built upon these foundations. In the early years, preventive and promotive strategies accomplish more and cost less than later-age therapeutic approaches. In countries across the socio-economic spectrum, on-going studies show that nutritional and psycho-social programs introduced in the initial years of life have important benefits for health and well-being, employment and earnings, personal relationships, and social life.

# 9: Conclusion

Nurturing care consists of five components: wellness, education, safety and security, early learning, and sensitive treatment. Children need all five areas of nursing care to understand their capacity for success. Many health and nutrition programs, as well as safety and security policies, are already in place in many countries, but there is a need to expand their scope and efficiency. Their importance from birth to encourage the development of human capital should be recognized. The emphasis on early learning, responsive care, and the mental health of careers in the current framework is new. As we grow older, the brain becomes increasingly complex, and while new connections continue to be made, the brain is only built once, and under exceptional conditions. Nurturing care is the set of circumstances that provide the best care for young children. This refers to a stable environment created by parents and cares with help from policies, programs, and communities that ensures good health and nutrition for children, protects them from risks, provides them with opportunities for early learning through emotionally supportive and sensitive interactions. Nursing is essential for child development and lays the foundation for life-long health and well-being and creates human capital in today's child, tomorrow's adolescent and adult, and in the future into the next generation. For successful implementation of early childhood development policies, programs, and services, evaluation and transparency are essential to track threats, engagement, resources, and effects. Sound monitoring systems need to cover inputs, outputs, and results comprehensively, and be the responsibility of stakeholders across all industries. Data collection, interpretation, and reporting metrics, resources, and processes need to be made available and streamlined.

A catalyst for continuous improvement will be the regular compilation of relevant data in health and other programs, complemented by frequent in-depth and valid assessments.

# Danish Way of Parenting

*Discover the Parenting Secrets of the Happiest People in the World*

**By Samuel Pattinson**

© **Copyright 2020 by (Samuel Pattinson) - All rights reserved.**

This document is geared towards providing exact and reliable information in regards to the topic and issue covered. The publication is sold with the idea that the publisher is not required to render accounting, officially permitted, or otherwise, qualified services. If advice is necessary, legal or professional, a practiced individual in the profession should be ordered.

- From a Declaration of Principles which was accepted and approved equally by a Committee of the American Bar Association and a Committee of Publishers and Associations.

In no way is it legal to reproduce, duplicate, or transmit any part of this document in either electronic means or in printed format. Recording of this publication is strictly prohibited and any storage of this document is not allowed unless with written permission from the publisher. All rights reserved.

The information provided herein is stated to be truthful and consistent, in that any liability, in terms of inattention or otherwise, by any usage or abuse of any policies, processes, or directions contained within is the solitary and utter responsibility of the recipient reader. Under no circumstances will any legal responsibility or blame be held against the publisher for any reparation, damages, or monetary loss due to the information herein, either directly or indirectly.

Respective authors own all copyrights not held by the publisher.

The information herein is offered for informational purposes solely, and is universal as so. The presentation of the information is without contract or any type of guarantee assurance.

The trademarks that are used are without any consent, and the publication of the trademark is without permission or backing by the trademark owner. All trademarks and brands within this book are for clarifying purposes only and are the owned by the owners themselves, not affiliated with this document.

# Introduction

Denmark, a small country in northern Europe known for the fairy tale by Hans Christian Andersen, The Little Mermaid, has been selected by the OECD (Organization for Economic Cooperation and Development) nearly every year since 1973 as the happiest people in the world. It's has been more than forty years since the happiest people in the world are regularly chosen! When you stop thinking about it for a second, it's a tremendous achievement. Even the latest United Nations Global Happiness Survey found Denmark at the top of the list every year since its launch. What is the secret to their success?

Countless papers and experiments were devoted to the resolution of this puzzle. Denmark? Denmark? What Denmark? Why Denmark? The documentary on this was entitled "The Discovery for Happiness" for 60 minutes. Oprah said, "Why are the Danes so happy?" And the findings are always inconclusive. Is it the scale of your social system, your houses or your government? It can't be high taxes, or the long, cold winters, so what does that give?

The United States, on the other hand, is not even among the top ten in its "pursuit of happiness" statement. It's just in the top 20, close to 17 after Mexico. Although we have a whole psychological area dedicated to the happiness and an infinite sea of self-help books, which tell us how to reach this mysterious condition, we are not so happy. Why is it? So, in fact, why are the Danes so happy?

I eventually discovered the secret of the Danes people. And the reason is in their upbringing, very obviously.

The Danish philosophy behind parenthood and their way of bringing up children produce some powerful results: resilient, emotionally safe, happy children who become resilient, emotionally secure and happy grown-ups who then reiterate this strong parenthood with their own children. The legacy is continued for over forty years.

Through exciting journey of discovery, I have decided to share with you this experience of the "Danish way." In this step-by-step guide, my goal is to help mothers and fathers who are about to start on or have started one of the most demanding and exceptional jobs in the world. It takes practice, persistence, determination and knowledge to implement this approach, but the results are worth the effort. Remember it's your legacy. Please read this book carefully if you want to create the happiest people in the world. The real secret to the prosperity of the Danes lies inside.

# Chapter 1: Our Default Settings (P.A.R.E.N.T)

For time to time, we've all pondered what it takes to be a dad. Whether it's before your first child's birth, a kid's meltdown, or a fight over your kid's not eating his or her peas at the dinner table, and we've all once thought, "Do I do that right? "Many of us are pointing to books and the Internet, or we're looking about advice and support for friends and family. Most of us just want to be told we really do things the right way.

Yet hast thou ever considered what the right way is? Where do we get our ideas about parenting the right way? If you go to Italy at nine p.m., you'll see kids eating dinner. Running playing around in restaurants until nearly midnight; kids in Norway are routinely left outside in less than twenty degrees to sleep; running children in Belgium are allowed to drink beer. Some of these actions sound strange to us, but it's the "right" path for these people.

Such tacit agreed assumptions we have about how to raise our children are what Sara Harkness, a professor of human development at Connecticut University, calls "parental ethno-theories." She's been researching this phenomenon across societies for decades, and what she's discovered is that these fundamental views about the right way to parent are so rooted in our environment. It just seems to us like things are the way they are.

And so, most of us have been thinking about what being a parent means, but have you ever thought about what it means to be an American parent? About how we wear colorful American glasses and desire to see what is "the right way"?

What if we take off those glasses for a moment and would we see? If we stared back and looked away at the U.S., what would be our impression?

## 1.1 An Epidemic of Stress

I have seen a growing problem with the happiness level of people across the board. According to the National Center for Health Statistics, antidepressant have been used by 40% of American between 2005 and 2008. Kids are being treated with medicine and recommended for a growing number of psychological disorders, some with no specific diagnosis process. For 2010 alone, there were at least 5.2 million children taking Ritalin for attention deficit disorder between the ages of three and seventeen.

They are battling obesity and early puberty initiation, or "precocious adolescence," as it is now called. Girls and boys as young as seven and eight have testosterone injections pumped to delay the puberty. Most of us don't really doubt this as odd; rather, it's just the way things are. "My daughter gets the kill," one mother stressed around her eight-year-old, who she felt hit puberty too fast, nonchalantly.

Most adults, without even knowing it, are overly aggressive with themselves, their children and other people. Not all people are like that, of course, nor do they want to be, but they can also feel pressured to live in this aggressive society. The vocabulary around them can be loud and intimidating, putting people on the defensive:

"At soccer, Kim is just amazing. The coach says she is among the teams brightest. Yet despite basketball, karate and diving she still gets straight A's. How she does it, I don't care! What's Olivia up to? How do they do? "We feel pressure to perform to deliver with our children, to do well in school, and to satisfy our perception of what a good child should be, what a successful parent should be. The degree of uncertainty is often high, and we feel judged by others and by ourselves.

This is part of human nature, and part of that is what it is to be American. What pushes us as a society to perform and compete, and be successful to a standard that does not ultimately seem to make us as adults very happy? What if some of the "answers" that we have are faulty to raise our children our parenting norms?

What if we discovered the glasses we wore had the wrong prescription, and we couldn't see things as clearly as we thought? We'd remove the glasses, fix our view and look at our planet again. We'd come across things looking different! The question arises simply when attempting to see life from a new perspective, through new lenses: Is there a better way?

Maria's and Joseph Story

I discovered from my friend Maria and from her Danish husband Joseph a philosophy of raising children which opened my eyes and completely changed my life. Happy children grow up into happy adults raising happy children, and so on. My good friend Joseph and I have been discussing the proposal. Joseph is a Danish psychotherapist with many years of experience working with families and children and we asked the question together: "Is there a Danish way of parenting?" To her knowledge, that was not the case. For some literature on the subject we looked high and low but there was nothing. She had never heard of a "Danish Way" during all her years of working in the Danish school system and being a family psychotherapist. She knew all the academic theories and research into parenting practices, many of which she used on a daily basis in her family life, but could there be a distinctive parenting style embedded in her very own culture that she had not seen?

# 1.2 Examining Our "Default Settings"

The other day Maria and her almost-three-year-old son were in the area. He was on a push-bike with no brakes, so he began pushing himself out into the street amid her several crying to him to stop. She ran frenzied after him, grabbing him by the neck and shaking him. She has been we sometimes forget that parenting is a verb, like love.

Furious and afraid, and he was about to scream, "If I tell you to stop, you'd better stop!" Maria could see that she was going to cry out of panic, and at that time, it took all her courage to collect the energy to go out and see what she was doing. She did not want to react like that. She scanned her mind for a different way, and there was an answer, miraculously. She paused, took a breath, and lowered to his floor. She held his arms and imploringly stared into his eyes. She said in a calm but concerned voice, "Want to go ow-ow? Mum doesn't want to go ow-ow! Look at those cars? "She was looking at the vehicles and smiling." Ow-ow cars go to Sebastian! "He smiled, then waited. "Motorcars. Ow-ow,' he repeated.

"That's how you stop when Mommy says to stop, Ok? So that you don't leave the cars ow-ow. "He nodded. In the end, he did not cry. They kissed, and Maria could sense on her shoulder, smiling at him. "Motorcars. Ow-ow. "They'd been at another crosswalk five minutes later. Maria kept telling him to stop, and he did. He pointed to the lane, shaking his head. "Cars ow-ow." She told him how pleased she was when she stood and knocked.

Not only was she pleased with him for leaving, you see. She was also happy with herself for stopping for stopping herself in a difficult moment and changing her natural behavior, her default settings. It wasn't easy, but doing so turned a tense and potentially explosive situation into a happy and secure one, and the outcome made both of them happier.

They occasionally forget that parenting is a verb, like marriage. To yield positive returns, it requires effort and work. Being a good parent requires an incredible amount of self-awareness. This demands that we look at what we are doing when we are tired and stressed and strained to our limits. Such behaviors are considered our "normal settings." The actions and reactions we have are our default settings when we are too lazy to choose a better way.

Our parents inherit most of our default settings. They're drilled into us and programmed like a machine motherboard. These are the industrial environments that we resort to when we are at the edge of our wit and not thinking; our culture has built them within us. It is when we hear ourselves saying things that we really don't want to be doing. It is when we behave and respond in situations that we aren't aware that we want to act and react. It's when we feel bad, and we know deep down that there's an easier way to get results from our babies, but we're not sure what it is. Anyone who has children understands the feeling.

That's why looking at the default settings, learning them and knowing them, is so critical. What do you like about how you interact with your children and how you react? What is it you don't like? What do you do is just a continuation of your own upbringing? What is it you want to change? And when you see what your parent's natural inclinations are your favorite settings can you determine how you want them to change for the better.

We'll allow you to see what some of those positive changes can be in the chapters that follow. Using the easy-to-remember acronym PARENT play, authenticity, reframing, empathy, no ultimatums, and juxtaposition we'll examine some of the tried-and-true methods that have been working for parents in Denmark for over 40 years.

Increasing our awareness of ourselves and taking conscious decisions about our actions and reactions are the first steps towards a powerful change in life. So we're better parents and better people. And this is how we build a well-being culture that can be carried on to the next generations. Is there a bigger gift you can bestow on your children than helping them grow up healthier? Healthy and more resilient adults? We don't believe that. So we believe that you will agree.

# Chapter 2: Play

## 2.1 P Is for Play

Have you found that the urge to coordinate events for your children is unspoken, or even spoken? Whether it's the pool, dance, T-ball, or soccer, if you don't have your kids sign up for at least three to four events a week, you just don't feel like you're doing your job. However, many times do you hear parents say they take up their Saturday by taking their children to various sports, lessons, or activities?

In comparison, when was the last time you heard anyone say, "My daughter will be playing on Saturday"?

And by "play," we don't mean playing the violin or playing a sport, or even going to a playdate where adults arrange events. We say "play" in which they are left to their own devices, with a partner or alone, to play for as long as they want, just as they see fit. And even though parents allow this free play to take place, there is often a nagging sense of guilt to accept it. Because in the end, we feel we're better parents by teaching them something, involving them in a sport, or giving some input to their little brains. Gaming often seems like a waste of worthwhile learning time. But are they?

The number of hours children are allowed to play in the United States in the past fifty years has dramatically decreased. Aside from TV and electronics, there is also the concern of parents that children will get injured combined with a need to "create" them all these considerations take much of the opportunity they once had to play.

As parents, when our children show visible signs of progress, we feel comforted. Parents like to watch them play soccer while others egg them on, or go to their piano or dance recitals. We're proud to say Billy won a medal or prize, or learned a new tune, or can read the Spanish alphabet. It makes us feel good parents. They do it with the best intentions, as they give them more guidance and organized opportunities and teach them to become more positive, productive people. Or do we?

The prevalence of anxiety disorders, insomnia, and concentration issues has skyrocketed in the U.S. is no wonder. Is it true that we leave our kids nervous by not encouraging them to play more without knowing it?

Are we over Programming Our Kids' Lives?

Most parents aim to get their kids started early at school or skip a grade. Children learn to read and do math's earlier and earlier, and we are proud that they are "smart" and that being smart or athletic is highly valued in American culture. Through tutors and fun equipment and programmers, we can go to great lengths to try to get them there. Progress is progress, and these signs are real, noticeable and observable. Free play sounds enjoyable for all intents and purposes but what does it actually tell them?

What if we told you free play gave kids less anxiety? It imparts endurance to them. Yet endurance has proved to be one of the key factors in forecasting success as an adult. In a healthy, functioning adult, the ability to "bounce back," regulate emotions and cope with stress is a key trait. They now know that resilience is important to avoid anxiety and depression, and for years, the Danes have been instilling it in their children. And one way they've done, that is by putting a lot of focus on the story.

In Denmark, which dates back to 1871, husband and wife Niels and Erna Juel-Hansen came up with the first developmental theory-based pedagogy that integrated play. We found that free play is important to the development of a child. In reality, Danish kids were not even allowed to begin school for many years before they were seven. Instructors and people who set the agenda for children's schools didn't want them to get involved in education because they felt kids should be kids, and play first and foremost.

Even now, at two p.m., children are ten years old, and regular school is under completion. And then have the option of going to what is known as "free-time school" (skolefritidsordning) for the rest of the day, where they are often encouraged to play. Splendid but real!

Throughout Denmark, the focus is not exclusively on schooling or sports but on the whole child. Parents and teachers concentrate on things such as socialization, individuality, unity, equality and self-esteem. We want their kids to learn endurance and to grow a strong inner compass to lead them through life. We know that their children will be well educated and that they will learn other skills. Yet true happiness doesn't only come from a good education. A kid who learns to cope with stress makes friends, and yet is pragmatic about the future, for instance, has a set of life skills which are very different from being a math genius. And the Danes speak about all aspects of life through life skills, not just work-life. For what is a master in mathematics without being able to cope with the ups and downs of life? All the Danish parents we talked to have said they find it very odd to rely constantly on bullying young children.

As they see it, if children are always performing to get something good grades, awards, or praise from teachers or parents then they're not getting their inner drive developed.

We believe that children fundamentally need room and confidence to allow them to learn issues on their own, to build and solve their own problems. It promotes genuine self-esteem and self-reliance because it comes from someone else's own internal cheerleader of the kid.

## 2.2 Internal vs. External Locus of Control

In psychology, this internal cheerleader or drive is called the control locus. In Latin, the word locus means "place" or "location," and thus the locus of control simply refers to the degree to which a person feels he has a sense of control over his own life and the events that affect him. Thus, persons with an internal control locus believe they have the power to control their lives and the things that happen to them. Their drive is internal, or personal; from within comes their place of control. Those with an external locus of control assume that external factors such as the world or destiny control their lives, which they have no power over, regulate. That makes them arrives from without, so they can't change it. We are all influenced by our environment, history, and social status, but the distinction between internal and external locus of control is how much we believe we can control our lives given those influences.

Research has shown consistently that infants, teenagers, and adults with a high external control locus are predisposed to anxiety and depression they become nervous when they feel they have little or no control over their life, and they become distressed when that sense of helplessness becomes too intense.

Research also shows that in the last fifty years, there has been a dramatic shift toward a more centralized influence locus for young people.

Psychologist Jean M. Twenge and colleagues looked over a fifty-year period for results from a test called the Children's Nowicki-Strickland Internal-External Control Scale. This test measures whether an individual has an inside or an outside control locus. The researchers found that in children of all ages, from primary school to college, there was a dramatic shift from an internal to an external locus of control. To give you an idea of how great a shift it was, in 1960, youth were 80 per cent more likely to claim that parents in Denmark would not try to intervene unless it was absolutely necessary.

They had control over their lives in 2002 compared with children who were more likely to say they lacked such personal control.

And what was even more striking being that the trend for elementary school kids was more pronounced than for middle and college kids. So there is a loss of control over their lives with younger and younger girls. Earlier and earlier, they experience a sense of helplessness. Over the years, this rise in external control locus has a linear correlation with the rise of depression and anxiety in our society. What could this change cause?

**Giving Kids the Space to Learn and Grow**

A concept called "proximal growth" is fundamental to the Danish parenting philosophy, first proposed by the Russian developmental psychologist Lev Vygotsky. It basically states that, with the right amount of help, a child needs the right amount of space to learn and grow in the ways that suit him or her.

Consider helping a child climb a fallen log in the forests. If he needs a hand at first, you give a hand, but then maybe just a finger to help him over, and when the time is right, you let him go. You don't move him or pull him over.

Parents in Denmark seek not to interfere unless it is absolutely necessary. Parents trust their kids to be able to do and try new things and give them room to develop their own self-confidence. In their growth, parents provide them with scaffolding to help them build their self-esteem, which is very necessary for the "whole person." When children feel so stressed, they will lose the excitement in what they do, and this can lead to fear and anxiety. Instead, Danish parents try to meet kids where they feel safe trying a new talent, then encourage them and invite them to go further or try something new while it still feels fun and strange.

Having this room and maintaining the proximal growth zone helps children to develop both maturity and confidence in their internal control locus as they know that they are in charge of their own problems and progress. Kids who are forced or pulled too much fear having an unconscious feedback locus because they do not control their development; then, there are external factors, and the foundation for their self-esteem is weak.

They often believe they help kids by forcing them to succeed or learn faster, but leading them in the right moment in their growth will produce even better results not only because of the learning itself, which will certainly be more pleasurable but because the kids will be more confident of the mastering of their talents because they are more in control of gaining them.

British researcher David Elkind agrees. For example, children who are forced to read earlier can read better than their peers at first, but those rates even out in a couple of years ' time and at what cost? In the long run, forced kids show higher levels of anxiety and lower self-esteem.

In the U.S., we find endless books on how fear and depression can be raising or diminished.

They want to reduce tension at all costs for our children in particular. Most parents helicopter over their kids and interfere with securing them at the time of the moment. Most of us are barricading staircases and securing and locking up anything we might find remotely dangerous. If we don't, we sound like we're bad parents and we're actually judging and being criticized by others for not doing enough to defend them. Many days need so many gizmos and inventions to be covered that one wonders how twenty years ago, children survived.

Not only do we want to protect our kids from tension, but we also want to develop their self-confidence and make them feel special too. The standard method of doing so is to congratulate them for trivial accomplishments, even unnecessarily. But in our attempt to increase confidence and reduce stress, in the long term, we could simply set them up for more stress. Creating self-esteem rather than trust is like making a nice house with little base. We both know what happens when the wolf arrives big bad.

**But How Can Play Help?**

For years, scientists have studied playing in animals, trying to understand its evolutionary purpose. So one thing they find is that gaming is key to understanding how to cope with stress. In studies done on domestic rats and rhesus monkeys, scientists found that these animals were stressed out as adults when they were deprived of playmates during a critical stage in their development. We would overreact to challenging situations and couldn't manage social settings well. They would either respond with extreme terror, fleeing often trembling into a corner or with intense anger, lashing out in frustration. The lack of play was probably the culprit, as they behaved more naturally and coped better as adults when the animals were allowed a playmate for even an hour a day.

Fight-or-flight behaviors that are normally experienced in play activate the same neurochemical brain pathways as stress. When you see dogs running around chasing each other for fun, think about it. Most animals participate in this kind of play, taking the position of subordinate or antagonist in a play fight, causing some form of tension. We know that introducing baby animals' brains to stress affects them in a way that makes them less susceptible to stress over time, making their brains better at controlling stress as they mature. Their ability to cope is constantly improving by play, and they are able to deal with increasingly difficult circumstances. You see, endurance isn't developed by escaping pain, but by learning how to master and control it.

Should we strip away the ability of our children to control the tension by not permitting them to play enough? Looking at the number of anxiety disorders in our culture and diagnosis of depression, one asks if something is wrong. As one of someone with an anxiety disorder's biggest reported fears is losing control over one's emotions, we can't help but ask: if we stand back and let our kids play more, will they be more resilient and happier adults? We believe that the answer is yes.

## 2.3 Play and Coping Skills

In a pilot study carried out at a child development center in Massachusetts on preschool children, researchers wanted to measure whether there was a positive correlation between the level of playfulness in preschoolers and their coping skills. Using a playfulness test and a coping inventory,

the investigators cross-checked the playfulness of the children and the quality of their coping skills.

What they observed was a direct positive link between the level of playfulness in children and their ability to cope. The more they played the more they got to learn social skills and engage in social / play contexts the more they coped. This prompted the researchers to conclude that playing had a direct impact on all their ability to adapt to life.

Another research, conducted by Professor Louise Hess of occupational therapy and colleagues at a health center in Palo Alto, California, sought to explore the association between playfulness and coping skills in adolescent boys. We also researched young boys naturally and those with emotional issues. As in the analysis of childhood, there was a strong and important link between the degree of playfulness and their ability to cope for both classes of students. The researchers concluded that play could be used to enhance coping skills, especially the ability to adapt and more flexibly approach issues and goals.

That does make sense. Look outside just to see kids swinging from the bars or climbing trees or jumping from the top. We are monitoring dangerous situations, and nobody knows the right dosage or how to treat it but the kid himself. But it's important that they feel the dose of stress they can handle is in control. That in itself makes them feel better at managing their lives. The same is true of young animals and primates. We deliberately put themselves in dangerous situations, diving and hanging from trees as we twist and turn to make it difficult to land. We hear about anxiety and how to cope with it. As mentioned earlier, it is the same as the battle for games. To understand the emotional complexities of both, the animals put themselves in both the subordinate and the intruder roles.

Socio-situations are also overwhelming for youngsters. Social play will offer rivalry as well as teamwork. Fear and anger are just a few of the feelings a kid has to learn to cope with in order to continue playing.

There is no such thing in play as receiving undue acclaim. Regulations need to be discussed and renegotiated, and players need to be mindful of the other players' mental state to avoid someone getting upset and leaving, and if too many players leave, the game is over. Since children simply want to play with each other, these situations require them to practice getting along with others as equals a critical later life ability for satisfaction.

Play is so important to the Danish concept of youth that many Danish schools have programs in place to allow all students to learn by activities, play, and exercise. For starters, Play Patrol focuses on the younger elementary school students and is encouraged by the older ones. These student-led programs encourage young and older students to play various activities such as hide-and-seek, firefighter, or pet family and encourage shy, lonely children to join the game as well. For different age groups, this form of enjoyable and imaginative play allows children to test themselves in a way they don't want with their parents or teachers. This significantly reduces bullying and fosters social skills and self-control.

**The Truth behind Lego and Playgrounds**

Almost everyone has heard of Lego and has played at least once in their lives with the iconic colorful building blocks. At the turn of the millennium, Lego, apparently one of the most famous toys in existence, was dubbed "the invention of the century" by Fortune magazine. Initially made of wood, Lego has never forgotten its simple understanding of building blocks. Like the proximal construction region, Lego will work for all ages. When the kid is willing to take the next step towards a more difficult building, Legos are designed for that. It's a perfect way to play with your child and help her slowly learn a new level. She will play on her own or with friends; she has spent countless hours playing with Lego around the globe.

Many people don't know about Lego the interesting fact is that it's from Denmark. Built-in 1932 by a Danish carpenter in his studio, it was dubbed Lego as a contraction of the words leg godt, meaning "play well." Even then, the notion of openly using creativity was in full bloom.

Another of the largest play facilitator providers in the world is another Danish company named Kompan. This produces natural playgrounds that have received multiple architecture awards in favor of children's play for their usability, consistency and functionality. The organization's mission has been to promote healthy play as important to children's learning. His first park was unintentionally built more than forty years ago when a young Danish artist found that his colorful art installation, which was designed to brighten up a drab housing complex, was used more by children to play on than by adults.

Kompan is now the world's number one manufacturer to the playground. It's interesting and quite revealing that the world leader in both indoor and outdoor play equipment is a nation of just five million people.

And note that this is their way of learning how much tension they will handle the next time you see your kids swing from the trees, leap off some rocks or play fighting with their mates and you want to try to save them. If they play in a group with some tough kids and you want to defend them, note that they are developing self-control and negotiating skills to keep the game alive with all sorts of different personalities. That is their way to test their own abilities and improve process adaptability skills. The more they play, the more resilient they become and become socially adept. It is an incredibly natural process. The building block for the construction of an empire of future happiness is able to leg godt or "play well."

## 2.4 Tips for Play

- Turn the TV and the electronics off! Imagination is an essential ingredient for the positive effects of play.

- Creating an enriching environment Studies show that a sensory-rich environment combined with play allows the brain to expand cortically. Using a variety of materials in which all the senses can be stimulated visual, auditory, tactile, etc. improves brain development through practice.

- Using creativity to expand the minds of children when they do make art. So don't teach them how to do it just set out the art supplies and let them spontaneously make them.

- Let them explore outdoors. Get them out to play in nature as much as possible the forests, the forest, the beach, wherever they may be. Try to find safe areas where you have no doubt of letting them be open and explore the world. These are ways they can use their imaginations and really have fun.

- Mix children of different ages try matching your kids with kids of different ages. This strengthens the proximal growth region, allowing one to promote learning for the other, ultimately encouraging each to reach a new level. Children learn to both lead in the game as well as work with older ones in this way. We learn to take part and contest the game as well. It teaches the necessary skills of self-control and persuasion in life.

- Let them be safe to forget the shame that they don't need any experience or unique toys guided by adults. The more you can let them have power over their own games, use their creativity, and do it on their own, the better they will get at it. The skills which they learn are invaluable. We are so caught up in thinking about how many organized activities our kids are involved in, or what they are talking about, that we forget the importance of encouraging them to play safe. Stop feeling guilty about letting them play does not mean you're a dad. All they miss is free play!

- Be true. If you want to play with your baby, in what you do, you have to be 100 per cent honest. Don't worry about looking foolish. Let them guide. Don't care what people think of you, or what you think of yourself. Sit down to their level and try letting go for just twenty minutes a day if that's hard for you. Even at their stage, a little playtime is worth more than any gift you might purchase.

- Let them play on their own to Playing alone is extremely important to children. It's often a way of processing new experiences, disagreements and daily things of their life as they play with their toys. We will re-enact what is happening in their imagination, which is incredibly relaxing, by engaging in fantasy play and using different voices. It's perfect for building their creativity and fantasy too.

- Build an obstacle course. Try to build obstacle courses using tiny stools and mattresses, or create space in the house by any other way so that children can run about and use their creativity. Let them play and climb and experiment and build freely and don't sweat it over.

- Get other parents involved in the movement for safe play. The more parents who do it, the freer the children can engage in non-adult-led games together. In the United States, podiatrists have established recommendations to reassure parents that playing is safe. It is fun for youth and should be promoted and shared with others.

- Do not intervene too fast. Try not to judge the other children too harshly and intervene too quickly because you want to protect your children from others. Sometimes it's learning how to deal with the tougher kids that provide them with the biggest lessons on self-control and endurance.

- Let your kids do things themselves. Just step back and take a breath when you feel the need to "save" them. Know they master some of the essential talents to help them through life.

# Chapter 3: Authenticity

## 3.1 A Is for Authenticity

Have you ever watched a happy ending movie that didn't really make you feel good? One in which you found, despite the great resolution, that you had the feeling somewhere deep inside yourself that your life wasn't so perfect? Wasn't your job terrific? Your friendship, home, car or clothes just weren't as good as the ones in the movie? Hadn't the whole thing really felt that realistic? Yet you set it aside because it was, after all, a feel-good movie, so there's no need to talk about it too much. Many Hollywood movies are supposed to get you feeling good. But when art imitates life, you wonder how realistic these syrupy-sweet endings are in fact.

In comparison, very often, Danish films have dreary, grim, or dramatic ends. Much rarer is one left with the happy endings we're used to. Maria has watched Danish films countless times and waited to hear the calming background music that would signal that her misery was about to stop and that after all, everything would work out well. The kid would get the girl, the hero would save the day, and the world would all be perfect. She almost felt like an American it was her right to have a happy ending. But the Danish films would focus upon delicate, actual, and painful topics time and time again that didn't tie it up with a nice bow. On the opposite, with their raw emotions triggered and unfinished, they left Maria and its fellow audience members behind. How could Danes be so happy watching films like this?

Communications professor Silvia Knobloch-Westerwick and colleagues at Ohio State

University have done research that has shown that, contrary to popular belief, seeing dramatic or sad movies often makes people happier by drawing attention to some of the more positive aspects of their own lives. This tends to make people think with appreciation and empathy on their own relationships, making them happier and more in harmony with our own humanity.

**Fairy-tale Endings**

Hans Christian Andersen is perhaps one of the best known Danish writers in history. He is the author and forefather of many fairy tales like "The Little Mermaid," "The Ugly Duckling," and "The Emperor's New Clothes," to name but a few. These are tales which were told throughout the world. But what most people don't realize is that there are many original fairy tales by Andersen that don't have our idea of a fairy-tale ending at all. They are dramas. As an example, the Little Mermaid does not get the prince but instead, due to sadness, transforms into sea foam. Many of the fairy tales by Andersen were merely tailored to fit our cultural ideal of how things should be.

In the English translations of Andersen's fairy tales, parents paid close attention to what they felt children should be spared from reading. For Denmark and the older versions, it is more up to the authors to come up with their own assumptions and decisions. Danes think that tragedies and upsetting events are also things we should be talking about. From our sufferings, we learn more about character than from our successes; therefore, it is important to look into all parts of life. This is more authentic, creating empathy and more profound respect for humanity. It also makes us feel gratitude for the ordinary things in our lives that we sometimes take for granted when relying too much on fairy-tale life.

Authenticity for the Danes starts with an awareness of our own emotions. When we teach our children to recognize and accept their real emotions, good or bad, and act in a way that's consistent with their beliefs, the struggles and rough patches of life won't undermine them. We should know that they have acted in accordance with what feels right. We should learn how to understand their own boundaries and value them. This internal compass, authentic value-based self-esteem, becomes the leading force in one's life, essentially immune to external pressures.

## 3.2 Parenting with Authenticity

Parenting with honesty is the first step to leading children to be courageously true to themselves and others. Being a model of emotional health is effective parenting. Emotional honesty, not perfection, is what children really need from their parents. Kids are always watching how you feel anger, happiness, disappointment, contentment, and accomplishment and how you express it in the world. We have to model authenticity for our children and let them know that it is OK to express all of their emotions. Most parents find it easier to handle their children's happy feelings, but when it comes to the more challenging ones, such as frustration, hostility, and fear, it becomes more difficult. As a result, children learn less about these feelings, which may affect their ability to control them in the future. Acknowledging and embracing all feelings, including hard ones, makes it easier to navigate in the world at an early stage.

When you go through a difficult time, for example, laughing and pretending that everything is OK is not always the best course of action. Self-deception is the worst kind of deceit and is a risky transmitting message to our children. They'll have to do likewise. Self-deception is misleading because it allows us to disregard our real feelings and may allow us to make

choices based on external factors rather than our own honest wishes. It takes us down roads to points in life that we don't really want to be. And that is how sad we end up.

It's that time when many people are looking at their life and thinking, "Hold tight, is this really what I wanted? Or was that what I felt I would ask for? "Authenticity, on the other hand, checks your heart and intestines for what is best for you and your children and is not afraid to follow it through. This helps you to be in contact with your own feelings, and move on them instead of suppressing them or numbing them. These things take courage and strength, but there's a huge payoff. Trying to focus on intrinsic desires, such as strengthening relationships or investing in activities that you enjoy, rather than on extrinsic goals, such as buying a new car, is what helps to create true well-being.

So it can be a self-deceptive pitfall to have a bigger house or more things or to engage the children in all the right sports. Instead of listening carefully to their wishes and respecting their unique pace of growth and development, pushing your own or other dreams onto your children is another pitfall. Children may learn to do things for outward attention rather than for inner gratification, which becomes a default setting for life because they are too stressed or rewarded. It encourages extrinsic goals: To make them happy, they need something outside of themselves. This can bring success by the standards of some people, but it will not necessarily bring them that deep sense of inner happiness and well-being that we are all striving for. It can potentially cause anxiety and depression, as we have seen earlier.

## 3.3 The Danish Way of Authentic Praise

In Denmark, humbleness is a very important value. This dates back long into history and is part of the cultural heritage of the Danes. This value of humility is about knowing who you are so well that to make you feel important. You don't need others. So they're trying not to flood their kids with compliments.

Joseph often tells her daughters that with hard work they can do whatever. They know they need to develop and grow, and she supports that.

Yet she attempts not to overpraise them, realizing that too many compliments can't make sense for kids because they can sound empty and hollow.

For e.g., if a Danish boy scribes a drawing really quickly and sends it to her father, the parent will probably not say, "Wow! Good job! You are such a good performer! "She has a greater chance of thinking about the drawing itself. "What are they? "When you wrote this, what were you talking about? "Why did you use colors like that? "Or maybe she'd just say thank you if it were a gift.

Focusing on the task is a much more Danish approach, rather than complimenting the child too much. It tends you focus on the work done, which encourages modesty as well. Helping children build on the feeling that they are capable of mastering a skill rather than being a master provides a more solid foundation from which to stand and grow. That encourages endurance and inner strength.

And, in reality, this concept is backed by new and fascinating work. The way we treat our children has a profound effect on resilience!

Fixed Mind-set vs. a Growth Mind-set

In the U.S., many parents believe that rewarding children for their intellect build their trust and learning motivation. American parents tend to complement their children and others openly and feel it increases their faith and growth. Yet three decades of Stanford psychologist Carol S. Deck's work has proven otherwise.

Praise is intimately related to how children perceive their intellect. Children acquire what is considered a "locked" mindset (their intellect is predetermined, and they have it) if they are continually rewarded for being inherently clever, creative, or gifted (sound familiar?).

In comparison, children who are advised they should improve their knowledge through work and education develop a mentality of development (they can develop their talents because they are working very hard).

Dweck's findings show that children with a fixed mindset, who have been constantly told they're clever, seem to be obsessed first and foremost with how they're going to be judged: smart or not. We are scared of having to expend too much effort because we feel stupid with effort. They think you shouldn't have to put effort into this if you have the potential. So since they have always been assured that they have the skill, they are scared that they will lose their status as "smart" by having to really try hard to do something. Kids with that mindset tend to care about studying, instead. Those inspired to rely on their efforts rather than their intellect see the initiative as a positive thing. This stimulates and encourages their intellect to rise. Such students are growing their attempts in the face of disappointment and looking for new ways in learning, rather than giving up. This is the durability epitome.

## 3.4 The Key to Lifelong Learning and Success

Growing research in psychology and neuroscience also supports the notion that growth mentality is the real catalyst for exceptional achievement. Brain studies indicate that over time, our consciousness has far more plasticity than we ever dreamed of. Through learning even into old age, the fundamental facets of our intellect can be increased. When faced with challenges, it's patience and determination that are the key ingredients of overall success in many fields.

That really is an eye-opener. How many smart and talented people do you know who never lived up to their potential because they had a predetermined mindset of being inherently clever so they stopped trying when success didn't come easily?

Several fascinating research by Dweck and collaborators on fifth-graders tried to see how the recognition influences the success of the pupils. Student groups were given specific assignments to work on, and then received various kinds of praise for their efforts. Several students heard things like "You must be clever to solve these problems" (encouraging a fixed mindset) and others heard "You must have worked hard to solve these problems" (encouraging the mindset). Afterwards, the students were asked to agree or disagree with some comments, such as "The intellect is something fundamental about you that you can't really alter." Students who were rewarded for being clever agreed with these statements much more than those who were congratulated for their initiative.

The students have been asked to give their definition of intelligence in a follow-up report. Those praised for intellect said they thought it was a set innate trait, whereas those praised for the initiative said it was something you could improve with training.

Afterwards, students were given the option to work on a simple or complicated problem. The students who have been lauded for intellect have preferred to do the easier question rather than the challenging one, possibly in order to ensure a perfect result. The ones lauded for the initiative have selected the difficult one with the chance to learn.

All the students were eventually given a complicated task to focus on. The children with fixed mind-set lost their confidence and happiness the minute they had difficulty solving the problem. The promotion meant being innately clever for them, and fighting meant that they did not.

On the other hand, the children with that mindsets did not lose their faith and were eager to try to solve the problem.

When the challenge was made easier again, the students appreciated the fact that their intellect had already lost their confidence and motivation in the hardest question and had gone badly overall. As a group, they fared worse on the same sort of mission they had been assigned at the outset, while the community appreciated their continued improvement in their performance and did an excellent job overall.

Perhaps the most interesting thing, however, was that when asked anonymously to submit their ratings, set minds over reported their results more than 40% of the time. Their self-image was so tied up with their ratings that they were reluctant to admit defeat, while the development mind-sets changed their scores upward by 10% of the time. Research on bullying in schools suggests that now, pupils are much more likely to cheat in order to get high grades than in previous generations, a result of intensified pressure to achieve combined, in many situations, with a fixed mindset.

They think telling kids how brilliant they are improving their morale, but it actually makes them lose confidence in the face of difficulties! Praising students for their intellect doesn't give them the critical incentive or stamina to be successful, but can give them a fixed, fragile mindset instead. Conversely, appreciation for commitment or "process" praise for dedication, perseverance, tactics, progress, etc. fosters inspiration and resilience. It highlights what they have done to be successful for children and what they need to do to be successful in the future.

Ironically, a recent article in the New York Times notes that even companies today look for people with a mentality of development rather than a fixed attitude.

Since individuals with an increasing mentality are better at promoting collaboration and overcoming problems without getting stressed out, they are much more appealing to most organizations. The innately creative, or predetermined mindsets, are more egocentric and concerned about being the organization's biggest star. It's the people who can handle a challenge with perseverance and persistence, attracting thankful friends, who will finally get the coveted position and even making it into CEO level.

Some examples of process praise:

"I like the way you tried to put together the pieces of the puzzle over and over again. You have not given up and have found a way to pull it together! "You have performed this dance so many times and today's dedication has really been seen! You danced so right! "How you shared your snack with your dad, I am so proud of you. It makes me so happy to see you sharing." "It's been a long, challenging task, but you stayed at it and got it done.

## 3.5 Tips for Authenticity

- Weed out self-deception in the first place be frank with yourself. Know how to look authentically at your own personality. It is a huge milestone to be able to detect and define your own emotions and how you feel really. It is a great gift to teach your children emotional honesty and to prevent them from becoming self-deceptive. Hearing one's own true thoughts and feelings and expressing them is what keeps us on the right path to follow what makes us happy in life. It's how we calibrate our inner compasses, to be frank with ourselves and place ourselves in the right direction.
- Respond frankly if your children ask a question, then give them an honest answer. Your responses will, of course, be age-appropriate and proportionate to their level of understanding. In all aspects of life, it is important, to be honest in your answers, even the tough ones. You are weakening the child's ability to know what is true and false by not being truthful.

- Using stories from your own life, whether it's a doctor's office or a difficult situation or just a fun time, kids like to hear about your experiences and how you feel when you were little, particularly when it's genuine and heartfelt. It gives them a better sense of who you are, which helps them to realize that even if they are afraid, happy or sad, their condition is normal.
- Teach integrity Talk to your kids about the value of honesty within your family. Render an interest to it. Let them know why you value integrity more than punishment for bad behavior. When you threaten your children with indignation or accusations accusingly and are harsh when they misbehave, they may be scared, to tell the truth. They'll be honest if you make it safe for them. Remember, it takes a lot for anyone at any age to confess or tell the truth. Apparently, it isn't always coming. It is up to us to encourage them to be bold enough to be truthful and insecure and to apologize if needed. Be non-committal. When fostered well, this kind of honest relationship will be of paramount importance during teenage years.
- Write stories expressing all emotions. Tell stories of all sorts to your kids. Don't worry if not all of them have happy endings. Actively select tales that also have difficult subjects, and stories that don't finish in a "storybook" way.
- Kids learn a lot from grief and loss (being of course age-appropriate), and they open up honest communication with you on different aspects of life that are just as important as the prince had the princess. Exposure to life's peaks and valleys fosters empathy, endurance and feelings of meaningfulness and appreciation for our own lives.
- Use process praise Keep in mind that the most meaningful and useful praise is based on quality, not quantity.

Hold your attention based on the method or initiative that children put in rather than on innate abilities: "You've studied hard for your exam, and your progress reflects that. Multiple times you walked over the material, made cue cards and questioned yourself. That did work! "Try to come up with some more Process Louise examples. Practice makes things perfect the more you try to use the praise of the process, the better you get it. See if you can avoid saying, "You're so smart." By focusing on the effort involved, you'll give your kids the tools to understand that what matters most is perseverance, not an innate ability. In the long run, because of it, they will have greater self-esteem.

- Do not use praise as a default response. Do not exaggerate appreciation for items that are too simple. This can teach your child that when he performs a mission quickly, easily, and beautifully, he's just praiseworthy and that doesn't inspire him to take on tasks. When, for instance, a child quickly gets an A without much effort, try saying, "Well that was too easy for you! Why don't we try to do something more demanding, from which you can learn? "The goal is not to make quickly completed things the basis for our admiration.

- Reflect on effort and hold it sincere be quick of credit for errors or shortcomings. Saying such things as "Well done! "You've done your best! "Next time, better luck! "Can be heard pitifully. Focus on what they did and how it can be accomplished "I know you missed the goal, but it was very close! Let's get out next week and practice so you'll get it next time! The practice is important, remember! "By concentrating on the learning effort, we build a mentality of development. This collection of minds is useful in all aspects of life, from work to interactions.

- Teach kids not to equate themselves with others. They need to know if they have done their best on a project or if they like they can do more. Not everyone can be the best at all, but for yourself, you can be the best. This emphasis fosters health as opposed to competition with others.

- Highlight your own and honest viewpoint, and that of your child, by saying "for me" Try to add "for me" after a statement to reinforce the awareness that your perception of a given situation is not exactly the same as that of your child. For example, if you have a disagreement with your child that food is too hot, consider that although it isn't too hot for you, it might be too hot for her. Saying, "I don't think the food is too spicy for me," let her know you appreciate this. Or instead of saying, "The weather isn't cool," you might say, "The weather isn't cold for me." This appreciation for the individual experience builds confidence and reverence which helps children understand and appreciate their own experience.

# Chapter 4: Reframing

## 4.1 R Is for Reframing

AS an American marrying a Dane, Maria recalls the first time she learned that her husband was doing something for their children differently than what she was. She tended to respond a little too quickly whenever there was a negative situation of some sort. She'd throw her hands up with exasperation. "We are not going to do it! She would never listen! "Meanwhile, her husband always had more courage, more grace, and a magical expression on hand for every circumstance that even Maria could be astonished. It was like a window opening into a darkened room, throwing new light on a conversation in which she had not seen any potential before. He might place a more positive light on something negative. He might make a black-and-white situation appear a bit greyer. Pain became less intense and more balanced with rage. Maria thought his family and friends were doing the same for their families. Where was this magical book of phrases used by these Danes?

One moment, listening to her husband delicately change the vocabulary of their daughter around her fear of spiders, it struck Maria just how important that effect would have been for the life of her family. When she watched her daughter study the spider closely with him and marvel at it, rather than crying in terror and shouting, "Eew!" It struck her that it was extremely important to use the" Danish style "of expression. Because it wasn't just the language; it was about using the language to create a shift in perception.

## Taking Off Your Old Glasses (again)

You know, the way we see life and process our daily experiences influences the overall way we feel. Many of us do not know that the way we see life is an implicit decision.

We know that reality is our experience of life. It is our veracity. We do not consider our perception as an acquired way of seeing things (often taken from our parents and our culture). They see that as being just the way things are. This fixed way of "the way things are" is called a "box," and our experience is that context in which we see the universe. And what we define as the truth is just how it feels.

But what if we could see a new way of looking at the truth? What if we could take the truth as we see it and hang it back on the wall in a new mental frame a broader, more open-minded frame? When we stared at that photo, we once again call it "the truth," how would we see that?

Only pretend you're in an art gallery. The image is hanging on the wall, and there is a guide pointing out to you its subtle details. You start noticing things you hadn't seen before. Before you see these new details were clearly there, but you missed them because you were too focused on what you thought was the most obvious theme. You decided it was a bad picture. The guy was the center, the woman was powerless, and the mood was bleak. You're about to move on, but now, with the help of the guide, you realize that there's a completely different line of the story to focus on in the picture. You see now that, behind the pair, there are jovial men bearing gifts entering in the room. A dog bit the man, which is why he looks mean and the woman is friendly and not powerless. The context you hadn't heard is a kid laughing, and the light coming through the glass is exceptional. There are many other things to focus on in the very same photo that you hadn't even seen. Experiencing this mental shift and experimentation, it feels exhilarating. The recollection of that image will be completely different now, and the way you express the thoughts with others about it will be likewise. Creating such alternate lines of stories with repetition becomes a talent, not a challenge. And in the future, you will be the reference that points out these alternative storylines.

## 4.2 Realistic Optimism

Would you believe that the opportunity to reframe a stressful situation a family question, a dispute with a coworker, a disobedient child like you did with this photo might actually change you are wellbeing? The response is a resounding yes! And for generations, it is something the Danes have been doing. They teach this invaluable skill to their children, and learning how to reframe early helps they grow up to be naturally better at it as adults. And being a reframe Master is a pillar of durability.

When it's snowy, rainy, and raining out, ask a Dane how he feels the weather is, and he will unintentionally answer: "Ok, it's a good thing I'm at work! "I'm happy I'm not on leave! "Tonight I'm looking forward to having a family at home." "There's no bad weather, just bad clothes! "In any subject, try to get a Dane to concentrate on something really bad, and you'll be mystified about how she can get a more positive outlook on the discussion.

"Yeah, but this is the last weekend of our lives!" And we don't mean to say the Danes have an overly positive outlook, using sugarcoat reframing of their lives. We don't float around on a bubble of hope frequently associated with super-happy people.

The "This is all so beautiful and perfect!" types," he said. Those who look like their eyes were stuck on and are still high on life. No, the Danes don't pretend there is no negativity. I just find out in a very matter-of-fact manner that there's also another aspect that you might never even have known of.

I choose to dwell of society on the positive, rather than on the negative. We shift their perspectives and reflect on the bigger picture instead of being stuck by one part of a debate, and we seem to be more balanced in their conclusions in general.

Danes are what psychologists call "realistic optimists." Realistic optimists with the glued-on eyes are different from those overly optimistic people those people who sometimes seem to be phone and life is so good. The problem of being excessively positive and optimistic is the same as at the opposite end of the spectrum, with the overly negative and depressive people. Very negative people tend to ignore positive information that can bring them down and make them unable to see a positive reality. On the other hand, overly positive people tend to ignore negative information, which can make them insensitive to significant negative realities. It's risky to force yourself to believe that it's all great, saying, "No, there's no problem at all," when it's really there. Underestimating negative situations can bring a much bigger blow when you're hit with one. It applies to the self-deception. It is much more in line with being a realistic optimist to be in touch with reality but to focus on the more positive angles.

Realistic optimists actually screen out needless negatives. We learn to tone down negative words and events and grow a pattern of viewing more objectively nuanced circumstances. They do not see what we think we feel.

Things just as bad or good or black or white, but realize instead that there are many shades in between. Focusing on circumstances with less negative aspects and seeking a middle ground reduces anxiety and increases well-being.

## 4.3 The expertise of Reframing

Most U.S. companies educate their staff in the ability to reinterpret or reframe details because it is seen as a key feature in resilience. Dean M. Becker, the founder of Adaptive Learning Systems, states in a Harvard Business Review article, "More than knowledge, more than practice, more than preparation, a person's level of endurance can decide who succeeds and who fails.

That is true in the cancer ward, in the Olympics and in the boardroom. "A key element to being successful is the ability to reframe negative situations.

Numerous studies indicate that when we consciously reinterpret an event to feel better about it, it decreases activity in areas of the brain involved in the production of negative emotions, and enhances activity in areas of the brain involved in cognitive control and adaptive integration. For one reframing study, images of angry faces were shown on two classes of participants. The first audience was advised to think that the people in the photos had just had a rough day and had nothing to do with their faces. The other party had been told to feel whatever feelings the faces elicited. What they discovered was that the group that had been taught to change their disposition toward the angry faces was not at all upset in reality, neural brain activity reported revealed that the reframing had washed out the unpleasant messages in their brain whereas the faces irritated the group that had been told to feel anything that had come to mind. Everything we think we feel.

Participants with phobias were introduced to spiders and snakes in a study done by academics at Stanford University. Each party had been educated to reframe their experience and not the other. The educated group displayed far less fear and panic than the control group and reported lasting changes in emotional responses when introduced to the spiders and snakes again later on. It shows the perceptual reframing's lasting impact.

Therefore, reframing not only affects our brain chemistry, but it also helps how we perceive pain, terror, anxiety, and the like. And this reframing relates directly to the words we use both clearly and in our ears.

## The Limitations of Language

Limiting language has the opposite effect. Saying things like "I hate flying," "I'm terrible at cooking," or "I don't have willpower; that's why I'm so fat" is language limiting. "I just love flying once I get off the plane," "I like to use recipes while I cook," and "I'm trying to eat better and exercise more now" offer entirely different ways of looking at the same things. It's less black and white and less restrictive, and it has an entirely different feel. You see, our language is a choice, and it's crucial because it forms the framework we see the world through. We are also changing the way we behave by reframing what we mean into something more positive and less punishing.

It's unclear where the Danish inclination to reframe stems from. Realistic optimism appears to be just the default setting in Denmark; these reframing-related language choices are passed down through generations. Many Danes don't know they have that gift it's so much a part of how they are. And we are convinced that it is one of the reasons why Danes are so pleased to be voted on all the time.

## 4.4 How Reframing Works with Children

Reframing with children is about helping the child change the attention from what it feels it cannot do to what it can do. The parent lets the child view things from different angles, which allows the child to reflect on the less negative results or assumptions. This can become a default setting with practice- for both parent and child.

When you use restrictive words like "I hate this," "I can't do it," "I'm not good at that," and so on, you create a negative storyline. The storyline may have persuaded us that we are not good at anything, or that we are doing all wrong.

A kid who is told to restrict myths on "how he is" or how he should do something or handle things in different circumstances, he starts building coping strategies based on a lack of trust in his own ability in the face of new obstacles. "In athletics, she's not very good;" "He's too messy;" "She's so emotional." All of these are quite distinguishing. The more children learn of these claims; the more misleading assumptions they draw for themselves.

This lets your kids find and create a different story to raising the issue. We are encouraged to reframe by bringing them to a different, deeper, or vaguer view about themselves and the world around them. And this skill will transfer to the way in which they learn to see and interpret life, as well as others.

She reflects a great deal on reframing in Joseph's work as a narrative psychotherapist and, even more profoundly, on "authoring." She helps people look at the expectations they hold about themselves and the perceptions they place on their children without knowing it. Statements like "He's antisocial," "She's not very smart," "He's terrible at math," and "She's too vain" all become habits with which the kids try to make sense and relate. Families can hear kids say these things much more often than you know. Soon, they believe it has to be the way they are. You don't even try to make sense of it when new behavior doesn't fall into this category because they've already described themselves as being uncoordinated, shy, or bad at math.

The language we are using is extremely potent. It is the lens we view and identify ourselves and our world-image into. Allan Holmgren, a renowned Danish psychologist, argues that the vocabulary we use determines our reality. Any transition entails a language change. A problem is only a problem when it's considered a question.

## The Influence of Labels

You know, many of these brands and stories bring us into adulthood. So much of what we think of ourselves as adults comes from the labels we were given as kids lazy, emotional, arrogant, dumb, and intellectual. Think about it: What are your beliefs about who you are, and how many of them come from what you were taught as a child? For the rest of our lives, many of us continue to live up to and unintentionally equate ourselves with those names. In breaking away from these stereotypes, we are opening new avenues of transformation for ourselves and our children.

Consider how common it is these days to hear people talking about children with disorders, even though they have never even seen a psychologist. It seems as though labelling babies, our own and others' as having psychological problems, has become completely natural. Shyness is named Asperger's, kids with a lot of energy are considered ADHD, kids who don't always grin must have depression symptoms, and the new thing we heard was a silent girl described as having sensory processing disorder. The parents were worried, the daughter was worried, and it was worrying to think that labelling her like that, without a diagnosis or a doctor's appointment, could have had an impact on her for the rest of her life.

It is very disturbing to say so nonchalantly that children suffer from a psychiatric or medical condition as if they are starving or cold. It not only ignores the extent and seriousness of those who are actually suffering from these disorders but it also wrongly marks them. Once they encounter a repetitive plotline in their lives, they continue to identify with those terms and draw conclusions about their identities from them. Such myths are becoming their story of life, and it is very difficult to get out of them. So by saying them, and then repeating them, we promote the very things we don't like in ourselves or in our children.

Through reframing, or authoring, we will continue to reinvent the future of our own and of our children.

Joseph shares an explanation of how she supports re-authoring in her work for adults and children. When someone comes to her who is unhappy with the way his life goes, she tries to talk about the things about himself that he is saying. She will discuss his negative conclusions on identity with him and try to separate him from those labels. One of her parents, for example, said she was idle and distracted and ruined her life. Then Joseph told her what this mark evoked and what sorts of emotions. The woman said it made her feel bad, particularly if she late forgets something or gets lost or sleeps. Those actions only made the bad mood deeper. Feeling sluggish made her feel as if she had lost, and she had no willpower. Therefore, once she said, "I am idle and distracted," she unintentionally repeated this plotline to others in her mind, and made it more prominent in her existence.

Joseph then used the language of externalization or language which separates the individual from the question. Laziness is not something in the genes; instead, it can influence people in different ways. Separating the individual from the issue makes us feel more capable of being active agents in our own lives to combat the crisis.

Joseph tried to help the customer imagine and explain laziness. Is that an unknown cloud? Is that just stifling you? What is it that makes you feel when it comes up? The woman said that it was like watching someone hold her down. It was hot air on top of her, and she was paralyzed; the alarm could not be turned off. As she attempted to read a map, it was foggy. If she wanted to exercise, it held her down. It made her feel weak, incompetent, and helpless.

We then went on to think about the feelings of laziness contrary. She spoke of what she cherished inside herself. She thought about what she wanted her future to be if she was able to shake off the heavy air that came upon her.

She then drew on past experiences and told another narrative about her life. It turns out she had outstanding communication skills and imagination. She was a funny friend and profoundly loyal. She was very talented in cooking and singing and had plenty of observations to choose from which she was not at all idle. She and Joseph have spoken about those encounters at length. So instead of concentrating on the negative character assumption of being weak and distracted, they focused on the ideals and talents of her story that they needed to "thicken." The more they focused on learning about the ideals and qualities she enjoyed about herself, the more the storyline about herself was optimistic and affectionate. Slowly, it began describing itself in a new way.

She was now imaginative, strong, and trustworthy, and found that she had the resources to reframe her outlook on her life and assumptions on her identity even more. Their outer voice was her inner voice of instruction. The problem was just the problem now; it was no longer who she was and it seemed impossible she would ever describe herself again as weak and dispersed. The strength of that vocabulary that characterized it was so much stronger than she ever knew.

Therefore, reframing or authorship is not about removing negative events in our life, but about putting less emphasis on these incidents and concentrating more on the aspects that we like. Just as in the painting from the beginning of the chapter: we can see a larger picture and practice concentrating on other aspects that tell a different story by being open to changing the background. We can transform our entire life experience into something better exactly the same for children. As adults, we are the guides to point out to them also a more positive and loving storyline.

## How to Limit Language

Saying things like "She's such a picky eater," "He hates reading" or

"He's never listening" causes that behavior to define who kids are. The truth is, there is an emotion or attitude behind every action. It's still not set. We may be sick of something, or thirsty, or angry. The more that we can distinguish the behavior from the child, the more that we can change the way we see her and hence the way she sees her. It lets her know she is OK, and the action is not her destiny. As we have seen, labels can become a prophecy which fulfils itself.

Sometimes a stubborn kid may be very hard but try to see the bigger picture and what contributed to that action. Instead of saying how impossible the child is, and making him a problem, try to notice the story's other sides.

The kid who refuses to eat maybe had a snack before dinner and isn't really that hungry. The child who won't get dressed maybe is at the boundary-pushing age and doesn't understand why socks are important. And what more, are the other sides of this stubborn behavior? The kid may be very diligent and aggressive and show great leadership skills. Persistence is an important attribute that moves us far in life. Perhaps the disturbed kid is very artistic and enjoys painting. In exploring and encouraging the positive aspects of the undesirable activity, we can help our child concentrate on the better storyline. This also avoids other fights for authority and leads to happy parents and children.

## 4.5 The Danish Way of Reframing

All in all, Danes use less formal words and do not tell children what they believe or what they should do in different situations. You don't hear many adult thoughts about babies. "You ought not to be this way."

"Don't weep." "You ought to be very good! "He's mean! He's mean! "That's not how he should be." "You ought to remind him next time! "They tend to focus more on the use of the vocabulary that helps children understand why they feel and act. Of starters, if they are angry or upset, they try to help a child to understand why it is like this rather than how it should or should not feel.

"What is wrong? What is wrong? "Nothing." "It looks like it is wrong is it there?" Hey." "What is happening? "I don't remember." "You're sad? Angry? Angry? Happy? Happy? "I'm sorry." "Why do you feel sorry? "I'm sorry that Gary took my doll at playtime." Why do you think your doll was taken? "Because he's mean." "Is he mean; you think? Is Gary ever mean? "Yeah." "But you said you were playing a lot with Gary last week, right?"Yeah." "So what does it mean? "No." "Alright, Gary is good sometimes? "Yes." Yes. Danish parents help their children conceptualize their feelings and then guide them to something more positive rather than a disdainful or restricted view. It's the core of reframing.

"So what happened when the doll was taken? "I screamed." "I was so sorry that he took your baby. I can understand that. I can understand that. What do you think you can do if Gary takes your doll next time so that you won't be sad? "I can tell him to return it. Or I can say to his counsellor." "I guess it sounds like a good idea to advise him to give it back. Was Gary interested in playing with dolls? "Yes." "Is anything else that you can do but inquire it back? "We can play with the toys." "It sounds like a great idea. We know that Gary is actually a sweet boy, so you can ask next time if he too wants to play dolls. "Yes! "The lighter side of things can be seen with all sorts of situations, not just men. It is much easier to search a scene with experience to locate the hidden details that turn a scene into something positive. It can even be fun.

When an infant finds a better line in memory, try to replicate it, so it lasts. But ultimately, the solution should come from the child. It develops true self-esteem by becoming the master of her own internal responses. She doesn't know how to feel and act.

When we hold to the good in people and isolate acts from the individual, we teach our children that when they misbehave, we forgive them. Imagine if we said Gary's acts were stupid and evil. Children ' going to remember that. When it comes to our own children every time, they know why we judge. If we trust others and know how to forgive, we teach our children that when they misbehave, we forgive them. When we believe it is natural to lose because, given the fact we can see more positive things, our children will also be more compassionate when they fail.

Humor is another means of reframing. If you're on the side of a football field and your kid has played bad and says," I've done terribly',' a common way to respond is," No, you haven't. You played great! You played great! The camp was slippery! Each time you're going to win! You're winning some, and you're losing some!

"There may be a Scandinavian way of reframing with humor:" I played awfully." "Did you break your leg? "No, but I'm an awful player." "But didn't you break your leg, didn't you? Are you sure? Are you sure?"

(Go down to check the hip) Ok, you haven't break your leg, at least! "Ha-ha, I'm bad at soccer. I ought to stop. "You hate it? I hate it." Yeah, today you played pretty poorly, but remember that you scored two goals last week? "

All right, but. "Remember when you scored these goals, how did you feel? "Pretty good." "I think I remember you dancing and singing around the room.

How hate you, soccer? "No." "Precisely. Remember how you felt last week, and let's talk about what we can do to make you play better next week." "Practice again, I suppose." "Yeah, and let's go have some pizza and compliment you've never hurt your hip. "Some days are bad; some are fine." Note that the parent does not overlook the fact that the child was playing badly in this case. The adult understands, however, uses satire to demonstrate how much worse the situation could be and to direct the kid to positive feelings about playing football the previous week. That's a realistic optimist. You recognize reality, but you still can remove the needless negative words and focus on positive, not bad, emotions by laughter or another moment of good feeling. You give him the tools to deal with his singularity if you choose to tap into the positive aspects of any child's behavior. Everything is in the way you frame it. And realistic experience makes it perfect!

## 4.6 Tips for Reframing

- Take care of your negative behavior when you have a pessimistic habit of thinking. Only check to see how often you use fear to see a scenario. Try to find new ways of looking at stuff like doubts or problems that bother you as an exercise. Try to step back into perspective and see whether you are able to find a way of seeing it or a way of thinking on a more positive aspect.

- Talk about how rational the ideas are and try to change the world. Take the following phrases: "I never have time to practice. "I'm a terrible writer" "My baby's so irritating." Try to turn them into another paragraph. "More or less once a week, I attempt to practice, and I try eating lunch salads that look good." "I'm a pretty decent author once I'm into the field." "I love my mother-in-law, even if our differences are significant. She is a great grandmother for the children. "It can be difficult to do, but we know it makes a difference in our brain chemistry. It can even feel dumb at first, but the more you reframe, the better you feel. All we think and say bad about ourselves, our families and our anxieties and worries transmit directly to our children, so allow

yourself and your children the blessing of retraining and helping them deal with the ups and downs of life.
- Use less restrictive words. Try to eliminate black and white, oppressive terminology. I love it, I always, I never, I never should, I shouldn't, I'm like that and so on. Limiting speech leaves little room for flexibility and only sees things from a different viewpoint. Seek to use less tense words. Use less judgment and tolerance, and your children and your wife will face fewer power struggles.
- Use the philosophy of externalization: isolate the behavior from the individual Rather than say "She is lazy" or "He is an aggressive person," use to see these issues as external rather than inherent. "It's laziness that is influenced by it," and "Moments of violence reaching him" are quite different from "how they are." 5. 5. Delete the story of your child for more love Make a list of the most negative qualities and actions of your child and write them down as a word. "I don't think he's got ADHD." "She's too persistent." And start editing the sentences to identify the source of these conducts. For instance, a person who is not very academic may like to read and be extremely social. The person with ADHD can be a strong and talented drummer. The stubborn man may be a hard-working patient who does not give up. Seek to focus on the positive side of the actions of your children, and they feel valued for their individuality rather than harshly identified. Rewrite your and your children's negative identification assumptions and isolate your actions from the boy. It encourages all parents and children to develop and compose their own love stories.
- Using language support Help your children by using language support rather than language constraint. Ask questions to help them identify their feelings. Enable them to recognize other people's intentions and actions so they can learn how to recover from difficult situations.
- Using comedy, listen to your kid and add fun to the situation to help transform things in a new way. Nevertheless, beware of not negating the thoughts or experience of the child.

# Chapter 5: Empathy

## 5.1 E Is for Empathy

Maria and her sister had a very strained relationship for many years. Together usually involves lots of rolling eyes and uncomfortable thoughts. Frankly, they didn't like each other so much. Maria thought her sister was overwhelming with her parents ' experience as children, and her sister thought Maria was spoiled and insensitive. Both of those views made them territorial and distrustful of the other, leading to friction, disputes and increasing alienation with little expectation that their strong connection would ever be restored.

Not until Maria saw the friendship of her husband with his brother did she wonder if there was perhaps a better way. The two Danish brothers had as many disagreements and issues as the two American sisters, but Maria's husband treated them always with empathy and compassion rather than eyes and exasperation and, despite their differences, had a good relationship. So one day, Maria tried to listen, without her preconceived filters. She wanted to really explain how her sister felt and how upset she was. And what she found was that the role she had played was a remarkable change when she met her sister like a friend, not as a bitter rival.

Finally, Maria really saw the face of her sister. So she started to feel true sympathy for her, so vice versa. We spoke to each other as real caring friends for the first time in their lives. In a year the friendship improved dramatically, and now it has become unbelievably close. Where once she felt they were destined to divorce, Maria is now like a sibling would rely on her, and she is thankful for her life. It is a positive sea change, triggered by love together.

It's amazing how many people don't know the meaning of the word empathy. "Is that like friendliness? Apathy? Apathy? Homoeopathy? Homoeopathy? What is empathy, exactly? "If so few people know what empathy means, how many people incorporate it into their day-to-day life, what is really surprising about this confusion? Empathy is the ability to understand and acknowledge others ' emotions. It's capable of feeling what someone else feels not just caring with them, but also connecting for them. Simply put, it runs a mile in the shoes of someone else. So saying is much better than doing. Why is it so hard? Has it anything to do with our culture?

A recent study showed that empathy for young people in the US had fallen almost 50% since the 1980s and 1990s. In the meantime, the narcissism degree has doubled. Narcissism is an abused image of the self that seeks to isolate the self and discourage meaningful relationships. The attributes of narcissists are such that people rely so much on themselves that they are losing attention to the interests of others. There are many reasons that this may be so, but no one seems entirely aware of why.

The Narcissistic Personality Indicator (NPI) was created in 1970 to measure narcissism, and a large number of tests have shown its validity. Jean Twenge and her associates examined NPI values for college students between 1982 and 2007 and found that narcissism increased significantly and consistently during that twenty-five-year period. The degree rose so drastically that almost 70 per cent of college students were arrogant higher than the average college student in 1982 by 2007. What might be the explanation for this?

**The Heart of America: Survival of the Fittest**

In the United States, individuals by humans have been considered to be fundamentally selfish, violent and competitive for many years. This began with the industrial revolution.

At least partially, the structure of the market economy and of the financial, legal and political systems is based on this concept, which essentially opposes each other. The message of covetousness on Wall Street is just one indication of this lack of empathy. For so many a year, evolutionary theorists, politicians and the general public have reflected on rivalry and on the imprudence of natural selection as the way people are drawn. Ayn Rand, whose philosophy many people admire, supports the belief that the human being is inherently egotistical and that the human being is here for his own sake. If you believe in this idea or not, the fact is that these ideas are so deeply rooted in American culture that most people don't know it. This penetrates daily life. Competition and desire to be number one are part of what Americans think.

Let's talk about the mothers you knew for a moment. How many really open up and share what happens to their children? How many are courageous enough to be honest and don't know if they're doing the right things? Currently, it seems that fewer moms are able to demonstrate their insecurity as the scope of what it means to be a "healthy" mother has gradually been applied to expectations which are able to live up to and even compare with other mothers. If you feed your child (breast milk, organic, healthy, etc.) or offspring events (how many they participate in and how good they are) or schooling, in what should be a simple everyday interaction, there's often a feeling of one-way. Naturally, this sense of increasing competition is not limited to childcare. It permeates all manner of expressions. It can be very discreet, but you might be shocked if you pay attention, how often you find it is just under the surface.

Many people are afraid that they are really open and vulnerable because they don't want to be judged or rejected. And many relationships are reduced to superficialities in this terror.

**Our Fear of Vulnerability and the Discovery of the Social Brain**

Brené Brown, a popular risk expert, says that people are scared of being vulnerable because they are actually afraid of being isolated. We want social connections so much that we are afraid to say something that someone else can reject us. Yet being weak and empathic helps to bring us closer. So we are switching from insecurity to the other side of the spectrum. Instead of attempting to use empathy and understand why a person chooses (to breast-feed, to work or not to work, to name only a few of the big ones), we regret her. "How can she work with foreigners and leave her child? I could never do that! I could never do that! "What can a housewife be like? I could never do that! I could never do that! "How long will she breast-feed? It is gross! It is filthy! "How couldn't she breast-feed? It's so egotistical! "And so it starts. The broad brush of judgment is swiped over another human. You're equal to all of your decisions, so naturally, you're a better parent. Because the highest is a commodity, we greatly admire. The cruel irony is that we would be much abler to feel encouraged, not manipulated by a linked social network.

The issue with guilt and always trying to be different is that we become extremely uncomfortable or nervous as we encounter our own feelings of insecurity. And what do people do when they experience some kind of fear or discomfort?

The most common reaction is to get stomached. Meat, Television, shopping, food, medicine and drink are all good treatments to stuff and feel all right at that moment. But it's just a band-help.

Nonetheless, everybody seems to have at their hands a box of these Band-Aids. Brown says in her TED address on poverty: "We are the most vulnerable society in the world, bloated, overweight and sick."

That makes us wonder: what if we sought a little more compassion and kindness rather than punishing others? What if we stop trying to achieve perfection which does not exist? What if we were trying to connect more?

Pioneering neuroscience research has shown what scientists call the' inner brain,' a brain region that lights up when we engage in social activities. Matthew Lieberman, a social cognitive neuroscientist, wrote: "This network is a reflection that enables us to think about the mind, thoughts, feelings and goals of other people. This encourages understanding and empathy, solidarity and compassion. "Lieberman is of the view that we are not only linked to self-interest, but also to other people's welfare.

**The Surprise of the Dilemma of Prisoners**

Lieberman set up a neuroimaging study with functional magnetic resonance imaging (fMRI), which examines human blood flow to various parts of the brain, to test human beings, while psychologically testing them called the "dilemma of a prisoner" How much each person gets depends on whether or not the other person splits things fairly. If both players decide to cooperate, then each player receives $5. If one works together, the other "defects" the cooperative player doesn't get anything, and the defector gets all 10 dollars. Each one gets one dollar if both defects. The challenge is to determine what you should do without understanding the opinion of your mate. It's safer to defect: you're going to get at least one dollar and perhaps ten. When you cooperate, if your friend loses, you lose nothing.

The findings showed that the players decided to collaborate more than allowing the selfish choice of injuries, contrary to what the researchers predicted.

However, the findings of fMRI show that activation in the ventral striatum (primary reward area for the brain) decreased as long as both participants interacted. And this award center was more prone to the total amount of both players than to one's own personal performances. This means that people have more satisfaction than their own joy from the happiness of others! What might this explain? The Danes have always had an underlying conviction that caring for the welfare of other people is important for their own happiness, and they judge on something by these scientific findings!

## 5.2 The Truth about Empathy

Empathy was historically considered to separate people from animals. Most thought that animals and primates showed no empathy. But in his book The Age of Empathy, the renowned primatologist Frans de Waal reveals that empathy is indeed evident in all kinds of animals. Research shows affection for rodents, priests, monkeys, dolphins, elephants and other species, but the general public learns little about them. This is because so many of our governing policies were founded on the conviction that nature is a "life fight" and that our societies should be built on competition and selfishness, not on the full spectrum of what it means to be human.

Empathy is a beneficial instinct from an evolutionary point of view, which helps us live in communities. Without empathy and solidarity, humans could not have survived. Unlike popular belief, most of us are concerned with the well-being of others. This impulse was just asleep because of lack of focus.

People thought babies were born without empathy. But that's just not true. We all have to be wired for empathy; just know how to link the wires and make them work.

Empathy resides in the limbic system of the brain. Memory, feelings and instinct are regulated. It is a fluid neural network of mirror neurons and insula. How many don't know is that we are physically susceptible to communicating with others. This is made possible by a large number of neuronal systems embedded in the right hemisphere of the brain, which is important to the mirror neurons.

You see, the self is not an independent person, but a connected structure.

"Empathy is not a privilege for people, and it is a need," Daniel Siegel, UCLA's clinical professor of psychology says. We're not living because we have claws and we don't have large fangs. We exist because we can connect and work together. "Empathy makes our relationship with others better. During infancy, it grows through the connection to the attachment figure. A kid first learns to respond to the feelings and moods of his parents and then to other men.

The infant should feel and imitate what the mother feels. This is why issues like eye contact, facial expressions and voice tone are so critical at the start of life. This is the first way we feel trust and connection and start to learn empathy.

For a fact, when the kids hear them cry, they often soothe other babies with pacifiers or a fuzzy animal. They respond by being frightened or afraid to cry from others, and some even start crying when they hear it. You may not understand why or the feeling behind this weeping, but you will know with time and experience.

Studies show that children aged eighteen months almost always try to help an adult who visibly struggles with a task. If the adult is asking for anything, the kid tries to give it to him, or if the child sees the parent slip, it picks it up.

On the other hand, if the same person drops it firmly to the table, the kid will not pick it up for him. She realizes it was intentional, and the adult doesn't want it. Even before children are taught to support or to be careful maybe before they realize that it is a duty they are less greedy than is often believed.

## 5.3 The Responsibility of Parents

Parents have a huge responsibility because they are the main example of empathy and have to be empathic. This can be achieved by using their vocabulary and actions. Children are continually focused on and mirroring their kin. Therefore, what you feel in your home is essential to your empathy.

The families in which children are exposed to physical, psychological or sexual abuse are the kinds of families which can quash their ability to empathize. Their healthy boundaries and their ability to feel for others are broken. Every child suffering from an attachment disorder is impaired by its empathy ability.

Other types of family that can affect the development of a child's empathy are overprotective. These are the parents who fear failure or the great emotion of their children and who do whatever they can to prevent conflict and fulfil all their children's wishes. Sometimes these parents conceal their logical, irrational and emotional reactions to "protect" their children. This hinders the children's ability to read their own feelings, which, in effect, will reduce their ability to empathize (because what they see and hear is not what parents confirm). Often, children from overprotective families are more susceptible to narcissism, anxiety and depression. You cannot self-regulate because of the difference between thought and behavior.

Kids that are consistently told how to act and behave will not grow into individuals that are respected and allowed to display their full range of emotions. We may be detached from how we feel, which makes it difficult to navigate the many decisions in life safely. You can experience persistent vacuity and frustration. What can we say when we don't know how we feel?

Encouraging childhood sensitivity early on helps to build healthy relationships in the future. So we believe that these loving relationships are the root of true happiness and well-being.

**How Do the Danes Learn to Be So Empathic?**

In the Danish school system, the nationwide standardized curriculum Step by Step was already introduced as a pre-school. Each child's pictures show different emotions: depression, terror, rage, disappointment, joy, etc. Kids speak about these cards and bring in words what the infant feels and tries to conceptualize the thoughts of one's own and others. We learn empathy, solve problems, monitor themselves and interpret facial expressions. An important part of the program is that facilitators and children do not evaluate their feelings. Instead, they just recognize and respect them.

CAT-kit is another system which is becoming more and more popular. The curriculum aims to enhance emotional awareness and understanding and reflects on how perceptions, thoughts, emotions and senses are communicated. Resources in the CAT kit include picture markers, emotionally-intensive measuring sticks and images of the body, in which participants are able to draw the physical and emotional dimensions. There's also a tool called My Circle, in which children draw their peers, family members, experts and outsiders to help them understand others.

The Mary Foundation has also greatly influenced empathy training in schools. Mary, the Crown Princess and the forthcoming Queen of Denmark have developed a country-wide anti-bullying program. Free of Bullying is a program where young people between three and eight talk about bullying and teasing so that they can learn to be more concerned about each other. It has produced positive results, which are recommended to other institutions by more than 98% of teachers.

Another less obvious example of Danish school empathy is how they combine children of different strengths and weaknesses. Students who are academically stronger are taught together with less strong children; shier children with gregarious children; and so on. This is quietly handled. The teacher gets to know the students over time and then sits them. The aim is to make sure that everyone has positive qualities and to help each other reach the next level. The math whiz may be bad in football, and vice versa. This system promotes collaboration, coordination and loyalty.

Studies show that in teaching others, there is an enormous learning curve. Students who instruct others have more difficulty understanding, remember and use the content more accurately. However, they must also try to understand other students ' perspectives to help them where they find themselves in trouble. The ability to explain complex topics to another student is not an easy task, but an invaluable ability to live.

And as Joseph observed in her teaching years, this kind of teamwork and sensitivity always gives children a strong degree of satisfaction and joy. It returns to the collective brain, and the problem of the inmate is what we saw at the fMRI. In reality, contrary to what we might believe, people's minds are more pleased that they partner than compete alone.

So it may not be shocking that empathy is one of the most important factors for successful managers, businessmen, administrators and businesses. This decreases abuse, increases our empathy and significantly improves partnerships and social connections. Empathy improves the quality of meaningful relationships, one of the most important factors in our sense of well-being, we learn. Empathetic teens are more successful because they are motivated by a greater purpose than their cynical peers. And it makes sense if you think about it. Successful people do not work alone; we each need the help of others to produce positive results in our lives.

Perhaps by concentrating on consciously teaching our children empathy as they do in Denmark, we will make our adults happy in the future.

## 5.4 The Power of Word

The prominent Danish philosopher and theologian Knud Ejler Løgstrup claims parents can nourish the minds of their children more than merely through amusement and language translation. We should also cultivate their empathy. He said that words or stories that we tell about others are essential in order to teach our kids how to put themselves in another's shoes.

Of starters, when Danes speak to their own children about other children, it is pretty extraordinary to hear the words they use. We don't talk about them consciously. These are essential words used by all parents when referring to others. They are phrases. Yet their propensity to point out the good character of other children is strong.

"He's such a sweet boy, isn't he?" is very common to hear "She's very kind, don't you believe that? "It's been very effective, haven't you thought so?

"He's good. You think so? You think so? "What makes it amazing is to think about how these word choices lay the groundwork for the positive of others as a potential norm. It is normal to see the positive in others by pointing out the good in others. Trust becomes more normal. Nevertheless, it is unusual for a Danish adult to talk critically about another child before their own.

Alternatively, they try to explain others ' actions and why they might have behaved disagreeably. "She was definitely really sleepy and missing her nap." "Did you think he was starving? We try to lead the children to think that a child's behavior is simply influenced by a situation instead of portraying the child as cruel, egotistical or strange.

This is actually how the ability to reframe starts. Being able to imagine quickly that someone might have trouble allows us to see his or her actions plainly. Instead of swiping a wide brush with a negative label, we should empathize. That also makes us feel better because it saves a lot of money. Otherwise, negative energy would be lost.

Løgstrup wasn't naive to believe that trusting others was necessarily rewarded. He simply believed that trust is a fundamental element of being people, like other "supreme manifestations of creation," such as speech honesty, love and compassion. "To show faith and confidence in others is to give oneself." And this is valid. Confidence is very easy.

**The Danish Way of Teaching Empathy**

One of the first things to consider when it comes to teaching empathy is to differentiate between the capacity for empathy and the consequences that is, how one should bring empathy into motion in relation to others. This needs to be learned, and many good examples from parents and others with children on a daily basis take a long time.

Just give us an example. Lisa plays with a shovel along the sea, and Mark, a little boy, wants to play with it, but Lisa doesn't want it. Mark starts crying. Mark starts crying. What is she going to do? What many people would do is give Mark the shovel as he cries. But what does this teach? What does it teach? Is it real that we always have to give others what they want just because they want it? Again, this is teaching how to do things because there is an extrinsic effect rather than an inner rationalization. Lisa works with the shovel and can tell that Mark gets upset. She needs an adult to help her balance her own needs and limitations and then to decide for herself and take responsibility for herself. What often occurs in such conflicts is that the adults have mercy on Mark and demand that Lisa carry out the compassion of the adult and force him to give Mark the shovel. It's not rational or empathetic. This does not mean that Lisa should not try to consider the feelings of other people not at all but it is also important to educate children that adults have empathy and sympathy for them, and to realize how they feel and what their desires are so that they can really appreciate them themselves. It also tells Mark that by crying, he does not actually do anything.

So what can the father of Lisa do? After the children let themselves find a solution, Lisa's mother or dad could read their body language and ask if she would like to share it. The parent may propose a plan Lisa spends another five minutes with the toy, and then Mark can borrow it while Lisa starts a new project. It's fun to chat and play together if you're in a mood for it. It's all right to say no at times, but it's also important to learn how to share and appreciate it.

In the long run, these exercises over sensitivity can be immense.

It becomes a powerful lesson in the long run as you teach a child not to be compelled to do something purely through appeasing another or making things simpler.

Teenagers subject to the wrong kind of peer pressure will easily stand up to what they think is right because their thoughts have been shown to be legitimate from the very beginning. When we educate our children with empathy, they can appreciate and apply it themselves even better. If your inner compass is good, it leads you in the right direction.

One way Danish parents encourage empathy is by pointing out the feelings of other people to their children. It's not unusual to hear stuff like this: "Aw, you can see that Victor cries? Why do you think he's weeping? "She looks angry. Why do you think she's furious? "You're angry, I can see. Can you try to explain why to me? "It's very rare to hear anyone say,' don't be like that. "Why is she mad? There's no need to be upset." That's absurd! "You don't have anything to cry stop crying! "Why are you so angry?!"You ought to be satisfied! "Do Danish parents tend to understand the feeling when talking to the kid at leastoh? Why are you crying? Why are you crying? "And they sit down to show them they're seeing them.

"You're mad, I see. What's worried about you? How did she take your toy? She's only a small baby. I don't believe she did so intentionally, do you? "There are not always good reasons for or easy solutions for a child's emotions, but we teach respect, at least by admitting them and not trying to judge them. Imagine if adult mental issues were constantly ignored as irrational, inappropriate or wrong and instead it asked us how to act.

One of the foundations of understanding in Danish is not judgment. The Danes try not to judge too harshly their children, friends, friends of their children or family. Both family members have the right to be heard and taken seriously, not just the one who yells loudly. It is important to be respectful of yourself and others.

So note that you will help your kids grow up to be less judgmental in the long term by fostering a more empathetic, less bullying so insecure, honest attitude in your family including yourself.

## 5.5 Tips for Empathy

- Understand your own empathic style. There are questions that you have to think and speak about: what is empathy for me? To my wife, what does empathy mean? Where are we in agreement and disagreement? What are our core values? How do I judge myself and others? How do you judge my other partner? How does this reflect our language style? How can I change my language style to a more empathetic and less judgmental style? Remember, this isn't easy, but you'll get better with practice. Seek first to listen to yourself and see what you're thinking about and then learn of different ways to express yourself with more sensitivity. Remember, your kids are reflecting you. Help your partner to do the same thing.

- Understand others to understand other people rather than to shame them. You'll be surprised how often you judge others and how much it takes to find a reason to defend them by putting yourself in their shoes. This is really a form of empathy.

- Notice and try to identify emotions. Help your child see the emotions of others and experience one's own without making a judgment. "Was Sally angry? Why was she furious? What happened? What happened? What do you think of what happened? What do you think? "Not' she ought not to be angry and have done it.' Read, read, read studies show that children's reading significantly increases their empathy. And reading books that cover all emotions, including negative and uncomfortable ones, not only good books. Dealing with reality, even at the level of infants, is truthful and genuine and has proved to boost sensitivity dramatically.

- Improve meaningful relationships Try to patch your own relationships with empathy. It has been shown that broken relationships cause physical and psychological damage. Empathy and compassion stimulate the same brain region, making it easier for you to forgive and be forgiven; the more your empathy skills are improved. Meaningful friendly relationships and family relationships are the main factors determining true happiness, far beyond money.

- Try to be more vulnerable and don't be afraid to be vulnerable. It's what we can do most connecting. Learn, be interested, think and use metaphors to respond carefully.

- Seek empathy in others, encourage friends and family who want to cultivate empathy and kindness. New mothers and parents can greatly benefit from this support.

# Chapter 6: No Ultimatums

## 6.1 N Is for No Ultimatums

We were all there. We're tired, our children disobey or not listen and, despite all our efforts, they're still misbehaving or annoying, and we're snapping. Many adults shout and scream, many people threaten to take time out, and some use physicality.

We saw many friends and fellow parents shouting or spreading their babies. It often comes from a child's anger that doesn't listen to an ultimatum. Normally the scene goes as follows: "You could do it better right now or else!" or" If you don't interrupt it now, you'll get it. Yes, I know it! I mean it! "When I ask you again, that's it! "And once the ultimatum is out and all options are expended, the parents feel that they have to go about it to gain control and the outcome results in some form of spanking, yelling or exercise.

Several studies suggest that up to 90% of Americans still use spanking on their children as a punishment. Like her twin, Maria was spanked as a child. Parents who usually spank only work from their own default settings based on their education, which is typically quite physical.

Maria has never been debating spanking as a form of punishment for many years. Just recently was teachers ' corporal punishment eliminated when she was in elementary school. She thought it was quite normal and never felt that she had a problem with it.

Only when she was pregnant with her first child did she realize how different her husband's perspective on discipline was from her own.

Her discussions on the topic and her increased understanding of the Danish upbringing of her husband prompted her to take another approach. Like so many aspects of understanding the Danish Way, the journey to this discovery opened the eyes.

As we read this book, we found that there are still nineteen states in the United States where physical punishment in schools is still permitted. This is to hit students with a paddle or a cane. Although corporal punishment is prohibited in schools in 31 states, it is still permitted in private schools in all 50 states. This may or may not surprise you. The point is: there is still a prevalence of spanking.

Nevertheless, a large-scale study carried out through parental methods in the United States by the Centers for Disease Control and Prevention (CDC) shows that we use physicality more than one could imagine. The study measured five cultural groups, consisting of 240 focus groups in six different cities (Asian, Hispanic, African American, Non-Hispanic Whites and American Indians), which found that all groups were claiming to be physically punished sometime or another.

The similarities between societies in terms of when and where the range was even more surprising. For examples, African American mothers said they spanked. On the other side, white and American Indian parents felt embarrassed in public. White parents often talked in a restaurant (which came up frequently during discussions) of taking the child into the bathroom to span the span, while Indian parents preferred to delay it until they got home. This just shows that behind closed doors, more spanking may occur.

## 6.2 Four Parenting Styles

Whether or not a parent uses a body sanction, social researchers categorize childhood styles into four distinct types.

**Authoritarian:** These parents are aggressive, not sensitive. They want obedience and high standards, the classic tiger mother. Authoritarian parents ' children tend to do well in school but sometimes experience poor self-esteem, depression and social skills.

**Authoritative:** These parents are authoritative and attentive (not to be confused with authoritarian). They also set high standards, but support their discipline. Authoritative parent children are more socially and intellectually competent than other parents.

**Allowable:** These parents are highly responsive but rarely need their child's behavior, based on their child's self-regulation. Kids of permissive parents tend to have academic issues and general behavior.

**Uninvolved:** These parents are not attentive or aggressive, but are not neglectful. Uninvolved parents ' children are the worst in all regions.

Authoritarian parents are characterized as poorly receptive and controlled. The abusive parents ' reaction to a child wondering why it would be "Because I've said that." Children are not expected to question why.

Authoritarian upbringing poses several problems. First of all, being highly controlled will make children revolt. Furthermore, not having any encouragement apart from' because I have said so," pull up your socks," straighten up,' and' it is my way or the lane' leaves children alone to control their feelings that can be both overwhelming and disturbing, combined with fear and shame.

Authoritarian parents usually behave this way because they have been raised and feel good. And perhaps they did. But if somebody claims that they smoked all their lives and were all right, does it mean that smoking is good for us?

# The Hard Truth about Spanking

A recent analysis of two decades of research on the long-term effects of physical punishment on children found that spanking is not only not effective, but can also wreak havoc on children's long-term health.

The study found that not one of over 80 studies, regardless of the age and sample size of the children, has found a positive relationship with physical punishment. Not one. Not one. What correlations he noticed were these: spanked children can feel depressed and devalued. We can suffer from their sense of self-worth. High penalties can lead to backfiring, as they can encourage children to lie in desperate order to avoid being released. Physical punishment is associated with problems of mental health later in life, including depression, anxiety and use of drugs and alcohol. Neuroimagery reveals that physical punishment will change parts of the brain that are involved in IQ tests and increase the likelihood of substance abuse. And there are data showing that spanking can affect areas of the brain that control feelings and stress.

Parents are wobbling because they think it is successful. And perhaps it's, in the short term. But beyond that, it's quite ineffective. Children learn to listen because they're frightened. Power struggles build isolation and animosity rather than proximity and belief. Distance and animosity produce anger (or obedience, but with diminished self-esteem), opposition and revolt. And where do you go after you hit them if the bad behavior continues? Hit them more? Hit them harder?

Scream more laudable? Hit some more of them? It is not shocking that violence is one of the most common long-term effects of spanking.

Case in point: A woman in a spanking study conducted by a parenting specialist George Holden struck or kicked her baby after the bachelor: "It's to make you learn not to hit your mother. "And let's not mention how many of us adults practice this activity unconsciously. Yet do we ever ask the question, "Is it appropriate to yell or stretch incessantly? "Many of us don't ask that question until it's too late.

What are the best feelings of the universe about spanking, yelling, and power struggles?

Spanking became illegal in Denmark in 1997. The majority of Danes agree that using spanking as a form of discipline of an infant is extremely strange and almost incomprehensible. It was discontinued in Sweden earlier, in 1979. More than 30 nations now have similar laws, including most of Asia, Costa Rica, Israel, Tunisia and Kenya.

Across Denmark, the parenting style is very egalitarian. It is closely connected with the style of authority. This ensures that they create rules and guidelines to be practiced by their children. Nevertheless, they are very open to questions about the rules for their babies. Danes regard children as inherently good and therefore react to them. Of example, what we call the younger years is an interesting difference in language between Danish and English. In English it's called "the terrible twos," while in Danish it's called the "border age" trod alder; it's natural and pleasant, not disruptive and horrible children pushing boundaries. When you look at it like this, the abuse is better to accept than to see it as evil and deserving of retribution.

You rarely hear this in Denmark when you yell and scream at your children.

A household full of yelling is indeed an extremely rare occurrence. How do they do? How do they? One of the parents we met expressed it quite well: "First of all, I think that we should keep quiet as parents and try not to lose control. How can we trust our children to control themselves if we can't? This does not mean that the Danes are weak or soft not at all, but steadfastness and kindness can replace a loss of temper and immediate power struggles and ultimatums. Avoiding these creates a quieter and safer atmosphere.

**Parenting with Respect**

The Danes expect their children to be polite, but respect goes in both ways. You must send it in order to receive it. Governance with fear is a problem because it does not encourage respect; it encourages fear. There is a distinction between solidity and terror. With panic, the kid won't ever know why he shouldn't do anything. He just wants to avoid getting hurt or yelled at. This does not make a strong sense of self simpler. A strong meaning of the heart is the asking and comprehension of which laws and why, and then the integration and recognition of them. Fear of what is known as a statute is very special. Working in a violent, shouting atmosphere does not help. And likewise, if she is afraid of you, you won't know if her kid is honest with you in the future. Maybe she'll tell you what she thinks you want to hear out of fear. Fear is strong but not conducive to an atmosphere of proximity and confidence. If you foster an atmosphere of respect and peace in which there is no fear of guilt, shame, or pain, you will have a much more positive influence and a true closer relationship.

In reality, studies show that children from trustworthy parents are more likely to be self-reliant, socially accepted, productive academically and behavioral.

Depression and anxiety are less likely to be reported, and antisocial behavior such as delinquency or alcohol use is less common. Research suggests that even one powerful parent could make an enormous difference. Children are also better adapted to their parents and less affected by their peers. A study of American students showed students a number of moral problems and asked them how they would solve them. Students from leading families were more likely than others to say that their parents should influence their decisions rather than their peers.

## 6.3 How Danish Practice No Ultimatums at School

One way Danish schools promote democracy is to encourage students, together with their teacher, to set up rules each year. At the beginning of school, teachers talk to their students about what it means to have a good class and what their principles and actions are structured to make it a good class. The laws can be anything from time to time, including consideration for others. However, what is important is that everyone decides jointly on the code of conduct. No set of rules is the same for any gender. And they do this each year because the graduates are older and more mature than the previous years and have different senses of obligation.

The results are amazing. For starters, if somebody was too disruptive or interrupting, in her daughter Julie's class one year, the entire class had to stand up and walk around the room to clap her hands ten times. They both discussed this at the beginning of the year. Children who are too loud find like their classmates have direct responsibility and influence, not just on their teachers. This can be a surprisingly strong incentive to stop.

Within Denmark, they spend much more time and money talking about how problems can be solved rather than disciplined.

Most Danish schools are fitted with various types of equipment for students to deal with different problems. Of starters, kids with ADHD or hyperactivity will sit on a ball coil, allowing them to concentrate in class. This ball coil has spicy relaxation buttons on one leg. It activates the postural muscles so that the student sits more upright and retains equilibrium and improves concentration unconsciously.

Schools also include "fidget packs" and "cuddle things" for children who have trouble keeping still, which can lead to distractions for others. Such packages contain items like stress balls and spaghetti-like loops, which can be used to relax and concentrate them on. Children who are too noisy or violent may be asked to spend time on their own to help them consume some of the excess energy.

Danish teachers are also trained to follow the principle of differentiation. This essentially means teachers learn to see each student as a person with specific needs. They plan with each student and keep track of their growth twice a year. Academic, personal and social objectives can be achieved. The hope is that the instructor is better able to understand their individual needs by "differentiating" the students so they can respond and react accordingly.

This is crucial because, as we saw in previous chapters, it makes a big difference in your response to them that you choose to see them. You will react accordingly if you see them as nonsense and exploitation. When you consider them as innocent, you are much more likely to react by feeding them and by loving them, even by encouraging them than by punishing them. When one sees benevolent intentions and kindness in another annoying child, patience is much easier to mobilize. This is a loop that returns to you. Better begets better. Worse begets worse. Peace gives birth to peace. Recall, it's not the bad child, it's the bad behavior. This differentiation is always significant.

## 6.4 Avoiding Power Struggles

Joseph tells us of how, when she was teaching, she stopped power struggles with a classmate. There was a kid who was very offensive and defiant in her class. He got the "disorder makes" mark. Many of the students thought that Joseph was perhaps too straightforward with him, but she believed it was incredibly important to stay away from making him a poor boy and having a lot of confrontation. She knew that he had a rough house life, and she saw him always as a cute, caring child. He was funny and smart, so she concentrated on his qualities and chose to ignore the rest so as not to reinforce his bad story. She listened kindly to him and focused on his ability to be a good guy.

Several years later, despite bad feelings, the student came to a school gathering. He turned his life entirely around and came to say thank you. He recalled that Joseph wasn't worrying about him, so she knew that he would do well in life. He said that her confidence in him gave him the power to support himself and become a better person. Joseph was deeply touched. She then realized how important it really is to separate the behavior from the person. Trusting, encouraging and treating people as actions rather than as the individual, helps to create a more caring tale of life.

We have, therefore, now seen why a more inclusive approach directly enhances our children's well-being, joy and resilience. How can we not follow the Danish way of ultimatums?

### Put a Mirror Up to Yourself

Think about the things that you do not like to hear about yourselves and then put up a mirror. That's what your child's going to get. If you don't like the shouting and the exasperating paws, don't do it. Don't do it if you don't like physicality.

## Stop Thinking About What Others Think

Stop thinking about what others say about you or about the actions of your kids. Yelling and physicality are often overshadowed by someone who is watching you. Regardless of whether you are at the home or a friend's house, in a restaurant or store, keep your actions in accordance with your beliefs. It's about honesty and conformity with what you believe. Don't think about how others raise their children or how your family believes you should raise their children. Concentrate on doing what is best for your kids and trust in that success. Some parents only replicate behaviors of their own. In making a change, you are doing something even bigger and harder. Try to form a group of parents who communicate and support each other in the Danish Way. Believe in your beliefs and stand by your sacrifices. The data is in the test to make us happy, more resilient and better adjusted.

The Danish Way works. Don't go there if you feel torn about a power struggle to eat or polite or belligerent with friends or family. Breathe, just stay calm, and remember. You are using satire. Use humor. Offer a way out. Offer a way out. Don't think about how a friend could judge you or your children or not. Your offspring will be happier and healthier in the long run, which is what matters.

## Chill Out and Remember the Big Lines

Know the difference between fighting and battle and don't fight. Does it really matter that your clothing or hair always look perfect? Is it really necessary that one day they don't wear the Batman shirt?

Do you really have to scrub your plate right now because you said so? Or are they trying to lettuce because they need to? Is it really valuable? It is what you and your friend must decode and determine whether broad lines are to be applied.

Maybe it's not the right time for a friend's house or a restaurant. What are your main lines, and when will you actually try to educate and enforce them? Ask yourself if it respects you and your child to make a scene public. You must be persistent, but you must not lift troops. Note, infants experience periods where they don't want to do/eat / wear / say those things. They emerge from them. They rise. When you follow the big lines, they will recognize them. The key is having patience and the courage to go through these periods without losing the coolness and concentrating on what is important.

Maria's father, for some time, refused to wear a sweater or shoes. It was exhausting, and nothing helped but to take it outside without a sweater or a scarf, and her daughter said, "Oh, I'm cold; I'll put that on! "It took a while, but she grew up. For a while, she didn't say hi to people either. People stopped and said hi, and she was looking away. Yet Maria never pushed it. Maria kept reminding her. She began to say hello one day, six months later, and from there on, she managed to do so.

Children are also checking things for themselves. If it becomes too much a power game, everyone loses, and life gets bad. If you're cool, they're cool.

**Examples of No Ultimatums: Offering a Way Out**

Typical answer: "Don't throw it! When you chuck it again, that's it! "Take it away. Take it away. Distract. Distract. Remove the child. Remove the child. You are using satire. Use humor. Stay cool about it when you say no. Tell the kid what it can do to chuck it. Mime to give it back an "ow-ow" from being struck by the rock. Show him again, shake your head and look distressed, if he throws it back. "Ow, ow, ow, ow! "The first time he may not be able to get it, but he will understand more and more over time.

It is wrong to beat or pinch someone, and you should be strict in those situations and hug the kid and tell them "No! "Forcibly. Let her smile at you and give you an apology and caress so that she knows the meaning of sadness and the lack of physicality at an early stage. Note, it needs to happen soon because children forget what they did immediately. You have to deal directly with this behavior. Children may not understand the meaning of grief at first, but they will become empathized with time and learning.

**Dinnertime Often Means Power Struggles**

How hungry a child responds to food? When, for example, he eats more in the day, he still isn't very hungry. Or he might be so hungry that he needs to regulate his blood sugar in order to feel better. Eating blood sugar controls the way a child functions. Empathy helps you understand from where he comes and reacts accordingly. Learning, instead of getting upset is a good starting point. Imagine how you'd feel if you were too hungry or over, either way and then leave there.

Something to remember: encouraging a kid to love and value food is an outstanding gift. Nutrition is what sustains us, and having a healthy, loving relationship will build a happy life. Check your own diet relationship and make sure it's as healthy as possible. Basically, meals should be a fun time for the family to come together.

Put a little of it all on the plates of your kids and allow them to eat the food they want. Food conditions will above all be nice and cozy, not tensioned and focused on children having to eat. Under these conditions, most people would lose their appetite!

If you do it a lot, it will be a lot.

There's milk.

They can come back for it if they want it. We don't always love food, we don't always scrub our dishes, or we don't want to

try things that we don't.

Occasionally we do, but not always. Give kids a way out if you can. You will be more valued when you find a guideline for yourself. Bear in mind also that you are the source.

Low stress uncharged everything, particularly nourishment. Remember, your children also have food phases. Giving healthy choices with food on the table, cutting out unhealthy snacks, and making meals more fun than a prison camp will teach your kid that food is lovely, pleasant.

Parents in Denmark sometimes say, to motivate children to eat, "You have to eat this food so that you are big and strong! You want to be big and powerful? "The parent tells the kid to flex her knees to show how strong she is and promises her that it comes from her greens and healthy foods. It works more frequently than you think!

**Explain the Rules and Demand for Awareness**

"Put your seat belt on." "No, I don't want that. "No." "Because you can be very hurt and have to go to the hospital if we have an accident. Want to go to the hospital? "No." (Put the seat belt firmly on.) The more you explain things, the better you can understand. This approach gives respect and helps you and your children to share a common goal (in this case, take a ride).

**Getting Started**

**1. Make a plan of action.**

What are your ideas for your kids? Include your partner and your own.

**2. Are you hitting or hitting?**

Hold a vow to stop. It is not appropriate and does not encourage faith and appreciation.

## 3. You shout too much?

Start vowing. Stop pledge. Only use it if appropriate. Yelling isn't good for anybody. Your kids are mirroring you; you are a model for them. If you want them to regulate and behave, you need to set the example of controlling yourself.

How can you stop screaming? Search for ways to reduce your own pain. Get more sleep. Get more sleep. Breathe. Breathe. Sleep more. Exercise more. Getaway some time. Getaway some time. Yelling and hitting are often the product of the absence of extra time to analyze and have the gap between the responses to help pick your answer.

If you feel close to bursting or shouting, take a deep breath. Go to another room and take a rest. If your friend will pass the baton, do it. Seek not to be in step with your punching and shouting values and always be firm on what you do or do not want your children to do. The partnership is important. It also helps because you can keep each other in check for your outbreaks more quickly. And if one of you is at the max and about to break, remind the other to take over peacefully. In a short time, you will begin to see your children behave more peacefully.

## 6.5 Tips for No Ultimatums

- Remember to differentiate the child's behavior. There's no bad child; there's only bad behavior. And there's bad parenting, too.
- Avoid power struggles. You won't find them if you don't look for power struggles. Win-win still say, not "How can I win? "Fourth. Don't blame the child for taking your own responsibility and next time trying to do better.
- Try to make sure children are inherently good Children should push limits and test rules. It's not terrible and deceptive. That's how they are rising.
- Learn to guide, nurture and educate your children. Do not just punish them and see them as more discipline is required. Try to find ways to handle complicated behavior. Do not call them "sneaky" or

"manipulative" or "terrible." The behavior is the actions; it is not the boy.
- Reframe Look for the best story about your kids and others. Learning how to reframe your children and showing them how to do so makes you more caring and healthier.
- Remember: the loop returns to you bad gets good. Poor begets poor. Worse begets worse. Power is out of power peace is quiet.
- Research shows that even one parent adopting the dominant style (not authoritarian) and maintaining her cool will make a big difference. Yet two are stronger yet!
- Write down all the ultimatums you use daily. Test the ultimatums. How are they identical to those used by your parents? How can you get them more positive?
- Consider always of your child's age. What can you expect of your child in relation to his or her age? Every era has a "style" of what is required of it. Kids aren't little people.
- Support all sorts of emotions Consider the feelings of your kid, whether or not she's in the mood you like. Everybody sometimes has a bad day, even babies. By not stressing it, you attract less attention to it and are more mindful of its self-regulation potential.
- Remember that opposition is a response to something Recall that protest is a way to communicate. It can also be a symbol of increased liberty. Instead of thinking of it as a horrible frustration, understand what it is.
- Put the wrong behavior into context has there been any changes in the life of your child that could lead to behavioral change?
- Know what snaps you It is important to know the causes. Where is your breaking point, and what can you do to get there? Do you need more food, relaxation or workout? Listen to your needs and ask for assistance.
- Say you are attentive, make sure you show your kid you are listening to her. For one, it's important to show her that she's heard and understood when she asks for something even though it can't. Say it, so she knows you heard it. You know. "I can tell that you want a lollipop, but I can imagine that. " Explain why something can't be done to your boy. Teach love, respect, and you will be valued more.

# Chapter 7: Togetherness and Hygge

## 7.1 T Is for Togetherness and Hygge

As Maria first met the family of her husband and spent time with her in Denmark 13 years ago, the feeling was, to say the least, shocking. Hygge sig, or hygge, (pronounced "hooga"), meaning "to sleep together" was for them a way of life. She is cozying together involved lighting candles, playing games, enjoying nice food, having cake and tea and typically in a comfortable setting with each other. This large family would come together for days only to be warm without a great break. In the beginning, Maria thought this party odd, but after 13 years of studying the trend, we finally worked out the key for hygiene.

Maria's culture, being American, was very different. As a rule, they could only be around for a limited amount of time, after which they would need a break. They did so professionally, but they knew it was part of their way of life to take breaks and to do their own thing. Feeling the need to be together for a long time would almost have seemed a violation of their rights as Americans. This looked like a catastrophe formula and claims. He could not actually understand how the Danish families seemed to live together without further family drama for so long. Sure, someone had issues, problems or at least a neurotic propensity to talk over with friends and family around. There seemed to be very little negativity and no resentment, and they ran together like a well-oiled machine given how many people came together. What was going on in the world?

Could this pleasant time together be part of why the Danes have been the happiest people in the world so consistently voted on? The answer is a complete, yes!

Research shows that quality time with friends and family is one of the top predictors of well-being and satisfaction. This is not always necessary in our modern world, but the Danish Way blends sanitation into everyday life to ensure that.

## 7.2 Hyggge as a means of living

The word hygge dates back to the XIX century and originates from the Germanic word hyggja meaning "to remember or to feel satisfied." Hygge is something Danes understand in practice as well as in being it is part of their cultural base.

Since the Danes see hygiene as a way of life, they all try to make a comfortable time with family and friends. For starters, they work together at Christmas to ensure maximum relaxation. It's a team effort. It includes stuff like lighting the room with candles and good food, but it's also in their way. I try to help so that one or a few people do not feel like the only people who do the work. Older children are encouraged to play with the younger ones to support them. We try to play games everybody can enjoy, and everybody makes an effort to play even if they don't want to. The choice out of the game was not huge-light, it would not be "comfortable." They're trying to leave their personal issues behind and be constructive to stay away from too much conflict, and together they enjoy this cozy moment and want it to be. We can be concerned about our lives and stressors at days, and happiness comes from putting those moments aside and being with those we enjoy at the moment. To Danes, the ultimate goal is to have a warm and beautiful experience together, and this is a great example to our children.

Feeling connected to others gives our lives meaning and purpose, and that is why hygiene by Danes is so respected. The person is also respected, but without engagement and support from others, none of us as a whole can really be satisfied.

The notion of unity, if you think about it, is quite distinct from the individualistic ethos that constitutes a large part of the American culture.

**The American Bedrock**

The US was built on the ideology of self-confidence. If we are strong enough to succeed on our own, we do not really need others. Why should we focus on help if we can do it ourselves? They glorify individual achievement and self-fulfillment with words like "the self-made guy" and idolize an individual hero from politics and sport in all walks of life. If you listen to sports, the team effort rarely comes to you; it is the person who stands out, namely the famous quarterback or pitcher. It is the light that shines from the others. People who help to assist the celebrity frequently transform into flouted background noise. It is the hard work and survival of the fittest we most respect. Then we are born to aspire to be the light, to succeed. Geert Hofstede, a world-famous cultural scientist, concluded that the US has the highest level of individualism in the world in a very famous study on cultural differences. That's quite incredible. We are so conditioned to talk about "I," we probably don't even know.

This does not mean that the US has no unbelievably, strong community spirit. This simply points out that we are more programmed to think individualistically in cultural terms. For example, it's much more common, during a family reunion, to talk about how I feel than how we feel. We talk about things like me time or how to meet my desires, or how it makes me feel rather than how it makes us feel.

It is also fair to say that most of us would like to be "winners." We want our kids to win or at least to be the best and to stand out. That's quite natural.

What would not want that?

Who would not?

Look for a number of creative reasons nowadays for the number of awards in schools. We aspire to gain praise for something, whether it was the hottest laugh, the sweetest grin or the best jump roper in the school. It has become the very foundation of our society.

Additionally, how many of us would actually find the "gang unity" trophy? How many of us would measure the success of our child not how well he played but how well others played or how well the children were playing together?

Where you replace "We" for "I," then "Illness" is "Wellness."

There are many consequences for the definition of cohabitation and sanitation, but it is ultimately for the good of everyone. It leaves the drama at the door and sacrifices your individual needs and desires to make a group meeting more enjoyable. This is a much more enjoyable experience for your children. Teen drama, negativity and divisiveness don't please them. Kids are very pleased to be warm and together! And if you learn to hygienic, you will also be able to pass it on to your children one day.

There are a famous heaven and hell fable that illustrates this concept well. In the hell is a long table with a beautiful champagne, food and candles party, but the atmosphere is freezing. The men around the table are frail and emaciated, and the air is overflowing with a cacophony of moaning and screaming. They have very long sticks rather than arms, which prevent them from getting food into their mouths. Seek it as you could, it's pointless. They are all starving, given the rich abundance of food.

There is much the same scenario in heaven. There is still a long table and the celebration and the candles, but there are ridiculous people around the table.

They sing, and they chew.

The environment is warm and vibrant, with cuisine, wine and business everyone enjoying. The irony is that they too have very long arms sticks. Yet they eat each other instead of trying to feed themselves. A shift of perspective substituting "us" with "me" or "I" has converted hell into paradise in this simple metaphor.

Across Denmark, from an early stage on, children work on projects across communities that enable them to learn to help others and partake in collaboration and team building.

**Teamwork in Denmark**

Children are taught to look for the strengths and weaknesses of others and see how they can help people move further than just on the surface. Danes are also promoting modesty of their star students so that they are compassionate and caring for others. It's not hyggeligt just to look for yourself. In reality, Danes are worldwide known for being quick and polite to deal with. That's because they're great team members. They help others to help themselves, and even when they are stars, they are humble. And who doesn't enjoy a humble start?

Social groups are also an important part of Danish culture. Such classes, known as "foreningsliv," are focused on a common passion or interest.

The target may be fiscal, financial, academic or cultural.

Their role can be to improve something in society, for example in a political association, or to express oneself in a manner that suits the social needs of the community, such as in the choir or bridge club.

Statistics show that 79% of business leaders in Denmark were participating before the age of thirty in partnerships. 94%, 92% and 88% of managers who have participated with organizations agree that these years of participation have gained and created a strong network for their social skills and behavioral competencies.

Ninety-nine per cent of the governors of Denmark agree that membership in these charitable organizations enhances the professional skills of young people.

The sense of cooperation and partnership is seen from the classroom, workplace and family life in all facets of Danish culture. Seeing the family as a team creates a deep sense of belonging. Eat together, clean up together, spend time with each other these are Danish families ' daily ways of fostering a feeling of well-being.

**Singing and Hygge**

An interesting way for Danes to establish hygge is their love of music. If there is a song-worthy gathering, they will most probably sing, from Christmas dinners and birthdays to baptisms and weddings.

The songs they sing are often written for a purpose that is circulated and sung in a common melody. These home-made texts are often hilarious, and everybody discovers the words together while singing. Songs they sing come from a national songbook entitled "Højskolesangbogen," which dates back to the royalty and aristocracy festivals of late Middle Ages, but was expanded over time and is now more popular than ever before.

Nick Stewart of the University of Oxford Brookes has studied choir singers and discovered that singing together not only makes people happy, and it also makes them feel that they are part of a cohesive community. The synchronicity of moving and singing creates a strong sense of connection. In fact, experiments have shown that groups of singers can indeed synchronize their heartbeats when singing. Together, the "good" hormone oxytocin is released, reducing stress and growing feelings of trust and bonding. One only needs to try singing (once you're stupid), to feel such powerful effects.

## Social Ties and Stress Levels

The level of happiness of the Danes is not the only evidence of the efficiency of unity and hygiene. A lot of research confirms this. Scientists at Brigham Young University and North Carolina University at Chapel Hill gathered data from 148 health outcomes experiments and their association with social relations. Together with more than 300,000 men and women across the developed world, these studies have shown that on average 50% more people with poor social links die earlier (approximately 7.5 years) than people with strong social ties. The lifespan gap is nearly as high as the mortality disparity between smokers and non-smokers. And the health risks associated with many other popular lifestyle factors such as lack of exercise, so obesity is greater than any.

Sheldon Cohen of Carnegie Mellon University subjected hundreds of healthy volunteers to the common cold virus, who had completed questionnaires describing their social lives and then quarantined them for several days, in another famous experiment in health and social relations. The findings have shown that the quarantined subjects with more social connections are less likely than those in their life to catch a cold.

The immune systems of people with many friends worked simply better. We could fight the cold virus better, often without symptoms. As stress hormones appear to influence the immune response, it is logical that a strong social life helps the immune system to remain strong physiological stress is monitored.

This influence was observed and validated by a research group in Chicago. Actually, social support helps to manage stress.

When we know that we have friends with whom we can speak or turn on support in difficult times, we are more willing to face challenges in life without breaking down. We're more durable. Feeling open to someone helps to lighten the burden we have. Most people strive to be stoic and to keep things close, but research shows that those who seek to be tough in a crisis suffer a great deal more than those who share feelings and are vulnerable to others.

**New Moms and the Danish Way of Togetherness**

In particular, the relaxing influence of the unification is noticeable in new mothers, who have unimaginable tension in line with their new role. There can be an overwhelming lack of sleep and all tasks in front of new parents. However, research shows that new mothers often react to this difficult period by reducing rather than increasing the amount of social support. This is paradoxical because it further aggravates the case. Support from friends, family members and parent groups was clearly demonstrated to help new mothers manage stress and thus to help them to see their children in a more positive light. This improves the quality of life of everyone, especially the growing child. The more parents get social support, and the healthier and happier the baby can develop.

When a woman gives birth in Denmark, a local sister gets her information and visits her for the first week to check in and see if she and the baby are safe.

More importantly, the midwife also gives her the names and contact data of all the women who have just had babies in her neighborhood, with information as to if she is the first, second, or third baby to make the women matched.

Such women form groups which meet once a week to discuss and support their experiences.

The other moms in the school are also supporters and test a mother if she doesn't.

They can call her or go home and ensure that she's all right and has contact with others with whom she can communicate. They are an important comfort in a very difficult time and an essential part of being a new mother in Denmark that makes all mothers and babies feel happy and safe.

## 7.3 The Danish Way of Hygge

We spoke a lot about social support, cohabitation and the value of hygge. But here is Maria's personal example because she knew what it is. It was a bright, fresh day. Maria lying under her husband's big plum tree in her baby sister's backyard, her young son and daughter were tucked between them. We were wrapped up like a swinging burrito, some with open eyes, and others with close doors. Maria put one foot out of the hammock lazily to hold them back and forth. The wind rocked the trees loudly; flickering rays of the sun shined in kaleidoscopic patterns on their faces through the leaves. It was a blend of touch, warm sounds and the smell of the downy hair of her baby son. The warmth of her husband's leg beside hers could feel her heartbeat. She held her daughter's foot, who was cuddled quietly with him. All of them were present.

"Oh, I see here you love some family hygge," she said as she came to welcome them for lunch. And that, Maria, felt it was hygge in a nutshell after thirteen years with her boyfriend.

It's both a feeling and a way of being. It eliminates all else's confusion and hysteria. He chooses to enjoy and respect the most important, meaningful moments of our lives those with our children and family and friends.

This keeps things easy, makes the mood optimistic and leaves our problems behind. It needs to be there at those moments, wants to be there and help to have a pleasant time.

With a large family, it takes effort, because, like all team projects, it works together to achieve a common goal. This is the opposite of being a person who stands out from the crowd. It must all be wanted and respected by everyone. Everyone has a part to play. It strengthens families significantly when we are all ready to contribute to having a comfortable moment together, which in turn affects our well-being and enjoyment drastically.

## 7.4 Tips for togetherness and hygge

- At the next meeting, make a pact with the whole team, not to "I," but to be at the moment to try to make things run smoothly and without argument. At the conclusion of this chapter, you can find the Hygge Oath or print it from thedanishway.com.
- All should agree to leave their everyday stressors at the door at this moment. Don't dwell on the bad things in your life or somebody else. Try not to dwell on problems or think too much about something. Everybody needs to make an effort to be together at that moment. Hold it bright, happy and accusative. Children embody this conduct and they feel safe and respected.
- Practice "pre-framing" Plan yourself and family for a meeting, so that you can make the most of it without throwing on your regular worldwide or personal drug glasses. Try to imagine what kind of interaction you will have and either consider or explore coping strategies, which will allow you to stay calm while you are there. Recall the stress-free family get-togethers greatly improve well-being. We are often trapped with different family members in our lives. Adjust it. Change it. Using empathy, reframing and preconception to help.
- Fun together when the entire family spends time together, play indoor and outdoor games in which everyone can participate. Set aside your personal preferences and just get out and play.
- Consider the room comfortable, with soft lighting, home-made decorations and décor, and food and drinks that you have cooked together.
- Just take a break anytime you feel the urge to lament, then, see where you can help. Alone, if everyone agrees, the level of happiness that you share as a family will make a big difference.

- Reframing is a truly powerful method if you get frustrated reframing. All can be reframed. Was the apple pie soggy? Everyone can use a spoon now! Has the football game rained out? Space for a Monopoly Fun Game! Recall that you pass it on to your children, allowing them to deal with their own emotional reactions.
- We also have so many toys (for adults and children), which drown simple things, as the wind sounds in the trees and the funny, sweet things our children do every day. Distractions take away the grooming, which deals with the most important and true issues. Keep it simple. Keep it simple.
- Stay current and inspire the children to remain present and useless games, DVDs, iPhones and iPads. These should be stopped in workshops so that the children can also be more involved. Play instead of games.
- Stay linked Seek to learn and practice together for a good time. Talking about sanitation together, the children can carry it on to better family interaction.
- Encourage play to Invite older children to play "in real life" with younger children, not on an electronic device. Give them pictures or allow them to play outside just make sure family playtime is free of technology or limited to certain times.
- Inspire team bonding. Organize more team building events to inspire children to work together. Build searches for scavengers, build a fort, and plan a tournament. Be imaginative. Be innovative.
- Confide and share when you're down or bad, rely on and share with your good friends and loved ones you trust. Note, this reduces stress and allows you to overcome it more easily. When the rough patch is over, share the story of how others helped you through with your kids.
- Start a mother community. Check your neighborhood for fellow moms and build a support network. This type of support has proven extremely beneficial, helping mothers face daily challenges and even see their children better.
- Teach your children that the family is a squad Instead of "everybody for themselves," allow all to join the family team, and teach your kids what role they can perform-how they can contribute and engage in various projects and events. This spirit of cooperation and co-operation makes everyone feel healthier and happier.
- . Celebrate everyday coexistence. Remember that hygge is not restricted to large family gatherings. It can be achieved with only one

or two people. Of example, one weekday you might announce a "hygge night." The concepts mentioned in this chapter are applied.

## Where Do We Go from Here?

And so, again, the question arises. What has kept the Danes so long in the top of the satisfaction list after 40 years of being chosen as the happiest people in the world? As we saw in The Danish Way of Parenting, it's quite simply how their children are raised. It's a tradition that persists over the decades leading to self-confident, trustworthy, concentrated, content and resilient people and it can work for anyone.

It is important as parents to first look at our default settings, our natural inclinations as parents, so that we can see better where change is needed.

Having time to look inside the mirror and see what we replicate from our own family patterns is the first step to successful parental reform.

Once we have identified our default settings, PARENT principles provide simple, effective instruments to increase the happiness of our children and of ourselves.

Play helps children to develop many vital skills in life. Resilience, expertise in communicating and dealing and self-control are only few of the valuable lessons gained in unstructured play as well as stress management, which decreases children's chances of battling fear as adults.

Practice helps to develop an internal control locus, giving children trust in their own capabilities that lay the foundation for happiness.

Authenticity helps children to build a strong internal compass by learning to trust their feelings. To teach ourselves and our children honesty promotes a strong value of character. And remember all emotions are all right. In addition, different kinds of praise affect children differently in the way they are seen worldwide. Giving empty praise or focusing too much on smartness can make children feel unsafe and risky. Through celebrating systems, we encourage a more stable, more optimistic and robust person rather than a set one.

Reframing is a powerful way to change the perceptions of our children and our lives. How we choose to look at things influences what we act. Realist optimists ignore bad news, but simply focus on the other facts they have at hand and write a better, more caring tale about themselves, their children and life in general. Reframing will improve our social experience and make our lives and the lives of our children happy in the process. Moving on to the ability to reframe our children can be one of the best gifts we can give, fostering their future happiness and future generations.

Empathy is a central and primarily human instinct. While empathy has fallen in our society and the level of narcissism has increased, research has demonstrated that we are more connected to empathy than to egoism. They can better understand the insecurity in ourselves and in others by being less judgmental and less judging, which brings us closer together, build healthier, compassionate relationships and makes us all happier. Empathy teaches children to respect others and themselves, which gives a deeper sense of well-being.

Some ultimatums remember the fights for dominance will cause us to lose our patience. Most adults yell or use disciplinary physical punishment. We lose control, but we do not expect our kids. Trust and closeness towards their children are replaced with apprehension in an oppressive parenting style. This works short-term, but can have long-term consequences. The Danish more relaxed form of parenthood encourages child trust and endurance. Children who are respected and understood, who are supported in turn to understand and follow rules, develop a much stronger sense of self-control and eventually become happier, more emotionally stable adults.

Togetherness and Hygge are ways to encourage our closest connections, which are one of a person's greatest predictors of happiness. Through learning how to clean or relax, we will develop our family to make our children fun and unforgettable experiences. When we leave the "I" at the door and focus on the "us," we will remove a great deal of the unnecessary drama and animosity related to families. Happy families and strong social support provide happier children.

As we said before, maybe you already know or may not have heard of some of the concepts in this book.

You may already practice or practice some of the Danish methods. We are confident that you are on a right track to raise happy babies, if you take even some of the approaches from this book and integrate them into your life.

To order to raise healthier, healthier babies, we believe that parents and teachers should help each other together. Support is needed for all of us. In building a community in order to practice these values, we will create some of the happiest people in our own backyards in the world. We hope you're going to get on board and help us to achieve it!

**Hygge Oath**

Hygge is the special Danish expression for a particular type of harmony. Picture hygge being a place the family will visit. The special room will be more hygienic if everybody knows and tries to conform to the hygiene laws. The hygiene can be discussed and thought about in advance, so everyone who enters the hygiene space for a family dinner, weekend barbeque, or simple family reunion will understand the "ground rules." If everyone knows that hygiene is time, everyone can work to foster proximity for the sake of the whole family. The foregoing is an example of a hygiene vow for the household. Adapt it to your own household and let the harmony continue.

We agree to hygge "Sunday dinner." As a team, we promise to help each other build a comfortable environment in which everyone feels safe, and nobody has to look out for them.

- We agree to try to do so.
- Turn mobile and iPads off.
- Leave us at the door to our drama. Some days we dwell on our issues. Hygge aims to create a safe place for relaxing and leaving stressful things outside.
- Don't complain unnecessarily.
- Seek ways to help so that nobody gets stuck to do all the job.
- If we're inside, light candles.
- Try to enjoy food and drink intentionally.
- Don't lift controversial issues such as elections. Everything that creates a struggle or an argument is not hygienic. At other moments, we can have these conversations.
- Say and say funny, wonderful and uplifting stories from the past.
- Don't praise too much. Subtly divisive praising can be.
- Not rivalry (think "us" not "me"). Not competition.
- Don't talk badly or dwell on negative.
- Play games that can be enjoyed by the whole community.
- Make a conscious effort to express gratitude to the people around us who love us.

# 8.Conclusion

Therefore, the question arises again. Despite 40 years of voting as the happiest people in the world, what has stopped the Danes in the top positions for so long? As I saw in The Danish way of parenting, it's the way they raise their children very clearly. It is a legacy that continues over the generations, which leads to self-confident, confident, centered, happy and resilient adults and that can work for anyone.

It is important, as parents that we first examine our default conditions, our natural inclinations as parents so that we can better see where changes are needed. The first step towards positive change and a happy childhood are taking the time to look in the mirror and see what we mimic from our own family experiences.

Once our default settings have been established, PARENT values offer simple and effective mechanisms for promoting joy in our children and ourselves.

As I stated earlier, you might already know or have not yet heard of some of the topics in this book. I am confident that you will be on the right track to raise happy kids if you take some of the methodologies from this book and integrate them into your life. I believe parents and teachers will work together to promote the Danish Way to bring up happier and more resilient children. Support is needed for all of us. In building a community in order to practice these values, we will create some of the happiest people in our own backyards in the world. I hope you are going to get on board and help us do it!

The Danish Way of Parenting provides a fantastic solution to contemporary parenting, which is a book that contributes to the true origins of family harmony.

Everybody around the globe will learn from the precious wisdom found in this book. Concepts like reframing and grooming are beneficial for communities of all backgrounds. It is great that Danish parenthood shares so much with Good Parenthood! This book I highly recommend! "The Danish Circulation allows parents worldwide to test their own preferences and take the entire infant into consideration.

An appreciation of the value of free playing is a breath of fresh air at a time of intense and overwhelming young children. I thought this book was a clear, very useful and intelligent guide on how to improve your own level of happiness as a parent, and how to encourage happier children in Danish. I would like to recommend this book to anyone who wants the best prospects of a happy life for themselves and/or their children.

# The Montessori Family

How to Become a more Mindful, Attentive and Easygoing Parent

**Samuel Pattinson**

# Introduction

Montessori hit the mainstream, and they're making headlines. I want you to read about the Montessori process, how to introduce Montessori to your home, and what it means to be a parent of Montessori. It can be difficult to navigate all the details.

The Montessori philosophy of education focuses on creating the whole self of the child and allowing the growth to be led by the child. At the root of this approach is reverence for the child.

A Montessori setting is designed carefully and prepared to meet the child's needs. Within that setting, the child has the right to choose materials based on interest and skill. The Director or Guide gives each material a lesson.

The Montessori curriculum has many positive aspects, and Montessori pre-schools are indeed a unique and beautiful thing

Practical Life, Sensorial, Science, Culture, Geography, and History are major areas. Art is very often a separate classroom area. Children start in Practical Life, then move on to the other areas and concurrently complete work. Montessori in home, including The Montessori environment, Montessori activities, Montessori bedrooms, and Montessori parenting approaches.

For babies and toddlers, it is especially important to prepare your environment for the child to have structure but a lot of liberty for self-directed and open play. Make the space kid-friendly so that the Montessori child can be independent and take responsibility for himself when it comes to eating, accessing his things, cleaning his body, turning on lights, and so on. Montessori in the home is an important part of Montessori. Plus, include

There is a need for research regarding how teachers can guide children to independence in the classroom and how parents can support that independence at home.

Montessori parents are willing to help, to reinforce Montessori skills at home, they don't know how. If the skills acquired at school are reinforced at home, children are likely to make more progress. If independence is to be achieved, teachers and parents must work together and support each other so skills acquired in the classroom can be reinforced at home.

The ultimate goal of every Montessori guide is to help children become independent. However, one of the biggest challenges is that the skills acquired in the Montessori classrooms are not reinforced at home. Classroom teachers can only enhance what the parent has nurtured at home. The purpose of this action research study is to determine if increased independence in the home will increase the level of independence in a Montessori classroom.

Within the Montessori philosophy, there is an underlying principle that all children are working towards becoming independent citizens that grow to become self-confident adults

Montessori ideals make kids more engaged and inquisitive while also fostering a lifetime love of learning without forcing them to learn.

Using the Montessori principles to encourage stimulating, self-paced, and positive learning works wonders in your home and everyday life! In fact, there are the added benefits of an active and confident child leading his or her own growth.

When you embark on this path from Montessori to Home, try to be careful. It will take time to change habits, and to incorporate a different philosophy on how you will run your home and be a family. There will be disappointment but you will also have victorious moments. Celebrate the moments and respect them, as fleeting or as transformative as they can be.

# Chapter 1: How Montessori Education Will Shape Your Child

If you're looking for a school environment that provides individualized, student-led learning with a focus on social justice, citizenship, and personal growth, then you've probably considered a Montessori school. Montessori schools are most common at the preschool level, but many parents end up sending their children through their elementary years, and even through high school, to Montessori schools.

So, what do you like about Montessori education, and how can you find out if it's the best match for your child? Let's look ahead.

The central tenant of Montessori learning is that children are capable of self-directed learning, deep focus, and the ability to work their own and at their own pace when given the opportunity, the right resources, and proper guidance.

While they are positively training teachers there to guide the students, if you walk into a Montessori classroom, you'd probably see a group of highly absorbed students some on the floor, some at a desk, each working on their individualized task.

What's in common with Google creators Larry Page and Sergey Brin, Sean "Diddy" Combs, Julia Child, Thomas Edison, Princes William and Harry, and Anne Frank? All educated in a school-based in Montessori.

There are many factors consider when deciding what program type to send your child. Daycare services, home-based schools, and preschools are available.

The school's approach to education and theory should be a part of your decision.

There are many different teaching styles: Montessori schools known for fostering independence. Waldorf schools are known for their creativity; the High/Scope method sets personal goals for children, Bank Street focuses on child-centered education, and the Reggio Emilia approach follows the natural development of a child. As the parent of a child receiving Montessori school, I'm amazed by his growth and the way his experiences shaped him.

If you're looking for a school environment that provides individualized, student-led learning with a focus on social justice, citizenship, and personal growth, then you've probably considered a Montessori school. Montessori schools are most common at the preschool level, but many parents end up sending their children through their elementary years, and even through high school, to Montessori schools.

Here are a few other primary Montessori components:

- Montessori classrooms are multi-age classrooms, usually in each school, with around three grades.
- The hope is that the older kids can educate the little kids when they are group, and the small kids can keep the bigger kids excited and inspired.
- Since everyone is working on their tasks and at their rate, children's rivalry reduced, and teamwork emphasized.
- Most Montessori schools do not use ratings or textbooks, but they give more holistic evaluations of teachers.
- Some student work happens independently and in small groups; apart from the initial explanation of a learning station, there is very little teacher-directed instruction.
- Using Montessori-specific learning resources such as wooden puzzles, colored counting beads, and deceptive geometric form, sticks, and blocks, much of the learning is hands-on.
- Children taught to pick up their area of play after they complete a project and engage in routine classroom tasks,

- such as washing, table setting, and preparing meals

## What Activities Do Montessori Students Typically Engage?

The main activity in which students participate in their job (called "free choice" or "uninterrupted work period") that is celebrated and taken seriously in classrooms in Montessori.

Work-time typically split into chunks of two to three hours, and children select their activity or activities based on interest with limited instructor guidance.

Although the students choose the job, it includes all the core subjects, including reading, math, science, and history.

Time provided for cleaning, caring for plants and animals in class, as well as learning and conflict resolution skills.

It's time for lunch and breaks after the first hour of work.

Younger kids usually have nap time after lunch and no more work; older kids typically engage in a second after lunchtime.

## Who Typically Attends Montessori Schools?

### Demographics and Diversity

Because Montessori schools are mostly private schools with higher-end tuition, they are usually desirable for wealthier families. Montessori colleges, however, generally offer scholarships that can open the door for families of varying economic means. Besides, there are about 500 public schools in Montessori that can care for children of lower-income brackets.

Montessori schools are becoming more diverse in terms of race, but they still have a way to go. As The Washington Post has pointed out, racial diversity continues to be a problem even among public Montessori schools. The cities post a study published in the Montessori Journal, which found that 6 out of 10 public schools in Montessori had proportionally fewer color students than school districts nearby .

**Tuition Costs**

Public Montessori schools are free to attend, and many Montessori schools provide scholarship. Tuition-based Montessori schools vary widely in terms of cost, as reported by The New York Times; for example, a Montessori preschool charges $6,970 in Peoria, Illinois, a year at the low end, and a Boston preschool costs $30,400, at the high end.

**Waldorf or Montessori?**

In addition to the Montessori programs, other parents searching for a less conventional, child-focused education for their child may be considering a Waldorf program. Waldorf schools, like Montessori, de-emphasize traditional grading systems, allow kids to "take the reins" when it comes to their educational programs, and generally provide more autonomy than conventional schooling.

Yet there are some critical differences between the two, including:

Waldorf education emphasizes creative playing much more than Montessori does; indeed, music, dancing, painting, and love of nature are core components of Waldorf education.

Waldorf teaching is more teacher-centric than Montessori.

Montessori classes are multi-grade; Waldorf classroom house just one grade at a time, and the same Teacher remains for all or most of the education of the pupil with the class.

Waldorf pupils do very little traditional academic learning in preschool or early grades, while Montessori starts the "study" of schooling as early as preschool.

Pros and Cons of Montessori Schools

**Pros**

The classrooms at Montessori allow children to be directed by their interests, which can be very exciting for curious children.

Montessori offers more "life skills" than most schools and aims to motivate students to become responsible world citizens.

Hands-on learning can be useful for children with different learning styles and who do not always do well in schools that are more conventional "textbook-based."

Montessori schools offer children versatility, improve self-confidence, and foster freedom.

**Cons**

For many parents, the cost of tuition may be prohibitive.

Many kids may not transition from the Montessori model as quickly into a more conventional educational program or school.

Many children are not doing well with individual learning, and are doing well in larger groups.

Many families do not want younger children to deeply immersed in "work" and prefer a school that is more play-based.

**How Does Montessori Resemble Playful Learning**

A routine in a classroom with its expectations of what happens when constitutes one component of an overall structure. Another dimension is the structural level within any given activity. At the time of painting, for example, drawing is free and unstructured, or a formal assignment with a specified set of steps exists

Conventional schooling appears to be less pre-school-structured and more tightly organized afterward, while preschools have become more standardized in recent years in

reaction to the 2001 federal law called No Child Left Behind (Hamre and Pianta 2007; Zigler and Bishop-Josef 2004 he traditional transition in educational approaches for children aged six from looser to more formal systems leads to an improvement in the obligations of a child and the expectations of adults in many cultures at this age.

Montessori schooling seems loose and amorphous to some researchers as regards the overall structure, and rigid to others. Indeed, Montessori education falls midway between these characteristics: it embodies freedom within freedom within structure and structure. The guiding theory calls for the child's behavior to be positive for its growth — and also for society.

Well-trained teachers at Montessori require that children behave constructively. Parents also ask children who misbehave to stay at their sides, where they can closely monitor the miscreants and, in turn, regulate the misbehavior externally. Gradually, teachers encourage the children to move away as the youngsters learn to control themselves and can, therefore, function more independently. Most kids do not stand like this, and those who never need to stay along for a long time. Montessori education, then, is very structured in this sense

A further standardized dimension of Montessori education provided in the Curriculum. Montessori has a collection of lessons and materials for each classroom level, and the teachers present the elements in a relatively ordered sequence in any given subject (for example, math or music)

. During teacher-training courses during Montessori, instructors move through the introduction of the materials and the philosophy that underlies them. Kids in Montessori programs can freely choose what to do within this sequence of particular lessons with specific materials, so it's at this stage that the Montessori Curriculum seems so unstructured.

Yet embedded even here, the work itself remains deeply organized within that free choice.

One may opt to wash a table, but one must follow specific steps in doing so. You have to bring a mat to a table, raise the table onto the carpet, fill a bucket with water to a specific level, and add a particular amount of soap. Also, carry the bucket and wash material to the cloth, place a sponge in the water, squeeze out the water with a taught squeezing motion, wipe the table from left to right (replicate the way needed to write), dry the table with a towel (from left to right).

And whether you see Montessori schooling as loose or rigid, depends on the level you concentrate. If one focuses on the table washing the micro level, it may sound overly static. If one focuses on the higher level of freedom, it seems loose to children to choose what they do when and with whom. However, if one reflects on (at least in some senses) higher levels of program and its behavioral expectations, it is again organized.

Playful learning, too, is, in some respects, organized but not in others. Teachers direct learning inside frameworks but do so in fun and loose manner, with particular emphasis on the goals they set out. By adhering to a rigid, general structure in some ways but not in others, Montessori teaching resembles playful learning

Conventional direct instruction on the use of objects generally lacks any materials which children manipulate for education. Teachers could picture a blackboard triangle, For example, use a real triangle but not. This training meant to learn through the eyes and ears, not by the hands.

## How Does Montessori Education Differ from Playful Learning

### Structure of the Material

Generally speaking, the kinds of materials used in creative learning don't have the complexity of structure Montessori materials have.

For example, we often see sets of commercially produced wooden or plastic blocks for building play in preschool classrooms. Usually, these comprise four or more block shapes with as many as one dozen of each type. Kids use the blocks to create an endless number of castles, villages, railroads, and other structures from their imaginations.

Children engage in free play with the blocks at will; a teacher can suggest different constructions in supervised play, pointing out how the contrast of the shapes

Children learn to use these products in order, beginning with the Pink Tower, because it seems easier to interpret differences in three dimensions. Next, they learn to perceive a variation in two sizes using the Brown Stair. Lastly, they move on to the Red Rods, which differ in one size only. From there, children take up the Red and Blue Rods, the first material on Montessori mathematics. The Red and Blue Rods are the Red Rods painted blue with alternating 10 cm parts. Children learn to number the sections "1," "2," and so on, leading to counting lengths by name. Montessori also created resources for a later sequence of learning in which the measures separated so that children learn to count objects

In brief, Montessori's block sets systematically differ in difficulty size and development, and inevitably cede into math materials. Such logical progressions govern and distinguish the entire collection of Montessori materials from the more freely formed materials often used in play. Montessori materials are each specifically designed to communicate specific information in a sequenced program at a particular place. Montessori education is thus different from playful learning by providing a broad set of highly structured materials to learn.

### Limits on Choice

Also, free play has certain limitations to it. Before crossing the line from game to violence, a child pretending to be a ferocious dog cannot bite his playmates (Bateson 1972). Therefore, imaginative learning has its limits. And instruction in Montessori is more restrictive. In Montessori classrooms, for example, children can't choose to play with things that teachers have not yet taught them how to use.

We undergo a lesson before children can take products from the shelves. We are using the products in such a way as to derive the desired benefits from the posts. It is doubtful that a playful-learning classroom will have that limitation.

More importantly, children cannot opt to engage in unconstructive practices in a Montessori classroom. An instructor must determine which actions are constructive and avoid non-constructive ones, and they typically recommend using resources for reasons other than unconstructive purposes. In other words, kids cannot take the blocks from the Brown Stair and build houses with the

There are at least three explanations for limitations of that kind. It may conflict with children learning the specific purpose of playing freely with materials that have a symbolic meaning. For instance, a model room in DeLoache's research (2000) serves as a representation of a real, larger office. If kids play as if it were a dollhouse with the model bed, they are less likely to see it as a representation of a real, bigger room. So, if a set of blocks meant to convey dimensional change, using them to explore dimensions systematically might serve their intended purpose and be useful, but using them to build a house might not be

The second reason why Montessori resources are limited includes classroom discipline. Extensive research indicates that children excel when their environments are more

organized, so this limitation on choice might be beneficial (Lillard 2005). That the Montessori approach calls for a particular orderly way of interacting with the materials probably contributes in itself to a sense of order in a classroom. This sense of law could break if children used the products in myriad ways

A third reason to restrict the use of materials relates to self-discipline. Students in traditional Montessori classrooms excel in executive function in looser Montessori classrooms and regular classrooms compared to children (Lillard 2012; Lillard and Else-Quest 2006). Maybe the requirement that children use each material precisely as shown may explain this increased executive ability, as the children will inhibit all other ways in which they can communicate with the object

What's in common with Google creators Larry Page and Sergey Brin, Sean "Diddy" Combs, Julia Child, Thomas Edison, Princes William and Harry, and Anne Frank? All educated in a school-based in Montessori.

There are many factors consider when deciding what program type to send your child. Daycare services, home-based schools, and preschools are available. The school's approach to education and theory should be a part of your decision. There are many different teaching styles: Montessori schools known for fostering independence. Waldorf schools are known for their creativity, the High/Scope method sets personal goals for children, Bank Street focuses on child-centered education, and the Reggio Emilia approach follows the natural development of a child. As the parent of a child receiving Montessori school, I'm amazed by his growth and the way his experiences shaped him.

If you're looking for a school environment that provides individualized, student-led learning with a focus on social justice, citizenship, and personal growth, then you've probably considered a Montessori school.

Montessori schools are most common at the preschool level, but many parents end up sending their children through their elementary years, and even through high school, to Montessori schools.

## 1.1 How did Montessori Education Develop

Italian physician and educator Maria Montessori developed Montessori education. Montessori developed many of her ideas while working with children who had mental challenges. Her first school, the Casa Dei Bambini, was opened to working-class children in a poor neighborhood in Rome. The approach to Montessori characterized by a focus on independence, freedom within limits, and respect for the natural psychological, social development of a child.

It was in this first Montessori school named Casa Dei Bambini by Dr. Montessori that many of the learning methods that are still used today in Montessori schools first developed. The emphasis placed on hands-on learning and the children taught to cook their meals and clean themselves.

Dr. Montessori's school, she had developed, along with the learning techniques, became widely popular in Italy, and soon more schools were opened.

The first American Montessori School opened in New York in 1911; as now, there are about 5,000 Montessori schools in America, with nearly one million children attending.

## 1.2 Montessori Approach

Montessori is an instructional approach based on self-driven practice, hands-on learning, and interactive play. Kids make creative choices in their knowledge in the Montessori classes, while the classroom and the instructor provide age-appropriate activities to direct the process. Children work both in group and individually to discover and explore the world's knowledge and to develop their maximum potential.

Two basic principles underpin the model. Next, through engaging with their surroundings, children and emerging adults engage in psychological self-construction. Second, there is an innate path of mental development for children, especially under the age of six. Maria Montessori believed that when children are allowed to make decisions and act freely within an environment that emphasizes the following qualities, they develop best:

- A structure for smoother movement and operation
- Beauty and harmony; environmental cleanliness
- Much of the instruction is hands-on, with learning materials common to Montessori, such as wooden puzzles, colored counting beads, and deceptive geometric form, sticks, and blocks.
- Construct concerning your child and his / her needs
- Limit materials, so that only materials included that support the development of the child
- Please order
- Most Montessori schools not use grades or textbooks, but they offer more holistic teacher evaluations.
- Nature inside and out of the classroom
- Children taught to pick up their area of play after they complete a project and engage in routine classroom activities, such as cleaning up, setting the table, and preparing meals.

## 1.3 Differences

Many schools follow strict laws on Montessori, while others follow guidelines on Montessori. In a Montessori school, the main difference is that the child is part of a group of 3-to-5 or 6-year-olds and has been with the same teachers for more than a year.

The aim is to create a family-like environment where children select activities at their own pace, and older children gain confidence by helping to teach younger children. Learning Montessori is based on self-directed practices, hands-on learning, and interactive play. Children choose what resources they want to work within Montessori classrooms, and the Teacher directs the process by providing activities that are suitable for the age. Children can work individually or in groups while they are discovering and exploring.

## 1.4 What Does a Montessori Classroom Look Like

While schools vary on how strictly they follow the techniques, the majority of preschool classrooms in Montessori are tidy, well-organized, and uncluttered. This welcoming room makes kids feel centered and relaxed. There are areas for group activities, as well as rugs and sofas, where a child can relax and rest. To order to promote independence, each object in the classroom is easily accessible to the children.

The room contains well-defined areas for various parts of the Curriculum, including:

- Practical life, which helps to build life skills
- Sensorial, which helps to develop sensory competences
- Math
- Language
- Culture, including music, art, geography, and science
- Classes are clean, with gentle, calming tones, and plants will be on show in many types or even a pet class.
-

Our place within the natural world is also a central theme in Montessori education, with many Montessori classrooms maintaining certain aspects of nature such as flowers or other living plants, a rock garden, or seashells.

## 1.5 Is a Montessori a Good Fit For Your Child

It is a personal decision to decide which educational approach best fits your child's personality and needs. Knowing your child is the first and most important step to figure out if your best match will be a Montessori school. Because there is self-directed learning, some may think that Montessori will not work well for a more unruly child. Still, the order and calmness may impose some stability on a child who has trouble slowing down otherwise.

## 1.6 Special Needs

Children with special needs, such as mental or physical handicaps, often excel in a Montessori community. The materials used in the environments of Montessori include all the senses. Kids are free to move around the classroom, which is a benefit for those kids who need a lot of physical activity. Every child learns at their rate, and there is no obligation for a set time to meet the structured standards.

## 1.7 What To Look On a Tour

It's essential to notice the classroom atmosphere and how teachers and the students are behaving with each other. Does it look like students are engaged? Seem bored the teachers? Check if an outdoor area exists and have a look at it. Playing areas of Montessori should allow large motor movements such as running, throwing, climbing, and balancing.

## 1.8 Transitioning To a Traditional School

Some kids spend their preschool years only in a Montessori classroom, while others go on for elementary and middle school. There will be some differences between the

Montessori Curriculum for your child and their conventional education. These differences may include: choosing his work versus learning the lesson plan of the Teacher,

moving freely around the classroom versus sitting in an assigned seat and learning in a mixed-age classroom versus learning with his age students. But don't be afraid, the children are adaptable. Children with Montessori education often learn to be self-reliant and calm, knowing how to work as part of a community in the classroom. Because of this, students switching from Montessori typically adapt to a more traditional approach very easily and quickly.

Consider the Space

A Montessori setting places great emphasis on order, harmony, and simplicity. A calm, peaceful atmosphere is paramount. A few choices of decoration will get the room closer to that ideal environment, such as choose neutral wall colors, dimmable lighting, and task lighting (like a sconce or table lamp in the place they love to read), and having as much natural light as possible. There should also be enough room for a child to play, so it's nice to have a large area rug on which to spread! Consider removing any unnecessary furniture (like the coffee table) even if it's only for a while, and getting more open spaces.

Prepare Their Surroundings

We all spend time and money proving the home for children, but consider their environment as a whole until your child is a baby. A Montessori space's goal is to be able to leave a room and be confident they're safe to play and explore by themselves. After all,

"Help me do it by myself" is the Montessori motto. Position toys, books, and even clothes at their eye level.

Consider a small wooden table and chairs, with low open shelve (the method's cornerstone) and some artwork at height so they can appreciate it better! Hang a mirror at their height so they can have fun watching themselves as they begin to develop responsibility for things such as dressing up.

Simplify

There is mention of the other open shelving; we automatically think about seeing a mess. But the guiding principle of Montessori is that it is in a calm and orderly environment that children learn best. Consider getting rid of all the waste, at the same time having just a few toys out in the racks. You should pick up a good chunk of toys and then turn on new ones once they get sick of them. Essentially, it is a more minimalist approach, which in turn keeps your house tidier and your child more active. Moreover, children tend to gravitate to just a few toys at a time, and never play with anything anyway. Should also help with excess spending because you are recycling what you already have instead of continually bringing in new products

Natural Is Key

We all know the benefits of fresh air, play outdoors, and get dirty.

Nevertheless, the Montessori approach does not confine nature to the outside. Bringing it inside is equally worthwhile! It's an excellent example to allow children to collect and view such items as rocks, pinecones, or seashells.

Hang the flowers they choose in your table setting or use that piece of driftwood. Natural elements are a component in your decor, too. Try to incorporate various textures, such as cotton, wool, lots of wood, or bamboo.

It also refers to toys–the Montessori approach meant to limit the amount of material that children play with, preferring more natural elements.

That could be the hardest part, what with the amount of technology now available. But even setting the aim of adding one wooden toy or shortening the screen time every day by a few minutes will make a difference.

## The Montessori Difference

What is the Montessori difference? Families that are new to Montessori ask: "What make A unique Montessori from other preschools? "The answer lies in the delivery of learning experiences. The prepared classroom environment, materials from Montessori and teaching concepts from Montessori provide children with the resources they need to succeed in their early formative years of education. Such firm foundations send Montessori students into the future as competent and enthusiastic learners who will aspire to achieve the only Montessori standard: "Excellence in anything you set your mind to." Reserving a tour is the best way to learn more about the Montessori distinction. For more information on the key differences between Montessori and child care services

## Main Differences

- Main difference based on relate to Montessori, These are as following:
- Prepared learning environments
- Montessori learning materials
- Child-focused instruction
- Active learning activities
- Adaptable curriculum are key differences in Montessori education

## Prepared Learning Environment

The first Montessori difference may observe In the Montessori classroom system which is a ready learning environment. Montessori learning resources inside the Montessori classroom displayed within their specific **Curriculum area**, including Practical Life, Sensorial, Mathematics, Language, and Culture. Each element presented in progression order, from most natural To the worst, then right to left. This rational framework allows children to coordinate their thought, make logical progress through the Montessori method, and learn the material outcome at their own rate. The Montessori materials' left to right orientation also helps children prepare for reading and writing, and the way that information is automatically interpreted by the brain. By contrast, play-based child care programs generally offer a classroom environment without a sense of order or structure that does not provide the harmonious learning environment with the same design.

Montessori Materials

The second Montessori difference may observe Looking round the classroom shelves. Each Montessori classroom provides a complete suite of authentic **Montessori learning materials** from Neinhaus and Bruins, Montessori's leading international materials suppliers. Montessori materials are tactile learning tools intended to isolate one particular skill or idea. The materials encourage hands-on learning, autonomous problem solving, and analytical thinking. The most unique thing about these hands-on learning tools is that every item is built with an error control. This encourages children to work with the materials, and through repetition and practice to discover the learning outcome. Learning with the Montessori materials teaches children how to improve' **Executive Function** ' skills such as critical thinking, teamwork, communication, imagination, independence and innate motivation. Play-based child care facilities, on the other hand, typically offer a range of activities that are primarily play-based toys, rather than instructional learning materials.

**Teachers' Roles**

A further Montessori difference is the role of the Teacher. In a Montessori preschool, the role of the Teacher is to provide students with learning experiences designed to animate their own "inner teacher." They will never say, "no, you're doing it wrong," or compare one child's progress to another. Instead, they observe, guide, and respect each child's unique development journey. This structure encourages students to develop the skills of independence, self-regulation, impulse control, and critical thinking, ultimately leading to a harmonious classroom environment, and the optimal learning space for children. Montessori Teachers also create daily lesson plans for each child, and teach at a child level, as opposed to a class level. This structure allows each child to progress according to their developmental needs and interests. In comparison, most traditional preschools deliver the same weekly plan, at the same pace, in the same order for all students.

Active vs. Passive

In the fourth place, Montessori lessons are interactive learning experiences that engage children's senses. Doctor Maria Montessori understood experiential education to be a crucial aspect of children's development because of its link to how children come to understand their world. Children first learn through their hands. Incorporating both gross and fine motor skills in learning activities is crucial to a balanced approach to each childhood education that includes

The social, mental, physical, and emotional aspects of child development. A lot of Montessori materials therefore encourage the development of these skills from a young age onwards.

The Montessori materials teach kids to become confident, self-motivated learners with the skills to succeed by encouraging them to explore learning through their senses.

Traditional pre-schools, on the other hand, generally promote learning through passive learning experiences such as listening and play-based activities.

## Montessori Work Cycle

A further Montessori difference is the three-hour work cycle. The Montessori work cycle is a structured period of learning at the beginning of the school day that allows children to direct and manage their learning. During the work cycle, children are free to choose from a tremendous range of Montessori activities from all areas of the Montessori Curriculum and develop critical Areas of knowledge via repetition and practice. Each child is free to pursue their interests, develop concentration skills and problem-solving skills and work at their own pace. By comparison, traditional preschools usually do not offer such services a large block of time for children to direct their developing and learning their concentration on activities.

## Mixed Age Groups

The sixth Montessori difference is mixed-age class groups. In Montessori, classrooms are flexible and determined by the child's developmental range, as opposed to chronological birth year. The structure allows children to work at their level when socializing with children of different ages and abilities in development. Mixed-age groupings promote unique learning opportunities, including imitative learning, peer tutoring, and collaboration throughout. Mixed-age classes often encourage students to develop a strong sense of community, as children spend 2-3 years in the same room. Classes are specified by chronological age within 12 months in most conventional pre-schools, rather than a stage of development for a child.

## Adaptable Curriculum

Further, the Montessori Curriculum covers five key developmental areas, including Practical Life, Sensorial, Mathematics, Language, and Culture. Culture also includes the study of Geography, Science, Music, and Art. Each Curriculum area contains a range of learning materials that progress in difficulty as children first master the necessary, then intermediate, and advanced foundations of the Montessori Curriculum. In each curriculum area, the activities were designed to teach specific learning goals while also offering a range of learning extensions to further strengthen key concepts. In this way the Montessori Curriculum can be adapted and expanded to meet the unique developmental needs and interests of each child. The program generally includes established learning goals in conventional pre-schools that do not provide learning extensions to fit individual needs of children.

## Self-Made Self-Esteem

The eighth Montessori difference is self-made self-esteem. One of the fundamental principles of Montessori education is that, as opposed to accomplishment, a child's self-esteem comes from a sense of pride, arising from the effort. There are no gold-star awards, universal expectations, or predetermined conceptions of what is considered "ordinary" or "common" in Montessori. Every child is free to develop their own talents and abilities, to flourish as well-rounded individuals, and to enjoy what is special about itself. Children are allowed to establish their independence in the Montessori classroom and accomplish this through their work with the Montessori materials. As the materials are self-correcting, children learn to master the activity through repetition, practice, and sheer effort. Such pillars are essential to the creation of self-made self-esteem, where the job reward is completing the case, not external recognition. For typical pre-schools, self-esteem is strengthened, as opposed to celebrating commitment, by public praise based on achievement.

## Love of learning

However, the goal of Montessori education is to promote a love of learning for a lifetime. Doctor Maria Montessori claimed that children were born with a natural desire to learn as this helped them to understand their environment and participate actively in it. Montessori education aims to nurture this passion by providing children with the environment, materials, and guidance they need to achieve their full potential. Each child considered in Montessori to be a natural scientist, and the world is their laboratory. Montessori teachers' job is to provide resources and encouragement for students to discover and master the knowledge and skills that will pave the way for their future successes. As a result, education at Montessori encourages each child's innate talents and abilities and prepares them to succeed in their educational careers. Children are encouraged to learn in conventional pre-schools because, as opposed to soul-fulfillment, it is important for school and work.

School and Life Success

Finally, Montessori views education as an aid and a preparation for life. It focused on the complete development of the child's emotional, social, cognitive, and physical self. Each child is free to develop their natural talents and abilities, to develop at their own pace, follow their interests, flourish as well-rounded individuals, and love what is unique about themselves. In this way, Montessori education aims to prepare children to become life-long learnings that are not only ready for school but life. In traditional preschools, training primarily focused on school readiness, as opposed to real-life skills.

Montessori Early Learning: Preparation for School and Life

The Montessori Training system based on scientific discoveries of Doctor Maria Montessori (1870-1952) on how children learn as they grow from birth to adulthood. Studies on child development by Montessori, and subsequent studies on how to build the ideal learning environment, came to form the basis of the' Montessori process.' The Montessori Curriculum, which is a child-centered learning method integrating comprehensive learning outcomes adapted to the developmental needs and interests of each individual, is central to the Montessori Approach.

The Montessori **Curriculum** covers five key learning areas, including Practical Life, Sensorial, Mathematics, Language, and Culture. In addition to these key areas of learning, Montessori Academy also covers the **Early Years Learning Framework** for the Australian Government, Health and Wellbeing, Science, Geography, **School Readiness**, and the **Arts**. In this way, Montessori Academy delivers a holistic education program tailored to each child's unique developmental needs and interests.

Practical Life

Practical Life activities help children learn how to care for themselves and their environment. These activities help the child to become more independent, leading to greater self-confidence and the ability to face new challenges. Practical Life exercises include lessons in grace and courtesy, care for self, and care for the environment. The purpose of these activities is to enhance coordination, concentration, independence, and indirectly prepare children for writing and reading. Activities often include cleaning, food preparation, polishing, and watering plants.

Sensorial

Sensorial materials were designed by Doctor Maria Montessori to help children express and classify their sensory experiences. The aim of sensory experiences to facilitate the development of a child's mental senses, which enhances the ability to observe and compare with accuracy. There are sensorial materials which focus on visual perception, tactile sensations, auditory sense, and perceptions of olfactory and taste. Matching and marking materials often include tasks that separate the sense of sight, sound, touch, taste, and smell.

Mathematics

Mathematical concepts are introduced to the child using concrete sensorial materials. Initial explorations with sensorial materials encourage children to understand basic math concepts such as learning number recognition, counting, and sequencing of numbers. Sensorial work prepares the child for a more formal introduction to mathematics, and the introduction of abstract mathematical concepts such as the decimal system and mathematical operations.

Language

Language materials are designed to enhance vocabulary and explore both written and spoken language. Through language-based activities, such as the sandpaper letters and the moveable alphabet, children learn phonetic sounds and how to compose words phonetically. We progress with tangible materials to create their written work, read others ' work, and learn to communicate their personal feelings and thoughts.

Culture

Cultural activities encourage the child to experience music, stories, artwork and objects from the culture, environment and cultural background of the child. The areas of geography, science, zoology, and botany are all included in this area. A range of globes, puzzle maps, and folders containing pictures from different countries all help to give the child an insight into different cultures. The culture area encourages children to develop their capacity for creation and develop excellent motor skills. While learning to express themselves freely. Through cultural activities, children develop an awareness and appreciation of the world around them.

# Chapter 2: Easy and Practical Montessori Practice

Mindfulness is not an easy practice to put in place, nor is it for all. It is even more difficult for children because it can be challenging to keep still and focused, as most meditation techniques require. Yet more and more work is continuing to show the positive effects of mindfulness on the lives of our children. Researchers found in one study that teaching respiratory exercises for seven to eight-year-olds significantly reduced their level of anxiety.

Practicing mindfulness can help children become more attentive and reduce stress and anxiety as well. There is now proof that carefulness can easily replace the traditional practices of the discipline.

However, few studies have explored the practices of mindfulness that work best with the children. There is also little evidence as to when the method of mindfulness practices is too soon to begin. However, Montessori education has always been aware of the benefits of exercising awareness of the overall well-being of children. Knowledge is a central aspect of Montessori education, according to Angeline Lillard. In Montessori classrooms, even the youngest children benefit from the practices of mindfulness.

Practicing mindfulness with children has many benefits – it helps to reduce anxiety and hyperactivity, it helps teach children to calm down, it helps improve focus and concentration, it helps children communicate with their inner self. It also teaches children how to control their emotions.

## 2.1 Produce Sensory Experience

Montessori education has always stressed the significant impact of sensory experiences on the well-being of children. Maria Montessori claimed that children become sensory seekers from age three, and thus, children can distinguish between different smells, sounds, and textures at Montessori schools. The finest sensory materials are aesthetically pleasing and bright, according to Montessori.

Montessori schools allow children to make connections and recognize interrelationships. Making comparisons helps children become more aware of the different senses which encourage them to distinguish sensory sensations. Teaching children how to identify sounds is also an everyday activity in Montessori. For example, teachers may set different bells around the classroom, and the children investigate to identify the corresponding sounds.

**How you can adopt Montessori's mindfulness approach**

- Provide materials to your child, which stimulate his senses. Substances that stimulate touch sensation are essential. e.g., encouraging your child to help you knead the dough by hand or providing grains with which he can experiment will help him practice awareness.
- Rouse your child with nature. Give openings for her to watch, touch, taste, and control the objects in her environment. The following time you're outside, energize your child to halt and scent the blossoms.

## 2.2 Encourage Your Child to Practice Deep Concentration

One of the fundamental principles of Montessori education is to provide children with opportunities to focus on them. Montessori believed that each child could focus and concentrate if the right atmosphere to him or her given by us. Concentration transforms children, calms them down, and brings out their spiritual qualities, according to Montessori. Exciting work is consuming, and this is consistent with mindfulness.

**How you can adopt Montessori's mindfulness approach**

- Montessori assumed that allowing children to choose the things they wanted to engage in would result in their complete absorption. Providing unstructured yet stimulating experiences at home offers a place for children to choose activities based on their interests.
- If your child has focused and concentrating issues, note that research has found simple and fun activities that can help reduce inattention.

## 2.3 Practice Walking Meditation

Young kids have not yet developed the skills to keep them still for long periods. So, they are likely to fight meditation. Walking meditation schools in Montessori is a form of mindfulness suitable for youngsters.

Young kids have not yet developed the skills to keep them still for long periods. So, they are likely to fight meditation. Walking meditation that in schools in Montessori is a form of mindfulness suitable for youngsters.

Upon discovering that children enjoyed walking along a line (rolling along with logs), Montessori came up with the "Walking on the line" practice. He felt reflecting on how one moves helped children work on their sense of balance. Montessori schools teach children to walk in the field on lines drawn, painted, or taped. Music can also accompany walking on the line practice, during which children expecting to move to the music rhythm.

How you can adopt Montessori's mindfulness approach

- Walking meditation is a high activity to help children become more aware.
  The development of strolling on line is simple to set up and utilize at domestic.
- You can also use a signal to practice meditation on walking with your kids. You can give him a sign, for example, and ask him to walk around the room while making sure the bell doesn't make any sound.

## 2.4 Take Advantage of "THE SILENCE GAMES"

One day I will be realized of using silence to test the ability of hearing of the girls, so I thought of calling them by name from a certain distance, in a whisper, as is the tradition in some medical tests. The child invited me to come up to me and walk so as not to make a sound. For forty children, this patient waiting exercise required patience that I thought was impossible, so I took some sweets with me as a reward for every child who came to me. The kids declined the candy, however. They seemed to say, "Don't ruin our lovely experience; we still filled with the joy of the spirit; don't distract us." And so, I noticed that children were responsive not only to silence but to a voice calling in silence imperceptibly. We came up slowly, sitting on tip-toe, taking care not to crash into anything, and they could barely hear their footsteps.

Montessori believed children loved quiet and wanted it. "The game of silence" is used in the Montessori classes in various ways. A bell is used in some schools to call for silence. Both children expected to remain silent, listening to their surroundings. The moment of silence is over; the kids are encouraged to share in the silence what they have heard.

How you can adopt Montessori's mindfulness approach
- Montessori's "Silence Match" can be used at home in many respects.
  You could come up with a "Peaceful Corner," for example, where the whole family gathers for a quiet moment. Mind to explain what your children expected to do-make your bodies as still as possible, what are you hearing?
- Keep in mind that allowing your child to have stand-and-stare time can also help her interact with the world around her.

## 2.5 Try Age Appropriate Essential Oils

Relatively new research suggests that inhalation of oil significantly improves meditation on consciousness. Though it can be challenging to use essential oils in classroom environments, some Montessori schools have integrated the use of essential oils into their daily routines. Evidence suggests that the right fats will help reduce anxiety and increase the feelings of relaxation and calmness.

How you can realize Montessori's mindfulness approach
- Essential oils might be poisonous for children, and there are some precautions to take when choosing the essential oils to use and how to use them to enhance feelings of calm and well-being in kids.

## 2.6 General Montessori Resources

- Montessori service provides lots of excellent tools for Montessori. You won't find the pink tower or math beads in this store, but in the Practical Life area and classroom set-ups, you can find a variety of starter kits. I provided a starter set of language objects and floored at the offering. I felt

ready and coordinated. You will discover Montessori classroom products and resources across all areas.
- To Earth, Montessori is worth checking out.
- Particularly noteworthy are the services and support this site offers, particularly at home schools.
- Montessori Books for Parents is a list of books I started my Montessori journey many years ago.
- To add to your learning environment, Etsy has unique and beautiful Montessori materials.
- Teachers pay teachers
- A rock-solid language program is all about learning.
- Perfect for homeschoolers and those kids that need an extra boost to read, write, and spell at home.
- My kids love it.
- Kid Advance online Montessori Courses is a great resource accessible via Amazon.
- The high quality of Andy's rates is fair.

Observe your Childs

Montessori activities help develop their interests, choose their work, and raise their own space. As Dr Maria Montessori said: "I researched the child. I took what the child showed me and articulated it, and that's what's called the Montessori Process."

Control of Error

Montessori materials designed with a power of error, which makes them auto-instructional. That means that the child can discover and correct their mistakes without adult intervention. The Montessori materials help to enhance independence, freedom of choice, and self-esteem.

Sensory Exploration

Maria Montessori discovered that children learn best when their senses are engaged in a learning activity. The child, to Montessori, is a "sensorial explorer."

Learn By Doing

Children learn by doing. Montessori education introduces complex and abstract concepts through hands-on activities that involve sensory-based learning materials.

# Chapter 3: Incorporating Montessori Principles At Home

Developed by Italian mathematician Maria Montessori more than 100 years ago, the Montessori Method of teaching and learning revolves around the idea that children can initiate their own learning experiences. If you're in any Montessori School or setting, you'll find a convincing combination of resources and activities specifically designed to build a well-rounded learner meaning students are physically, cognitively, emotionally, and socially challenged.

Many people have heard of Montessori education programs, but many do not know that Montessori's teachings are also ideas that you can implement quickly at home. In reality, Dr. Montessori first began to develop her theories on how kids learn while working with kids living in low-income apartments.

Why should a parent consider having Montessori values applied at home? There are numerous explications for this, but the most one is that it is an immaculate way to apperceive and develop the intrinsically facility of your child to memorize almost the world around them through significant play. Through making a few improvements to your home environment, you can help to encourage the natural curiosity and learning ability of your child

Many parents are intrigued by the idea when it comes to adopting Montessori concepts at home, but they aren't sure where to start. Nevertheless, it begins with a change in mentality.

As a parent, you must begin by realizing that children, even the smallest ones, are more capable than you know.

When you understand this, then you can make some improvements in your home to set up yourself and your child for success in Montessori.

The following are the priorities and values that Maria Montessori holds about her approach to children's education.

Maria Montessori Theory Principles

Independence

"Never help a child with a task he feels he can be successful at." – Maria Montessori.

Montessori education in the classrooms is always the aim of making the child confident and being able to do things for itself. That done by giving opportunities to the students. Opportunities for peregrinating, dressing up, deciding what to do, and fortifying the adults with the jobs. When the children can do things for themselves, their self-belief, self-confidence, and esteem improve that they can carry on throughout their lives.

Observation

It's easy for parents to track or watch the infant. We can spend countless hours just watching the kids and see how they enjoy themselves, exploring their surroundings. It was the simple method of how Maria Montessori thought about the children and developed her child development theories. Without preconceived ideas, she found that helped her create materials which the kids needed and were interested in that. Observation is also how parents can learn about what the child needs.

For instance, if a kid starts banging on things, it means he needs the gross motor exercise, so give him a drum.

When kids push things around the room and need to walk but still can't do it on their own, support them, or provide them with a wagon to travel there.

It is how insight can help to create peace, to meet the present needs of the child.

## Following the Child

Follow the kid, and they'll show you what they need to do, what needs to improve within themselves, and in which field they need to challenge by them. The purpose of the children who persevere with an object in their work is not to "learn;" they are drawn to it by the needs of their inner life, which must be understood and formed by their means. "–Maria Montessori.

Follow them through what you've observed from the children's actions in what they need to do. Don't be overprotective if they want to climb; give them the chance to climb carefully. Therefore, following the child means being non-directive, don't tell them what to do all the time. Make your child able to select what will good for them.

Do not tell them what to do, but instead provide them with options of various materials/toys. Avoid interfering all the time unless they are become violent and are about to harm them. Understanding when to interfere is a skill that parents learn as they get to know their child and as parents set the child's boundaries.

## Correcting the Child

Babies make mistakes. They can spill stuff, accidentally drop food, and so on. In cases like these, there is no need to raise your voice. Then, politely accept the mistake, "oh, you spilled the water... why don't we get a cloth to clean it up." The opportunity to ask the child to do some legitimate practical work for you. You will find that kids like cleaning up as they see it as something that adults do. There's no need to point out a glaring error of a kid, and there's a way to make them know it.

For instance, a child who knows how to drink from a bottle will find out with a cloth bib that if he tips the glass a little too early, the water will spill over him, and he will feel it. There is no need to correct them if they mispronounce a word but instead say the word correctly. We may be afraid to try anything in fear of making another mistake by adjusting them.

Children are going to make mistakes, and we got to teach them correctly. They are giving children freedom and choice. Encourage your child in their decision by ensuring that they are healthy, feeding their inquiring minds in such a way that they can appreciate and identify their needs to develop their full potential.

Prepared Environment

The first responsibility of the instructor is to watch over the community, and that takes precedence over everything else. The influence is indirect, but there will be no real and lasting effects of any kind, physical, mental or spiritual unless it has done properly.-Maria "Montessori.

An essential part of Montessori is the prepared climate. Learning from adults is the bond for a child. Rooms are child-sized, with success-built activities that require freedom of movement and choice. For the child to explore freely, the world has to be safe. The atmosphere has to be beautiful and ready for the kids, so it encourages them to work.

Montessori refers to work like the child's task, or what other people would call playing. She calls this work because they build themselves through this, and it's not just a task. Their playing is their work, and they love it still. The mission of the adult then is to create the atmosphere they will be learning in. Therefore, the child's growth depends on the world in which she or he lives, and that context always involves the parents.

Absorbent Mind

Montessori watched the children learn the language without anybody teaching them. Which ignited her "absorbent mind" idea Children under three years of age need not have lessons to learn; they absorb everything in the environment by experiencing it and being part of it. Therefore, the setting up atmosphere must be pleasant, friendly, and positive as that is what the child will absorb whether or not he chooses to.

The adult language is one that a kid can easily pick up from there. Pay attention to what you're doing about them. Even though you think they don't listen, because they might not be able to express themselves yet, you won't want them shouting back at you when they do. That's why one shouldn't try to say "No" to a boy. We don't want them to tell us, "No, rudely." Alternatively, when we want to tell the kids that what they are doing is wrong, we say, "Stop."

## 3.1 Organize Environment

One of Montessori's fundamental values at home is "a place for everything and everything in its place." If you assign a place for it all, your child will quickly learn where it all goes. It is an essential tool to teach them to be responsible for their belongings and to clean up messes that they may make. The significant changes can make you to order your environment effectively is to make things more accessible to your child.

**We recommend that parents do this:**

- Place clothes in low drawers or baskets and push the rod in the closet down to eye level so that your child can touch his or her clothes
- Step stools place in both the kitchen and the bathroom to allow them to wash their hands and help with the preparation of meals in the kitchen

- Place toys, games and art supplies on low shelves where your child can easily access them, then divide these toys into different baskets and bins so that the products remain separate and are easy to find without sifting through piles of other toys
- Store healthy snacks down low in your refrigerator or pantry so your child can help themselves
- Keep drinks in small pitchers located in the fridge on the lower shelf, with cups that are child-friendly nearby. Allow them to relieve themselves when your child is thirsty; be sure to keep a sponge nearby so that they can clean up any mess they do too.

Parents are also encouraged to change the toys and books for their children every few weeks. It is for keeping their focus alive and preventing boredom. Sometimes parents may find daunting, and the best way for it is to rotate the products on your shelves depending on the seasons and the real interests of your child. Are they curious about dinosaurs? Then include a dinosaur box and a couple of age-appropriate books on the shelves. Whatever topics your children are interested in, the aim is to promote creativity and creativeness.

## 3.2 Emphasize Life Skill

Even young kids can pitch in around the house. You will set your child up to be a considerate, competent adult later by encouraging them to take care of themselves and the environment around them at a young age. It will mean that you may need to stop as a parent and take the time to teach your child how to wipe the table properly after a meal or which cabinet to put their cups in, but their minds are so absorbent that it won't take long before they can do it independently.

Try to balance age and skill with their assignments. Younger children, for example, are well able to learn water plants, feed pets, clean the table after a meal and pick up their toys. Older kids will integrate more complex tasks into their routines, such as clearing the garbage, preparing meals, and essential home maintenance. In your family, too, you can have them teach the younger children.

## 3.3 Teach Concentration

Many adults don't think young kids can concentrate, and, indeed, kids can't focus on something for the same time as adults. But this is an ability under the Montessori philosophy of learning that you can start to cultivate in your child when they are young. Through knowing what they are interested in, you can do this by setting them up with the tools and resources they need to explore it more thoroughly.

Once people first start, they sometimes mistakenly assume that giving their child space means they have to have a secluded area away from the rest of the family. It is not real. While some kids need more isolation than others, it is crucial to figure out how best your child works, and then promote that. Many kids enjoy working right in the middle of the house at the kitchen table. Some prefer their bedroom's isolation or a peaceful corner of a playroom.

## 3.4 Focus on Inner Motivation, Not Reward

The Montessori philosophy is not focused on handing out extrinsic rewards for success to children, such as stickers or candy. Verbal praise is valued, although it is essential to ensure that they gave moderation. The goal is to teach your kids to appreciate and seek out the sensations of enjoyment and satisfaction that come with learning something new or completing a mission.

Creating a Montessori environment shouldn't wait until your kids are older. Also, babies respond well to a home Montessori environment. It's a great time to start this process because you're just starting with your child, and you can slowly implement ideas and change as your child grows.

## 3.5 Baby-proof Your Home

Secure electrical outlets put safety latches on doors and avoid things that might harm your baby or that could hurt your baby. We need to create an atmosphere where they can move and frequently explore when they continue to be mobile

## 3.6 Use Baby Gates to Create Areas for Exploration

Many people think of gates as a way of limiting their little ones, but you can use them for mapping their playing spaces and keeping them in areas built for learning and exploring.

## 3.7 Make Their Bedroom Child-Friendly

Try to put a mattress on the floor and age-friendly toys within reach. It helps them to switch from sleeping to playing without your aid once they can crawl and finally go walking. You're going to want to have a baby gate across the door so that they remain in this area.

## 3.8 Utilized Child Size Furniture

Consider using a small table and chairs for mealtimes rather than using a high chair. Place it in the kitchen or dining room — next to the table where the adults are eating — and use it as well for mealtime, snack time, and exercise. Once your baby can sit, they should do this with an adult close by to provide support and help.

Once you've built a safe space to explore for your kid, there are many ways you can stimulate their curiosity about the world around them. Babies react well to a low-hung mirror and other small toys when they are too young to travel about by themselves. Use toys and objects which help them make use of all five of their senses as they grow. Give them a box and some items to bring in and take out of the box to practice. Help develop their sensory abilities by playing with sand, water, and other textured objects.

The "Treasure Box" is a staple of a Montessori curriculum for younger children. That is something you can make at very little expense on your own. Once again, the goal is to help your little one grow their five senses. The basket can contain wood, leather, fur, feather, metal, and any other natural materials. Please ensure that the objects do not pose a hazard of falling, or have sharp edges. Avoid placing plastic items in the tub, too.

## 3.9 Keep Books and Toys on Low shelves

Place on low shelves a small selection of age-appropriate books and toys— but no plastic toys. Holding them on a little shelf will encourage your kid to help himself with anything that catches his eye. Place each form of a toy in another basket or bin so they can start learning everything has a rightful place. Rotate your collection of toys and books every few weeks to keep things fresh and new.

## 3.10 Hang Interesting Art Work

Whether it's a print from one of the greats, or a framed picture, your child or an older sibling drew, exposing your kid to beauty and art is a great way to stimulate their mind.

## 3.11 Create Seasonal Nature Trays

For your child to experience and discover, arrange a tray of things you've found each season outdoors. If you include your child in gathering objects from your yard, this will even become another learning and discovery moment. Always remember to make sure there's nothing in the trays that could be a shock hazard or make them sick if it ends up in their mouths.

If you are not sure where to start with a nature tray, take some of these seasonal ideas into account:

- Spring: Green leaves, moss, different plants and flowers, seeds, fake eggs
- Summer: shells, small boats, trees, starfish, nuts, herbs
- Fall: gourds, apples, berries, acorns, dried grain, fall books, actual or artificial mummies
- Winter: Paper snowflakes, evergreen trees, snow globe, winter scenic pictures

## 3.12 Recommended Montessori Resources

The principle behind the Montessori approach is that as your child grows and develops, you can build on what you've already begun. So ideally, you'd have already started to adapt your home and lifestyle to the Montessori Method long before your child starts primary education. If this is the case, you will expand on what you have already begun. Don't worry if you haven't, and it's never too late to get going.

It is essential to note that it takes some advanced planning to implement the Montessori Method for your child at any age,

but perhaps even more so with school-age children. It is vital to integrate daily activities such as cooking, cleaning, and reading into your home.

Continue to use the low shelves that you used when your child was younger but swap the toys for puzzles, books, and other age-appropriate activities as they grow. You should add elements that reinforce what they've learned in school — but the point of your efforts isn't to overwhelm them with book knowledge but to find realistic ways to teach them daily abilities.

**A Montessori Home:**

When a family becomes grown-up, you have made choices along the way that affect how the family communicates with each other, and the degree to which the children can be a part of the family unit. With a different set of circumstances, each family is unique. But a Montessori home has many common components-and this is not about the materials you see in classrooms at Montessori.

### What is a Montessori Home?

Simply put-it's that a home built with the children's needs in mind. It is a home where children can touch and discover and use and master everyday items used in daily life. The adults stepped back and looked through a child's eyes into the home. They used this dream to help them create a home that completely engages the kids

### Why a Montessori home

Teach me to do these things myself! "This is the most frequently heard call from children. They suppressed their deep inner desire to understand and be part of their environment. In their early years, home is most often the center of their world. There are so many tasks that children can learn to do in their own homes. There is no better place to help young children grow and learn than in their homes.

### How to make a Montessori home

Ensure your furniture welcomes your children and the spaces you make. Render them ideal in size, if possible. All your home furniture has not to be replaced. You may make adjustments or consider adding a few items to the furniture you already have.

Kitchen: kids will help prepare food (adapt the cooking and children's recipes), set the table, clear the plates, wash the dishes, load the dishwasher, and sweep the floor. Give the little ones a weaning table and chair so they can become more comfortable with their eating habits.

Bathroom: make available for use with the toilet and sink a small platform stool. You are using more miniature towels, which are hanging low enough to accommodate the boy. Make a drawer available for easily accessible personal hygiene items. Provide sufficient time for activities of self-care.

Bedroom: find a floor bed or add a platform stool to make it easy for young children to get off the couch. Lower shelves in the cupboard and a short rod in the wardrobe mean they can hang their clothing. A dresser at the height of the infant, with easily accessible and openable drawers, enables flexibility in the selection of their clothing. Shelves, baskets, and drawers help a child organize their toys-they can learn to clean up their belongings in return.

Good habits in a Montessori home

Young children need to start helping around the house as soon as you have the appropriate materials/furniture for them to manage with that. No task is too small, and it's never too early to start, including children in the care and cleaning of the family home.

These experiences form good household contributory habits. These are good for muscle strength and agility, visual and spatial perception, flexibility, and transparency. Young kids love to do those activities right next to you.

Kids seek out freedom and fight for it, whether we support them or not. Through involving your child in these regular home activities, you will help create a positive, confident person's self-image for your child.

## 3.13 Montessori Method at Home

### Montessori Playroom

- Look around that playroom. Ask yourself, "We have a place for everything? "That is my signature word. Plus, it makes life much more comfortable (sort of) with a young child. Make a rule "if there is no space, store it or hand it away."
- Next up, spinning the toy & book is essential. Take the time to rotate every 3-4 weeks, and even delete a few things. Wonders how to determine which toys to recycle or also

throw into the trash, one maxim I like to stand by is "if it's broken or if it's a duplicate, get rid of it."
- Playroom with soothing and aesthetically pleasing furniture
- Single jars with liquid watercolors are one of my favorite and easy to put together materials for a Montessori room.

Let's create an enjoyable and welcoming environment for my sons in terms of their hobbies, their materials, and their room decor. This addition to their space is straightforward and cheap to do. All you need, for example, are tiny glass bottles. At a local craft shop, I found some great ones for $1. You can also use Glass Spice Jars, as an alternative.

So, fill the bottle around 3/4 full, I added Liquid Watercolor Paint and some more water. As an example, I chose to use blue, red, and yellow to make purple and orange in two variations. I used clear water, blue, yellow, red, and "black" in addition to those colors. Then display the jars on a window sill, or the light can catch the beautiful colors somewhere.

Montessori Bedroom

- Start by giving your child the freedom to decorate his room, but encourage the less approach is more. In other words, include your child in setting up his spaces at home, and the Montessori Method will be buy-in.
- Provide a child some Place artwork (maybe even your child's work) at the child's eye level Accessible clothing with low shelves, lines, and hooks Relaxing lighting but don't completely block out natural light Make sure to make your child's room with books and even a few toys.
- But keep it simple. Evite the noise!
- Calm and soothing colors An essential oil diffuser is a right touch

Montessori Method at Home Shared Spaces

Montessori Bathroom

Next, beware of the development of the child. What I mean by this assertion is that they think concretely of young children. Just saying, "clean your face," for instance, might not resonate with a child. Unless he can't see the ketchup on his nose, does that exist? Therefore, including a mirror at bath time is one way to achieve the Montessori approach in the bathroom. Thus, the child can fully recognize the difference between dirty and clean.

Next, use a Faucet Extender, light switch extender, and stools to make the bathroom accessible to children. As a parent, I want from my child to wash his hands. I do this because it's necessary, but why don't I find a way to help the child help? Gain. Gain. There are ways to do this without having to rebuild your bathroom in adult size. Kids will enjoy washing hands and turning on / off the lights on their own.

## Montessori Kitchen

A critical component of the Montessori approach is the development of a personalized setting for children. Nevertheless, for most of us parents, using authentic dishware and glasses is a tough transition. However, if you want to match your kitchen with the Montessori principles, using real kitchen utensils, glass cups, and plates is the way to go.

One way to avoid losing all your cute plates and glasses is to search for perfect glasses and plates with goodwill. You will come across great deals! For a fact, if kids are practicing grace & courtesy, you don't feel too guilty about an accident happening. Montessori Services is an excellent resource for kid-sized kitchen, greenhouse, and equipment for cleaning. You are using real image visuals in learning charts and routine charts too.

## Peace Corner

First, I'll be able to tell you about one of my favorites, easy ways to integrate the Montessori approach with a peace corner in your home. That is, this room is intended for quiet contemplation, to calm down or to be. So, you can include a plant to look after and enjoy, a fish tank to watch, or just a window to see the outdoor wonders.

- Gathering practices to promote childhood understanding is through journaling, meditation, deep breathing exercises, and yoga and positioning them inaccessible areas of the house.
- Find the Labyrinth of a Cretan or ABC Yoga Cards in a basket.
- Write this beautiful book entitled Nurturing the Spirit: In Classrooms Non-Sectarian. The author shares ideas you should incorporate into your home to foster stillness.

# Chapter 4: Mind-Minded Parenting

Mental parenting is an approach that recognizes children's independent thoughts and feelings. Parents assume that the actions of their children are important and respond to the feelings, preferences, and expectations of their children. We interpret the communicative signals of their children correctly and talk to kids about the mind world.

The approach is linked to significant developmental advantages, such as forging secure attachment relationships, strengthening social skills, and possibly improving self-control.

Is it too early to start anyway? Is it really too early to treat a child as a partner in conversation, and seek sense in what he says or does?

Elizabeth Meins, psychologists, and Charles Ferny Hough say no. Yes, there is reason to believe that this strategy is particularly important in the first year of a baby.

Babies flourish as their parents believe they have their minds, and take the time to find out what their babies think and feel. Children seem to benefit from having "mentally stable" parents who correctly communicate about the mental and emotional condition.

I see that toy bored you, a mother might say.

Does this count as relevant, mind-minded talk? This depends on whether the kid is tired or not.

When he shows signs of interest staring at the toy, reaching for it, it is not appropriate to make a statement. Practice minded parenting requires parents to do more than chat about thoughts and feelings. They need to make comments that are tailored to what is happening.

# 4.1 Help Children Develop Secure Attachments

Meins and her colleagues looked at 6-month-old babies playing with their mothers and gathered examples of spontaneous mental talk (Meins et al. 2001). In particular, the researchers were interested in acceptable remarks, i.e., maternal speaking, which provided an accurate understanding of what a baby thought.

Six months later, the researchers tested the relationships of attachment of the babies and found a clear relation between parenting and attachment. Babies were more likely to have been securely attached at 12 months by mothers who made more frequent, adequate comments at six months.

Many studies have confirmed early minded behaviors predict the stability of attachment (Laranjo et al. 2008; Meins et al. 2012). Appropriate mental experiences have been related to stable attachments to both fathers and mothers (Lundy, 2003). These were also connected to stable attachments to daycare service providers.

When Netherlands researchers studied three-year-olds at childcare centers, they found that children were more likely to be firmly attached to a caregiver if they made frequent, mind-minded remarks (Colonnesi et al. 2017).

# 4.2 Help Kids Develop Social Survey

Besides secure attachments, children with mind-minded parents are also more likely to show advanced reasoning about other people's mental states — what psychologists call "theory of mind" abilities. How do researchers measure that?

An important test is the challenge of false beliefs, which requires a child to differentiate between what is true and what another (false) person thinks is true.

Consider, for example, this false belief assignment that Meins and Ferny Hough (1999) implement. We asked 5-year-olds to watch a puppet show and answer questions afterward.

On stage alone, the show started with Charlie the Crocodile. He emptied a carton of milk and replenished it with soda pop.

Next comes Penny the Penguin. She hadn't been around to witness the actions of Charlie. The prosecutors told kids that Penny prefers milk, not soda pop. They then asked the children to guess how Penny would feel when she first saw the carton of milk. Would Penny want to be happy or sad? How would Penny feel after looking inside the cardboard and finding inside there was soda pop, not milk?

Many preschoolers correctly predict Penny's feelings (i.e., at first she would be excited, and then disappointed), and these kids were more likely to have heard positive, mind-minded remarks when they were younger.

Many researches repeated the findings

For example, in study, researchers observed mothers playing with their 12-month-old children and noticed how often relevant, mind-minded comments were made by parents. So, when the children were four years old, they measured the theory of mind abilities. Appropriate 12-month-old mind-minded talk predicted a child's mastery of the false belief challenge at age 4 (Naranjo et al. 2014).

In a similarly designed test, researchers found that sufficient mind-minded talk in infancy predicted both the comprehension of a child's emotion and its success on a false belief task at 51 months (Centifanti et al. 2015).

And other work has shown that the early use of positive, mind-minded remarks by a mother improves the capacity of her child to take mental perspective during pre-school and early primary school years (Meins et al. 2003; Taumoepeau and Ruffman 2008; Meins et al. 2013; Kirk et al. 2015).

Is it the talk that matters? Or that attitude? In a recent study on mind development theory, Rory Devine and Clair Hughes tackled this issue.

The researchers spent 13 months monitoring 117 preschoolers and their guardians. They also assessed "parental mental chat" and "the tendency of parents to see children as mental agents" (Devine and Hughes, 2017). They have also tested the understanding of false beliefs among children. -parenting variable affected child outcomes more? As it turned out, only talking— talking about thoughts and emotions— predicted better mental skills theory.

## 4.3 What About Cautions?

Those studies are reporting only correlations. They don't allow us to conclude that mind-minded parenting causes children to form more secure attachments or develop better mind-skill theory.

Perhaps these results reflect certain genes that parents share with their biological children, genes that facilitate the development of all three phenomena— mind-mindedness, the security of attachment, and early childhood mental reading. If so, mind-mindedness is not so much the cause of the security of attachment and early skill in the task of false creed. It is a shared action.

But against that, there is evidence. Preschoolers were not genetically related to their caregivers in the daycare mentioned above research. Yet the correlation between mentally thoughtful comments and secure attachment was maintained (Colonnesi et al. 2017). And a twin study using behavioral genetics tools found genetic factors had a negligible impact on the development of mental skills theory (Hughes et al. 2005).

Furthermore, some points argue in favor of children honing intellectual perspective-taking through access to mental debate.

For instance, when researchers studied children's development with siblings, they found a telling pattern: having an older sibling encourages the development of mind theory. It doesn't have a younger sibling. This is what we would expect if children learn from older, more socially-savvy people's mental language when they play (Ruffman et al. 1998)

It's also indicative of cross-cultural evidence. Children show substantial lags in the development of mind theory in cultures where speech regarding mental states is discouraged (Mayer and Träuble 2013; Mayer and Träuble 2014). Ultimately they get there, but it may take years.

And researchers performed at least one randomized, controlled subject matter experiment. Heidemarie Lohman and Michael Tomasello divided the children into two classes, after collecting baseline measurements of false belief task success in some 3-year-olds.

Children in both groups spoke to an adult who showed them some strange, tricky-looking objects, like a pen that took the form of a flower. But the talk was somewhat different.

The adult spoke to the children in one group about the deceptive nature of the objects, using words such as "think" and "know." For example, the adult might say, "What do you think this is? ... You thought it was a flower ...."

The person in the other community spoke about the objects but did not use words of mental state ("What is this? ... It's a flower ... you can write with it ...").

After those sessions, the researchers re-tested the grasp of false beliefs by the participants.

Children trained with the vocabulary of the mental state performed better on the test of false beliefs. They also showed a greater understanding of the difference between appearance and fact (Lohman and Tomasello, 2003).

## 4.5 Mind-minded parenting: The takeaway

Some of the behavioral differences that we see within families illustrate genetic differences. Our genes will give us a greater or lesser chance of developing those skills.

But there is good evidence that matters relating to parenting and caregiving, and this is especially true for stable relationships and mind skills theory.

Mind-minded parenting tuning in, and making thoughtful mental state observations strengthen social bonds and help children understand other people's thoughts and feelings. Therefore, there is reason to think that focused parenting will help children to develop better self-control.

## 4.6 What is Montessori Parenting

Parenting at Montessori? Ahhh. Yes, this is one thing. One early morning sitting at my laptop as my oldest son (then a kid) and my husband is asleep, I breathed in the silence and started reading an article explaining Montessori. I stopped and loudly laughed. You see, my family adopted Montessori, and we never knew "it"-the parenting style of my mom-had a tag. I was instantly profoundly attracted to Montessori.

The moment I read the line "Never help a child with a mission that he thinks he will lose," I felt like Dr. Montessori was an instant kindred spirit. Everything I kept reading about the Montessori theory resonated with me as an adult, as a teacher, and as a parent.

## 4.7 Montessori at Home and Montessori Parenting

The parenting of Montessori is a big part of the Montessori philosophy. To raising a Montessori child the bridging gap between school and home is key. Consult with the teachers in your child to make this happen.

Life offers children moments of encouragement. Let them put those shoes on their own. Offer support for them without doing so. Don't take for granted that you have the solution or can solve their problem. Children can do so much and to be so. Respecting our children's potential for growth and development based on their impulses and preferences is just as much a part of the Montessori classroom as it is part of the Montessori home environment.

Opening our eyes to that possibility is crucial to Montessori integration at home. The universe is our classroom at the risk of sounding out cliché. What Dr. Montessori stressed included an approach to engaging with children, disciplining children, directing children, and preparing the atmosphere to ensure a child's development is successful.

## 4.8 Ways to Montessori Parenting

1. Embrace the idea that Montessori lifestyle and not just a method that begins and ends at classroom doors
2. Invest in stools so that the child can access the sink, cabinets, and shelves
3. Using real dishware; avoid plastic toys, cups, plates
4. Embrace the Montessori Coat Flip
5. Practice Simplicity
6. Be a model of action no matter what you're doing in life
7. Help a child learn about scientific thinking
8. Could be interesting to teach children about time
9. Using REAL pictures (aka cartoons with AVOID)
10. Hang a coat rack at the level of your child
11. Allow children to be creative
12. Consider a faucet extender
13. Create a culture basket
14. Wait for child to put his coat on
15. Give your child room and time to put on his shoes
16. Practice Letter Writing

17. Explore the nature with these books about rocks, ants, bears, and seeds.
18. Teach children to code (Maria Montessori will agree to move with the times)
19. Focus on words, not memorizing, letters
20. Using tangible things that children can get their hands on while learning
21. Tell children about what it means to be brave
22. Talk about constructive discipline and good parenting
23. Learn about ways to encourage children to write
24. Build an environment for learning how to read and write.
25. Cook with your children
26. Put together a simple letter of sound for your children
27. Just switch from left to right
28. Allow your child to fly onto his own
29. Make smelling bottles
30. Don't speak to your child.
31. Speak in a firm, respectful tone.
32. Explore photography with your children
33. Subscribe to one of these awesome monthly kits Read (a lot) with your child
34. Commit to these 5 Rock Star
35. Responses to children at Challenging Moments Build a music basket
36. Talk about Electricity with Children
37. Learn the 3 Period Lesson Develop object boxes
38. Expect a lot from your child as she can take Sensory Activities outside
39. Leave her room to grow at her pace
40. Allow him to make his discoveries because then he will continue to talk for life
41. Practice mindfulness
42. Build yoga with your kids into your daily routine
43. Listen to your kids
44. Kneel at the level of the child's eye while talking to him
45. Using words other than "What's wrong?"

46. Learn math outside
47. Better connect with your child with these rock star tips
48. Don't be afraid of insects
49. Take Language lessons outside
50. Help create a sense of awe and wonder in a child by using questions to help them learn
51. Garden with kids
52. Make time for dinner & family time.
53. Know that all children live in the continuum of education.
54. No two children are alike
55. Children want a gentle, confident leader
56. Focus on developing the emotional intelligence of a child
57. Be a role model in your relationship with your partner
58. Listening to children
59. Take Practical Life Outside
60. Buy Garden Tools for Children Practice inquiry-based learning
61. Read Madeline Levine's book "Teach Children Well" on redefining success

**What Will Your Child Learn?**

During first three years of life, your child develops more rapidly than at any other time. During this phase, your child adapt large amounts of information from the environment through observation and experiences. These are the years that laid the foundation for later learning — and the stronger the foundation, the more the child will be able to build upon it.

Montessori Infant and Toddler programs offer a curriculum that join from each child's unique skills and interests. Based on daily monitoring, teachers introduce new materials and activities that pique curiosity and stimulate learning. Learning aims for your child at this age involve developing skills such as language, concentration, problem-solving, visual discrimination, and physical coordination.

The routines of everyday living are the foundation of Montessori Infant & Toddler programs. Activities promote independence, order, coordination, and concentration, as well as support social, emotional, physical, and cognitive development. These learning activities include:

- Self-care: washing, dressing, toileting, and eating, according to each child's capacity
- Care of the environment: cleaning, food preparation, and food service; plant care and animal care
- Large-motor activities (indoors and out): walking, climbing, running, jumping, balancing, climbing steps, and more
- Fine-motor skills: reaching, grasping, picking up objects, transferring objects, using tools and utensils, doing artwork
- Language: naming objects, describing actions and intentions, discussing pictures, conversation, music, and singing

# Chapter 5: Montessori Parenting Habit Practice

Working with children at home, the Montessori Method can seem overwhelming. After all, educators get dedicated training in this program, so you might be asking yourself, "Why can I use this philosophy at home if I don't have a special degree?"

While it's true that educators need a well-rounded and comprehensive understanding of pedagogy to run a classroom, there are some things that you can do at home without years of study.

## 5.1 Respect Your Children as a Person

We respect our parents, we respect our friends, but at first, it seems a little strange to think of respecting the babies. They're all new to this country, after all! Yet that is all the more reason to show reverence for children in day-to-day experiences. They'll feel heard; they'll feel loved, and through your example, they'll learn how to treat others.

Example: If your child wants your attention, but you are asking them to wait for a moment, make sure you turn to them at the end of your task. Say, "What can I help you with? Thank you for waiting?" This shows them that you respect what they've to say.

When one cares deeply about a child or family member, watching them suffer is difficult, we want to step in to help! But in a child's learning process, their self-confidence and intrinsic motivation, this isn't always helpful.

Most of the materials in the Montessori classroom, including the kitchen and bathroom areas, are designed to allow children to use them independently.

Children love having control and freedom over basic tasks such as washing their hands or using the toilet!

Check for places at home where you can allow your child freedom. Maybe a shelf with a small snack that's all it is own? Lower coat loops, to enter them?

Example: Let your kid dress himself. It may take longer, and the clothes may not suit each other, but they eventually develop fine motor skills, step-by-step reasoning, and decision-making.

**Respect your child in every facts of their life**

Only put yourself in their shoes, why are they doing something like that? Why would they cry? It can be as easy as they're waking up this morning on the wrong side of the bed, which we also encounter as adults. Donate extra hugs to them.

If you're limited to a room or space, you will get frustrated as well as have the freedom to move places and not be pushed. Although acknowledging that sometimes they don't want to feed, we also have days that we don't have huge appetites.

Respect that as we do, they have needs. Being compliant with their needs can also extend by setting good examples to teach them respect and courtesy. Be gracious and kind to your children, and also to others. If it's used in education, this is the best way for them to understand. Love can also surpass other kids, adults, and other living things. When we show them how to take care of stuff, they will understand it and make it part of their very young age being.

## 5.2 Give Them Freedom But in Limits

A delicate principle of Montessori, independence within limits means allowing your child to lead his or her daily activities based on their interests. It's important to set boundaries,

though, because they help your child understand what's appropriate and not. Any action that harms itself or others would represent an indication of when to set limits.

Example: Let your child decide how they'd like to play in the park. Set some limits before you go, "It's not okay (it's unsafe) to go on a busy road outside the fence."

Freedom of Movement

Give them space and a chance to move about. Do not necessarily "cage" them or have them unable to discover their surroundings or try new possibilities of travel in one restricted area. (Tummy time, pulling up, walking, etc.) As kids get older, encourage them to climb in safe areas. As children learn to move it expands their learning possibilities by exploring their surroundings freely

Freedom of Choice

Just let them pick. This is best when it comes to coping with children, and you are engaged in a fight for power. Give them only two options that will require them for stuff. They can have dinner now, or with everyone else they can have it later, they can wear blue or red shorts with the green top.

## 5.3 Slow Down and Give Them Space

One part of the Montessori theory you can use at home is to give your child plenty of time and space to explore. Children run on an internal clock other than grown-ups, and to understand this, it can be difficult to take a step back. When making your daily schedule, make sure you consider your kids!

Example: Instead of hurrying through a trip to the library, give your child enough time to explore the books in the stacks or ask questions from the librarian.

## 5.4 Use Big Words Even With Little Kids

Use "big words" isn't just a Montessori term, but is applied in the classroom every day. Most of a classroom's first-time students are surprised to hear the teacher say, "I see some debris on the floor, which needs to be picked up before lunch!"

At home, you will continue to incorporate new vocabulary. Children can pick up the definition of new words by using contextual hints or by asking you, "What does that mean?" Your child will use vivid and descriptive vocabulary in everyday life very early.

Example: You should not censor your language. If a fire truck is really big, try to describe it using words such as "enormous," "gigantic," or "impressive."

Teach independence

Allow them to do things their way. Kids are not to be regarded as mini-adults who are willing to do everything for themselves but are not helpless human beings. Make things easier or simpler for them so they can do things on their own. Use elastic trousers instead of cotton, for example, so they can try to dress, rather than ask you to zip up their jeans. At a young age, encourage them to feed themselves, although it may be messy, you allow them to practice.

**Communication**

Speak properly with them always in a clearly articulated voice. Give them item names around them to increase their vocabulary. Talking to them also includes modeling communication and communicating with other adults. Be polite as you converse with them. Do not only talk to them to tell them to do something or not, but have a daily conversation about how the day went.

Teach not by correcting but by modeling

Do not teach by deciding whether the child is doing good or bad. If a mistake is made, then model how to do it correctly. Do not build a big deal out of it, quietly make them conscious of their errors. If they mispronounce, repeat what they have said in language, and pronounce it correctly. You don't have to say it was incorrect, plan on how it should be done.

## 5.5 Always Making Observation of Your Little One

Finally, for moms and dads, here's a Montessori reminder to take the time to observe your kid. In the classroom, teachers spend a lot of time studying how children communicate with learning materials and with each other. This knowledge gives the tutor insights into each child's special and complex character.

Example: Watch your child play on their own. Look at what gives them real joy, frustrates them, or easily tires them. Cater to your home activities based on the preferences of your child.

**Keep to natural, simple materials/toys**

There's no need for expensive or flashy toys to do all the work for the kids, and leave them to watch and have fun for a short time. Get toys that encourage kids to do something with their hands, drop the ball into a box or stack rings to perform a task. It can amuse them as they replicate the action over and over again for long periods. Don't get toys where they have to press one button and have nothing else left. Have materials to concentrate for more than 2 seconds, which involve children deeply! The TV may have long been attentive but does not require interaction/manipulation. Montessori felt the handwork was very important for the development of the infant. Give them toys they can manipulate things in.

While the Montessori program is best left to a school

environment, that doesn't mean that you can't use those philosophy elements at home. By using some of the above tips, such as appreciation, freedom, and observation, you will create a caring and supportive atmosphere that contributes to the happiness of the entire family.

Use common sense

It doesn't take rocket science to raise a child; some issues have to include the common sense that some don't seem so normal. If it feels right, trust yourself that you are doing the right thing. Most of the Montessori ideals often involve common sense and rational thought.

Patience

In the long run, what you are telling them now will benefit you. Don't give up having quiet for a few moments each day to encounter the question. Alternatively, when having a child to learn something may take a longer time when they do, it no longer becomes a concern. Do not make your child rely on you to rock or hold them or use a dummy for sleep, it may take time for them to get used to sleeping alone, but you don't need to spend long periods getting them to sleep in the long run.

**Lastly, love and support them**

If you do this, no parenting style you introduce can go wrong! It will be good enough. Note that it can never be flawless, and errors and mistakes are all part of the growing cycle.

## 5.6 Fun Family Time with Children

As parents and caretakers, we can make choices to ensure the time spent with our children is high-quality.

- Have a routine time to "talk" with your kids. If possible, do this face-to-face; but if this is not an option, create a routine to do so in other ways, such as leaving a note in your child's lunch bag, posting a note through his toothbrush, or writing an encouraging saying on a shared whiteboard in the house.
- Create a special routine, something that can be done every day, for you and your kids. Let your child pick and read one book with you at bedtime, for example.
- Tell your child that you always love her. And tell her how valuable she is to you, and how she feels to you.

- Strengthen good behavior. For instance, if your child completes his or her chores without asking you to do so, acknowledge it with words of appreciation— even if you don't have the chance until the next day.
- Whenever possible, make and eat meals with your family. Look for simple meals that need very little planning if time is limited, or grab a healthy snack like an apple and sit down for a couple of minutes and talk with your kids.
- Schedule the time to do your child's activity of choice. Be sure to carry on and complete the activity without distractions.
- Play with your child until you drop her off at the nursery, even if it's during bath time or outside. Each little bit of time is making a positive impact.
- Laugh with your dad, and be dumb.
- When you're spending time with your child, shut off technology. Try not to email, respond to calls, click via social media or watch TV.

Significant interconnections are about time quality, not time quantity. Keep it simple, and attach with your child in ways that make lifestyle and relationship meaningful. Each link has a lasting effect and provides the support and reassurance your child needs

## 5.7 Montessori Child Ages

### Montessori Child Age 0 – 6 Months

The bedroom will be the principal space for your baby at this age. It's important to note that before the outside world, the baby's setting was the womb. It was quiet in the womb of the baby, dark, and there were sedated sounds.

For the first eight weeks, this can be attempted to replicate in the baby's bedroom to help the child respond favorably to the new world.

Soft art music can be played in the room as this can help the young baby feel calm. Have some natural lighting and have a window where a child can see the wind blowing through the leaves or trees, if possible.

Montessori Environment 0-6 Months

Baby, this young person will mostly be drawn to mobile phones with great contrast in color, like black and white. One can even clearly draw the attention of a child, eye-tracking, by creating shadows by placing the light source behind the hands of a parent. Hanging mobile devices can also be effective; they have to be placed around 30 cm away from your baby as they can only see this far in the beginning.

Such mobiles may also have mother, father, or other sibling's pictures as babies are generally drawn to the human face. Mobile phones can also consist of a glass ball that can reflect light in various ways. There is no need for commercially purchased brightly colored mobile phones with too many distracting colors. The same applies to colorful cartoon characters in a room for a boy, although this does not mean that they cannot be decorated. It can still be decorated with simple, elegant, functional artworks.

In this room, a mother can feed her baby in a comfortable gliding/rocking chair with a nearby table for whatever she needs while her feeds. Mothers should concentrate on the baby while breastfeeding and not too concerned about doing other things.

A child's bed need not be a cradle, but for a very young baby, it can be a Moses basket that provides comfort and warmth. As children get older, it is valuable to allow them to have opportunities for movement. This is essential to make sure a child gets tummy time during the day so they can exercise and develop their muscle strength. This can be done at around three months.

To let the child to be part of the family, one can have a small flat mat that the child can be placed in, e.g., a small woolen blanket in the family room. The child need not be leave alone in their bedroom while he is awake. Hearing the family sound and voices will also help the children to learn as they observe their surroundings.

Absorbent Mind

Maria Montessori noted how children mastered a language without being instructed by anyone. This ignited her "absorbent mind" theory. There is no need for lessons to be learned for children under the age of three because they understand everything in the world by witnessing it and being a part of it. Therefore, the set-up of the environment must be decent, pleasant, and optimistic, as that is what the child can absorb whether or not he wants to.

Montessori Materials / 'Toys'

- A simple wooden A-frame would be enough to see a child up and try to understand it. There is no essential for fancy plastic ones that can break easily.
- Fluffy toys, fabric books, tiny rattles, and crocheted softballs will allow the child to practice grasping and hand use.
- A silver rattle is particularly fantastic for a young baby as it engages many of the senses. It has to be small and light sufficient for the baby to grasp it at first for a couple of moments, then longer and later. It can also give auditory stimulation, as it makes a soft sound, and as the child's mouths, it can give a sense of hot and cold.
- Especially wooden toys and rattles are aesthetically beautiful, last long and give a different, more natural texture to the child than would most plastic toys. A kid with the toys is going to mouth, knock and do a lot of different things. Educational / engaging toys must be strong enough to stand the growing years of the infant.

- Crocheted soft balls are perfect for hooking and gripping their tiny fingers. Kids will watch the ball's movement with their heads, too.
  - To children of this generation, mobiles are also particularly great. These mobiles can have contrasting colors in a banner to attract the gaze, black and white of the child, or even simply of different colors. Mobile phones that display natural light will attract babies too.

**Montessori Toys / Materials We Like for 0-6 Months**

**Baby Clothing**

Babies ' skin is delicate, so it's safer to use natural fibers, like pure cotton, as the material that directly affects the skin. Keeping most clothes in white or light pastel colors is also good, as strong dyes can react with the skin of the child. For a child's health, it is best not to have any tight clothes or garments around their arms or legs that may be tiny or tight. Dress up your child according to the weather, with coats and socks when necessary.

Montessori Child Age 6 – 12 Months

Kids are going around more at this point, and they have gained strength in the back, arms, hands, and legs. Ideally, your child has had opportunities to move about easily in the early months (a floor bed will support that).

At this point in your child's development, this can be applied further. Montessori claimed that motion is related to brain development. Thus, working with the hands can be helpful for the child's development.

Montessori Environment 6 – 12 Months

We need a movement mat at 6–12 months that can be placed in the family room. Having had enough tummy time to develop energy, if the child has had the freedom to move as he pleases, he/she and may have the movement that will amaze parents, if we watch and observe. We still need the wooden toys we had before, plus a few more softballs that can be grasped by the child if it rolls, may motivate a child on his tummies to try to reach for it.

That can be the start of crawling. In general, a child slithers and pulls up at around eight months on average. If it is later, don't worry as each child has its development blueprint. However, if children have the opportunity to move openly, then they will never stop shocking us with their skills. One can place a mirror with the movement mat in which the children can watch themselves and see their reflection to learn more about their bodies and movement.

When a child learns to generate movement in their environment, they will feel they have control which can develop into strong self-esteem in turn later. As the child gain knowledge to move around the room and explores his or her surroundings, this is a time when parents have the safety debate versus allowing the child to move.

This can be helped by childproofing the home-starting with the parent on the hands and knees and going around the room to get a better idea of the child's point of view.

Be attentive of anything that can be pulled down, wires and table cloths, anything that is light enough to be overturned-light tables, floor lamps, etc., anything that can be inserted into things, power points, cracks in walls, sofas, etc.

Always make sure the kid doesn't find anything they can drink. This is the time that the household needs childproofing without the risk of confining the child to a small space (e.g., playpen). An infant does not need to have cot/cribs in this same philosophy (freedom of movement).

These may limit the child's movement. They feel confined when a child wakes up and can cry out to be "let out." This allows them the freedom to play with any toy they choose when they wake up when a kid is on the floor bed that they can get off themselves. The toys/materials a child has can be put in low shelves that will allow the child to reach them and in small baskets that do cleaning and picking easy. Don't bring all the toys in one big box because there's no order. It will also make it difficult for kids to look for things they want, especially if they need to rummage through many other items.

Montessori Materials / 'Toys'

- Have a low heavy table/shelf for a child to pull on. Also, a low sofa is going to do. If they do, a child will try to pull up on anything. Try to make sure they pull up things that won't come down on them, as discussed earlier in childproofing.
- It will be nice to have a weighted down wagon as the child learns to pull up and perhaps even practice walking. You will also enjoy this content as the child grows older and puts things in the wagon to hold toys.
- Balls are amazing things every child enjoys playing with. Whether they're chasing it while crawling, grasping it, or rolling it to the ground, it's always a lot of fun. Do have a basket containing the balls. It will make it not difficult for your child to handle and connect. Some that can be used are a variety of different textured balls like crocheted balls, rubber balls with protrusions, a soft beach ball, and practice golf balls.
- There is no need for a walker for a boy. Research has shown that children who use walkers may be delayed in learning to walk by a couple of weeks, and the child learns to walk on their toes instead of using their entire foot. Walkers have also been involved in accidents, as children will roll over them and strike objects/walls. Let your child run around in their own time.

- Appliances that limit children must be evaluated in use and profit. Baby backpacks, slings, prams, wagons are ideal for transportation of children temporarily, as a parent may need free hands to do other things. The child is never given the opportunity to move as long as the child is not always put in it, or trapped in it for long periods of time.
- Baby swings, beautiful jumpers, baby seats are not good for the child's development as they allow the child to be put in it and forgotten while the parent is busy. These allow the child to observe their surroundings passively, rather than exploring their environment actively.

Montessori Toys/Materials We Like for children 6-12 Months

Weaning

In this age that the child will begin to get weaned. Some advice six months, but when they are ready, you can observe your infant. It can be as easy as being eaten by the adult watching boy. Montessori has a few tips to help with that process. Let the child have a clean environment with which to eat, to identify with the meal times and location.

A young child may eat before than the family at mealtimes but may still be part of family mealtimes sitting on a high chair pushed up on the family table without a small table confining him to his own space.

Choose a time you are not in a hurry when preparing the first meal, and the meal can be enjoyed at a leisurely pace. This will allow for a positive experience.

Language

The language at this age is that children start talking back and experiment from the sound they hear with their vocalization. Communicating with the kids is necessary, then. Communication dance may be that the adult talks in silence, then the child talks. This is to model the way communication happens to them.

The adult can mimic what the child said or say something else. There's also no need to talk to him/her in a high-pitch voice when talking to your child like you'd talk to another person, in a well-articulated manner. For the child to learn a real language, there is no need for baby talk. We will learn language from the way we speak to them, so speak properly to them.

Speak to them about how things are all around you; explain what they see, and not just directions on what you want them to do. When reading a book, point one time to things and name them. This will teach kids that each thing has a name, and if they say it to them regularly they will know that.

Sleep

Respect sleeping patterns for the infant. Allow them to sleep peacefully when they are sleepy or tired. It means that your infant is not concerned with sleeping with something like a pacifier/dummy, pillow, or rocking or spinning.

It's better to get your child used to earlier rather than later sleeping independently. One may sit with the child or away it to fall asleep on its own. Montessori also recommends that it is not appropriate for children to be wrapped or covered in a sleeping blanket as this hinders their movement.

As mentioned earlier, a child also does not need to be in a cot and can be put in a low bed on the floor. The child can then choose to sleep or play in their own house, or not.

Montessori Child Age 12 - 24 Months

Children are more flexible at the end of this period and can walk with confidence. If the children are given the right to action, their gross motor development can grow when they are younger. Kids will now be able to do more with their hands as they are starting to crawl now.

Space must be childproofed, and also ensure that the child can not touch sharp objects as they can now stand more securely and have greater reach. At this age, children would love to climb as they try to test their gross motor abilities.

## Montessori Environment 1-2 Years

A beneficial outdoor environment. There are things in this outdoor environment that encourage them to climb or let them run. And parents, let them climb, guide them from a short distance, independently. Low swings are good too. Allow the child to ascend on its own, and even if it falls it will only be a short distance away. Do not allow falls and trips to stop your child from trying new things, and its part of growing up and learning.

At this stage, you should buy a small table and chair sized for them to eat from their snacks, and do activities/work on. It can be put inside the living area. Please refer to the climate for 24-36 months for additional information.

## Montessori Materials / 'Toys'

- Kids can understand items at this stage and their eye-hand coordination is improving further. Donate one or two pieces of wooden puzzles to your kids. Don't give them things that are too hard, give them stuff they can do with a bit of effort / trying.
- Even offer them well rings of various sizes to be mounted on a rocking base according to scale.
- Wooden blocks are always in good condition. They'll enjoy watching you build them at first, and knocking them down. They'll be lining them up higher and higher a bit later. The blocks have to be not just cubes but also other shapes to encourage creativity.
- Give your kid a paper and a crayon. Have a small tray where the child can hold their paper in and a small cup with a big crayon or crayon block for easy handling. This will also encourage clean-up if they draw out of the

paper. Have the tray background in a dark color, so that they can see the paper's contrast.
- You may offer other tools, such as thick toxic-free markers, and colored pencils, as a progression. Show how to handle the pens properly and concentrate only on paper drawing.
- Drop boxes use balls or different shapes as they exercise their grip and deliberate release to put things in.
- Have a pin with a stable base, and have rings around the room, such as bangles and variety napkin rings.
- At this point, a child loves to incorporate things into things. The best for them would be an actual key with a lock in a room which is important. Locks at the fridge, and others. This will also empower the child to stand up to the lock with encouragement / leaning on the door. One will always be surprised when a child shows a commitment to be able to get that activity right.
- When the child becomes more skilled at using their hands, they give the child a basket or box of items to open and close. This can be a tiny zip pack, a stud jar, Velcro and snaps.
- Add small screw tops bottles from old recycled plastic bottles/containers as an added challenge when the child gets older.

Montessori Toys / Materials We Like for 1-2 Years

Language

Kids are learning to interact at this level. At 12 months, they may be speaking their first deliberate term. We need to encourage this development by constantly speaking to the child, not AT the child. We're not just talking to them about what to do but also asking them about the things around them and how things are going.

- To promote their language using books, music, and rhymes. Slowly and clearly speak to them this helps them to hear any sound they have made.
- One should strive not to over-anticipate their needs to promote expression.
- Give the child a reason to interact and their needs/food would often be the first.
- Do not always respond when they point to your child and scream at something they want.
- Call the object you want before you send it to them then later they'll know what it's called and use the right word for it.
- As the child learns that each item has a name, they that start pointing at items and waiting for an adult's response as to what it is called.

Children's favorite subjects at this age are animals and the sounds they produce, food, parts of the body, and transport. There's also no need for baby talk, properly and specifically, name things. It's not a flower alone, but a red rose. The sooner you expose the child to such vocabulary, the easier it will be for them to absorb such language as will become evident in later years.

It's also a good time to teach manners to your kids, saying "please" and "thank you," if appropriate. You will also find that a child's receptive language is more than their expressive language, a language they understand. So, keep talking to them and at this point, you can already ask them to do things for you as the child becomes more confident and their skills in the movement have improved.

Montessori Three Period Lesson

Maria Montessori had a way to teach children vocabulary-she called it the 3-period tutorial. This is best done with real objects, e.g., having three types of seasonal fruit, vegetables, clothes or utensils. Other objects that can be found in any toy shop can be realistic (animal miniatures). Have a mat on the floor to lay the items on, or sit down at their table with the boy. For easy handling, one can place certain items on a tray or basket.

- **Fist time is object presentation.** Show the child the object and say "This is an (object name)." Place it on the mat or let the child touch it and hold it, even feel it if possible, then repeat the object's name. Repeat with the other objects' operation. This allows a more tangible experience for them by allowing the child to feel and smell the object.
- **The second period is to ask the child to point to the object you mentioned**: "Can you point the (name of the thing) to me? "And move the object to another location so that you know the child is aware of the object's name and not its placement. This time brings the lesson to life and to be interesting. You might also ask the child to shift the items to various spots on the floor. This stage can be expanded to under 3's by asking the children to place the item you have called (another way of naming whether they know the object's name) in another region of the floor, or to remove or put it in the basket, or to hand it over to you. For positioning, you can include vocabulary words like' first," top," left," back,' etc.
- **The third period is to ask the kid,** as you point out, to name the object. Mostly this is done with older kids who can talk fluently.

Depending on the assistance your child needs, the number of items can increase.

Montessori Child Age 24 – 36 Months

The terrible twos, in which they are called dawn! But for your kids, you don't have to fear this transformative shift, and it can be done. Some techniques can help make a smooth transition through this time.

This can be accomplished by giving children choices to avoid power struggles and allowing them to do the suggested tasks and enabling them to do things independently.

Kids need to be given more independence at this stage as they grow up. The setting will significantly help with this.

Montessori Environment 2-3 Years

How one arranges the atmosphere so the child can do something for himself independently. That then gives him/her a sense of accomplishment and high self-esteem grows in turn. The trick is setting up an environment where he can excel in being able to do things safely by himself. Everything may have to be set up step by step for young children, which can be slow and boring for adults but is invaluable for a learning kid.

Bedroom Setup

The child may have his own bed at this age. If it's too big and you're afraid they can fall, you can still put a mattress on the floor for if when the child falls, but you may find that once the child learns from that experience when it happens.

Toys can be divided into a basket containing all of its parts by their size. Let your child see what they choose to play without really making a mess. At this age, children need external order to establish their own sense of internal order. Put his toys on a shelf where, if they choose, they can easily access it. Teach your child to put away stuff at this point when they're done. This also helps them in their setting to contribute to the order. They are making a habit clean as early as now as these are healthy lifetime habits.

Have a tiny drawer for clothes for your kids. This will encourage them to choose what to wear for the day as they may start showing their preference. Give your limited child choices so that they will dress suitably for the weather. Give them a choice for example, between a red and a blue winter jumper. When they can't choose then just pick them.

Bathroom Setup

Including a bathroom, time should be a bedtime routine by now. This is the time they are allowed to sit on the potty, wash their hands and brush their teeth. Have a small light foot stool that the kid can stand on to have access to the sink and potty. Have this lightweight to push it where they need it.

Place your toothbrush and toothpaste so they can access it on their own. Have a toothbrush and toothpaste of child size put in a tray in order of use series. The toothpaste then the toothbrush and a cup are put smoothly on a tray for the child to use from left to right.

Have a small soap and bottle of shampoo for the baby to use for himself at bath time. Children love to pour/squeeze soap out of a bottle and see bubbles made. Put a small amount of shampoo or soap into the tubes, so that if they want to dump it all out there will be no waste. When the child is in the tub, he or she has a little bag/net hanging over the bath to dry their toys. Also, this bag will be good at teaching your child to put his toys away by himself. Have a towel rack that is small enough to place your child's towel in for use.

Living Area Setup

One can have another small shelf in this area for his toys that he/she can use when with the kids. We can also have a wooden table and chair suitable for the child to use for his / her work/play. We can use crayons or other mediums of large sizes for crafts that are also available to the boy. One may want to have available painting, but this may be better for outdoors as the mess may be more difficult to clean for indoors. You can also provide the child with a small rug or mat to work on, rather than the table. This then includes a certain area of their work.

Dining Area Setup

The child will eat the food which the family has at this point. The child may also have meals with the family so that the proper social dimension of eating meals can be observed as well. To have a sense of belonging, your child can be placed in a high chair along with the family near the table. Have the child use the same table as the family when possible. Remove the secluding table and push it up onto the family table.

The child also has the choice of eating in his table and chair. In the kitchen, a child can have access to a low drawer that can hold its utensils and dishes.

The plates and utensils don't need to be plastic and can be very lightweight crockery. The glass can be genuine too. If the child is taught how to take care of things correctly, handle things carefully, they might surprise you.

If the child chooses to eat at the low table there should be no risk of losing glasses as it is a short distance to the plate. This can also teach the child how to take care of its plates and bottles, spoons and forks. A placemat with board, spoon, fork, and glass sketches can be drawn on it as a table setting guide. See Pouring operation on a beer.

Montessori Materials / 'Toys'

For any stage of the child's development books are always a must. Select books that may contain one or two sentences describing the scene on the page. Long storybooks may not keep their attention for quite a long time. Select books that are important to your daily lives. If it is something that appeals to them and they see every day, their attention will be kept. This can include issues relating to their daily routine.

As always choose realistic books that have the entire picture or illustration. That'll teach the kid how things really are. Montessori suggests that after age 3, imagination can be introduced to the children.

**Montessori Toddlers**

Many Montessori schools have a toddler program. The Montessori toddler program is absolutely unbelievable to watch. These human beings may be small but they can sure do a lot for themselves. As they continue to hone their hand-eye coordination there are so many resources to use in your home or classroom.

Montessori toddlers learn by truly mortifying the multi-sensory approach to discovering the world. Montessori toddlers begin the beautiful grace & polite, practical life, & sensorial lessons. Math and language also perform a role in a Montessori toddler's environment particularly through practical life and pre-reading lessons. Furthermore, toddlers are ripe for developing fine motor skills.

A Normal Day in the Toddlers Room (2 - 3 years)

**7.30 am – Montessori Academy Opens**

Good Morning! Welcome to another day of learning and searching with Montessori Academy. Upon arrival all parents are involve to sign in at the beginning of the day. Please place your child's own in their locker. When entering the classroom, please to not forget knock on the door, and wait to be greeted by your child's teachers. We motivate families to say goodbye at the door so as not to disturb the children's work.

## 7:45 am – Montessori Work Cycle Begins

For the three hours of the day, our toddlers participate in the Montessori work cycle. During this time children choose to work as wish with a Montessori activity from one of the **five curriculum areas**. Children may work with one substance for the whole work cycle, or they may move freely from one activity to another. New children are guided through the projects and lessons by the Montessori trained Educators.

## 9.30 am – Progressive Morning Tea

Morning Tea is given by Montessori Academy and is usually fruit, vegetable sticks, cheese and milk or another healthy snack. It is working during the Montessori work cycle, let children to continue working on the materials if they choose to do so. Children may work single or in small groups as long as they are productive.

## 10.00 am – The Montessori Work Cycle Ends

Children summarize their Montessori activities and pack away the materials. Packing away is a valuable part of learning to take care of the materials and their classroom environment. Children know the order of the environment and take pride in returning objects to their rightful place.

## 10.30 am – Outdoor Play

After the Montessori work cycle is outdoor playtime! Our ready outdoor environments are designed to invite interest and projects. This environment is set up daily with go around projects to meet children's developmental needs and interests. Outdoor enjoyment is a time for the toddlers to socialize with other age groups and exercise their gross motor skills.

## 11.30 am – Group Time

Group time let the class to develop a **strong sense of community** through shared learning and experiences. Group time projects for our toddlers typically include: show and tell, walking on the line, grace and courtesy, story time, interest-based projects, music and movement, language activities, geography study, and art and craft.

## Noon – midday Time

Working hard is hungry work! Most Montessori Academy services involve families to pack a lunch for your child. Homemade food motivate children to learn about foods from different cultures, encourages food-based discussions, and fosters a greater understanding of healthy eating. Our staff is happy to heat any meals that should be served warm.

## 12.40 pm – breathing Time

After lunch is breathing time for our toddlers. Each child has their own ground bed and goes to sleep listing to soft music. Children who do not need a day's sleep participate in quiet activities such as story time, coloring, or working with the Montessori materials.

## 2.30 pm – Toddlers Wake Up

Children begin to wake up and clean away their bedding. Educators make sure each child's bedding is packed away in their own bag, ready for the tomorrow. Once everyone has packed away, the children ready for afternoon tea and open-air play. Children bedding goes home at the end of every week.

### 3.00 pm – Communal Afternoon Tea & Outdoor enjoyment

Montessori Academy give a nutritious afternoon tea that usually consists of , rice crackers fruit, other healthy snacks, or vegetable sticks . Afternoon tea may be detained in the classroom, or as an open-air meal. Once children have ending eating they participate in outdoor activities such as gross motor games, dramatic play, and gardening activities.

### 5.00 pm – behind time Snack and inside enjoyment

Toddlers return for a late snack in the classroom about 4.30 p.m. and start winding down for the day. Kids are again given the opportunity to continue working with the Montessori materials. Otherwise, they engage in peaceful community time events or focus on interest projects

### 6.00 pm – Montessori Closes Academy

Good night and welcome back! After a great day of learning and fun your little one is now ready to go home. The Educators of your child will meet you at the door and help you collect the belongings of your family. If you have any concerns about how your child has done, or how much they have eaten, our helpful team will be happy to help.

The children are scheduled to receive daily toilet times and nappy changes throughout the day, and our educators regularly check if your child needs an extra nappy change.

Kids are provided with facilities to wash their hands before and after each meal and toilet break, and as required. Type Bottom

## 5.8 Teachers ' Position at Montessori

Teachers are an important part of any Montessori classroom, but their role in a traditional classroom setting is different from what you might be accustomed to. In a traditional setting, you'll see an instructor standing at a fast pace before the class exchanging information and instructions. Their role is to provide their students with information and encourage them to memorize it in time for their next test. Teaching this way can often turn the excitement of learning into a children's chore, taking away the enjoyment of exploration.

The Teacher's position in the Montessori setting is to promote the natural capacity of the children to explore and develop. The approach to Montessori recognizes that children learn best when teachers encourage them to use their natural creativity and intelligence to gather information and discover. Their reward is their sense of pride in learning a new concept.

A Montessori instructor, rather than standing in front of the details of class sharing, conducts exercises designed to introduce and reinforce concepts. These are selected based on the students ' ages and skills in the class, and often take a hands-on approach to learning. The instructor then assumes the role of a guide once the child selects their practice, answering questions or gently guiding the student to exploration.

## 5.9 ACCREDITED VS. NON-ACCREDITED MONTESSORI

Just as you will see in more traditional school environments, "accreditation" is an important consideration when you search for your child at a school.

The name and curriculum of Montessori are not trademarked, meaning any school can claim to be a Montessori school.

While there are many schools using aspects of the Montessori system, the only way to ensure that the school you are considering is certified is to check that the school is a member of a governing body like the Montessori International Association (AMI).

Membership in AMI and its U.S. affiliate AMI-USA means that the school is held accountable for the implementation of authentic Montessori principles and is reviewed regularly to ensure that its program continues to follow those principles over time.

## WHY DOES MONTESSORI ACCREDITATION MATTER?

Accreditation means a school has transparency and its true implementation of Montessori values has been accepted. Most schools take the Montessori curriculum bits and pieces, but when a school is certified, that ensures they follow the entire curriculum without deviation. This means you are sure to get the full Montessori program, in other words.

Accreditation is simply there to give you peace of mind. This assures you that your child's school is subject to regular review of its activities and has been recognized and accredited for adherence to the Montessori philosophy and best practices by an independent organization.

## HOW TO TELL IF A SCHOOL IS NOT AUTHENTIQUE

Although each school is entitled to some variation in practice and curriculum, an authentic set of principles will be followed by a true Montessori school. Ask these four questions if you are not sure if you are looking at a true Montessori environment.

1. **ARE CHILDREN ENGAGING IN ACTIVE LEARNING PRACTICES?**

   The authentic classroom in Montessori must focus on positive, hands-on learning.

Children are not going to watch videos or do endless worksheets. They will instead sort objects, conduct scientific experiments and engage in a variety of other multi-sensory activities.

## 2. IS THE CLASSROOM SET UP FOR SELF-DIRECTED LEARNING?

Montessori classrooms are designed to take over the reins of exploration for children. Furniture is sized to their age, all resources are child-friendly, and the instructor spends most of their time helping students in learning rather than usually "teaching." You won't find students from Montessori sitting quietly listening to lecture from their instructor. We will be interested in some realistic tasks tailored to their individual needs and skills.

## 3. IS THERE AN OVERARCHING CULTURAL EMPHASIS IN THE CURRICULUM?

One notable difference between Montessori and mainstream education is that there's a strong cultural dimension in the Montessori curriculum. The belief that every culture is unique and special is interwoven in traditional subjects— such as math, science, reading, and history. When children grow up, they are taught to value peace in the world and inspired to change the world when they grow into adults

## 4. DOES THE CLASSROOM CONTAIN MULTIPLE AGE GROUPS?

A true classroom of Montessori allows the children to learn at their own pace. It also emphasizes older children were helping with learning for younger ones. You'll find a range of ages in every classroom to accomplish this.

You will also see them working to solve problems and discover new things.

Note, however, that usually Montessori does not pair a three-year-old with a twelve-year-old. Combining ages is meant to assist in the learning process and not to inhibit it.

Older and younger kids can learn a lot from each other but limitations still exist. The authentic Montessori school will bring children closer to their age and stage of development amongst others.

## 5.10 ADVANTAGES OF MONTESSORI EDUCATION

Now that you know what a Montessori education entails, then your next question is probably: What are the advantages of Montessori?

- **MONTESSORI EDUCATION CREATES ENTHUSIASTICS, SELFMOTIVATE LEARNERS**

    We enjoy learning when children are allowed to learn at their own speed and in their own ways! Montessori approaches are designed to help your child grow a lifelong of love and insatiable curiosity about their environment. In 1907, Dr. Montessori founded the curriculum which means it's been around for over 100 years. The popularity speaks volumes towards its effectiveness in teaching more than just basic reading, writing and arithmetic to students.

- **MONTESSORI EDUCATION RESULTS IN IMPROVED SOCIAL AND PROBLEM-SOLVING SKILLS**

    Kids who learn under a Montessori curriculum usually communicate well with their peers because of the multi-age classroom environment. Through their mutual search of exploration, they learn constructive ways to solve conflicts and find communication and camaraderie. Children often grow up to learn the value of communicating with others from different perspectives and cultures because of Montessori's focus on cultural diversity, a skill that will serve them well for the rest of their lives.

- **MONTESSORI STUDENTS POSSESS ADVANCE READING AND MATHEMATICAL ABILITIES**

    Reading is a substantial part of Montessori education. Children love to read Montessori! We place tremendous importance on literacy, because it is a fundamental component of exploration. You will also note that students at Montessori demonstrate an advanced understanding of abstract and concrete mathematical concepts. Students enrolled in Montessori programs demonstrated a more advanced range of reading and math skills than their non-Montessori peers by the end of their third year in a Montessori program in a 2017 survey of 140 children— some in Montessori schools, others in conventional classrooms.

- **MONTESSORI STUDENTS BECOME COMPASSIONATE, CONFIDENT AND POLITE CHILDREN**

    Montessori is meant to do more than just teach kids to read and write. Students of Montessori usually show high self-esteem and great respect for others around them. We are not only more self-confident but also show more kindness and compassion for their peers. An interesting aspect of our focus on those school areas is that it also extends into their home life. Montessori student parents say their kids show great improvement in organizational, cooking, and household chores. When they develop their ability to help and hold their home spaces grows.

## 5.11 DISADVANTAGES OF MONTESSORI

This is not to suggest that any Montessori education experience is going to be good. On the one side, instructors, peers and administration may be able to influence your experience for better or worse. On the other hand, some Montessori values considerations may trigger some concerns. These are a few of the drawbacks of Montessori education:

- **It's Expensive**

   It is very difficult for Montessori schools to keep their prices down. It is an expensive undertaking to acquire many long-lasting and first-class learning materials along with lengthy and thorough training in the use of these items for young children. Hence the Montessori education programs are so costly.

- **Independence is not always helpful**

   Montessori education is very strong when it comes to developing a sense of independence and self-directed learning. But the cases aren't always this way. The mindset it provides can be valuable in some ways but, on the other hand, it can also make working in groups and working under a severe authority difficult as well.

- **There is not Enough Opportunity**

   The interaction in the classrooms of Montessori is different from the traditional classrooms. The interaction that it provides, however, is far more significant. The learning environment that the classroom uses allows children to interact more freely compared to traditional classrooms. But the interaction, by contrast, is far less structured and spontaneous.

- **Small Student Community**

Small Student Community in Montessori, students in the classroom environment are in a small community and spend time with the same peers. This can turn into a child development of great friendships or it can be a barrier to social skills growth. The social activities within the Montessori education system are limited to students. Montessori is a lifestyle, and is not just an educational form. Once you agree to go to Montessori, make sure that you fully embrace the philosophy and are willing to change the environment and make a decision about a Montessori community that requires consideration and dedication, but it will ultimately be beneficial for both children and their parents. Upon weighing the advantages and disadvantages of Montessori education parents should make a decision. Finding the right school is very important, because they can vary in different ways. Make sure that you are diligent in your research to find the right school that will help your child succeed.

## Criticisms of the Montessori Method

**Criticism #1: There isn't enough space for social development and engagement by a group activity.**

The interaction in Montessori classrooms certainly differs from that of a regular day public school or a non-Montessori-based school, but the students ' interaction is far more meaningful than that. The structured atmosphere used in the classroom allows students to engage more openly, rather than at set times of the day as they would in a classroom that is usually modeled.

Compared to Waldorf, the approach is more informal and far less organized–while the way teachers set up their classes is still structured. Students at Montessori are treated as individuals and the approach honors that by avoiding the rigidity and hierarchy found in conventional colloquiums.

**Criticism # 2: The imagination is quenched and the childhood stripped from the students because of the early use of cognitive thinking – and too much time spent on practical life**

The true potential of a child can be triggered in the early years of his or her life (up to age six is said to be children's most formative years), and for an infant, learning is a natural thing. Even in idle play, kids learn about social interaction, sharing, counting, and the fundamentals that will form the foundation they are going to take into the classroom.

Montessori does not take away childhoods but enriches them through early education which helps to ignite the development of a child. In these early years, children will learn with great ease, and will grow at a faster rate by giving them a Montessori classroom to engage and learn. This is important for experienced learners as well as those who still fail.

Children love imitating the world they see moving around them and Montessori takes advantage of the opportunity to help him or her work in their surroundings. Early-age sensory learning experiences will help to build a base for intellectual growth later in their lives: hand-eye coordination, small-and large-scale muscle control, and subsequent skills training required for writing and reading.

**Criticism # 3: The child has far too much space to choose in the classroom-and the classroom is far too organized.**

These two arguments contradict each other in some ways: how can there be too much flexibility and too much order at the same time. The way a student communicates with the world will help respond to both of these criticisms.

"A place for all and everything in its place" is part of Montessori's philosophy in the classroom. The approach is not organized in itself, since students are free to learn as they wish and what they are curious about at any given moment. In order to achieve this independence best, however, teachers will in some way organize classrooms to optimize the student potential.

Within the organized class the child can work freely and each child gains confidence in knowing things will be in the same place each time. In many ways the system of independence and class functions in a mutual way.

**Criticism # 4: Montessori school is for family only of the upper class.**

That is entirely untrue. Unlike private schools, Montessori schools don't choose students based on how much money, reputation or popularity a family has: they want the best students to help their students create the best educational and social environments.

Several schools have been working to improve mobility from the full range of socioeconomic statuses for students. If you want your child to be enrolled in a Montessori kindergarten, in Toronto, Ontario, or elsewhere, there are a variety of steps you can take to help ensure that you can afford to pay tuition costs and make a dream come true.

**Criticism #5: No research proves Montessori education has an advantage for children over public school.**

This is true: there is no evidence clearly showing that Montessori education is better than any other public or private education. This can be hard to determine for some reasons: mainly due to many variables that cannot be monitored in scientific study.

Students attending Montessori schools, however, are more than likely to emerge better prepared for life:

more structured approaches to life and learning; independence development; self-discipline and a strong interest in learning.

All educational methods are met with scrutiny and rigorous work for and against the particular kind of education. And similarly, the Montessori approach has both advantages and disadvantages. It may not suit you well your child, besides. It's all about finding a school and a system that works for what you and your child need.

Even when choosing a Montessori school, finding the school is crucial, because they can differ in many ways. So be sure to be vigilant in your research to find the best school that will help your kid excel.

Montessori preschools, primary schools, middle schools and high schools can be found on OurKids.net. You can also find our nursery, daycare, pre-school programs, incentives, training, and cost guides.

## 5.12 MYTHS ABOUT MONTESSORI

Montessori education is one of those things many people have heard of, but they equate the word "Montessori" with false or distorted details many times over. So, let's have a few misunderstandings clear up.

**MYTH:** Montessori Schools Are Faith-based

**FACT programs:** Montessori is not a program based on faith, nor is it based on philosophies of the new age. The Montessori program, in reality, is more than 100 years old and was developed by a psychiatrist whose medical and educational experience influenced her ideas about how children learn and develop.

**MYTH:** All Montessori schools are the same

**FACT program:** while Montessori certified schools follow similar concepts and guidelines, depending on how a particular school approaches the principles defined by Dr. Montessori, you are sure to find some difference between each Montessori school. That's why making sure you understand what a real Montessori curriculum looks like and the principles behind its methods are crucial. Learning the basics will allow you to choose your child's best environment, regardless of age.

**MYTH:** Young Children Won't Grasp Montessori Concepts

**FACT program:** parents sometimes ask us, "What's the best time to start my child in a Montessori program?" While there's no age limit, it's the perfect time to introduce Montessori concepts to a child anywhere between 18 and 36 months. Children spend much time on sensory experiences in the early years of Montessori schooling, intended to improve their senses of seeing, hearing, smelling, touching and tasting. That is what drives the Sapient Montessori School curriculum.

Montessori pupils will venture into more complex subjects as they progress through their elementary school years, applying what they are studying to real-world situations. We will benefit from this effort to help them coordinate their thoughts while we keep growing. The Montessori curriculum depends on this cornerstone during the teenage years to prepare students to integrate rationality and emotion to grasp the wider principles of equality, justice and freedom.

**MYTH**: Montessori Teachers Don't Have the Same Rates of Traditional Teacher Education and Training Do

**FACT program**: Montessori Teachers are some of the best and brightest teachers out there. They come to us with a remarkable mix of experience and advanced degrees that endorse their success in leading a classroom. What makes Montessori teachers unique is that they can concentrate first and foremost on fostering an environment of imagination and exploration that will inspire children of all ages and abilities to learn and grow. I have incredible endurance and imagination and their love of learning knows no boundaries.

## COMMUNICATION WITH CHILD DURING CONFLICT

A large proportion of my Montessori training involved taking time to reflect and be introspective about the teacher's role in the classroom. The significance of leaving our luggage at the door of the classroom, to be plain. Why? For what? Children take in profound and precise forms the vitality of the people around them. Knowing what baggage, you might bring to the classroom and learning how to handle it to help the kids in the classroom AND give you the ability to observe and guide the kids properly.

My children's affection, respect and trust was the sweetest reward I could earn for my efforts to be the woman I'd copy to them."

### Clearing up Child conflicts

Consider this one moment that an ongoing problem you have with a child is a reflection of an unresolved issue you have about that particular challenge or stage of life as a parent and caretaker. Crazy, huh? So, if we can take time to get clarification about our own problems, it will be easier to help our child-particularly with direct communication.

- Right now, I feel scared about something. I want to tell you this.
- I'm mad about something... I'm feeling sad about something right now.
- I want to tell you something.
- There's something I feel frustrated about right now.
- I want to tell you something.
- I want you to halt doing something right in the moment.
- I want you to do "this" instead of "that" Something I love about you. I'd like to tell you what this is like.
- I love watching you... I want you to do something right now.

- I'm not looking forward to watching you...

## 5 Simple Way to Make Your Home More Montessori

The classroom design is one of the striking things about a Montessori school. On the shelves, one will always find beautiful items laid out in a tidy, uncompromising setting.

The kids can move freely and have access to what they need. The environment is intended to foster independence. Montessori classrooms give off the energy of tranquility, but they are still busy with activity; it is a productive yet peaceful environment to be in.

### 1) Remove the Clutter and Show a Sense of Order

I know. I know. It doesn't happen overnight, it's easier than it sounds and usually the clutter in our homes takes years to accumulate. So, start off small and choose one place that will make it beautiful and free of clutter. The best way to do this is first, set a timer, I suggest 30 minutes depending on the area size.

Remove everything from the area except the furniture, give it a quick clean and think about what you add back to that space as you put things back.

Do you need it for real?

Is it pretty?

Does it please you?

Is it properly repaired?

Is this your' home?'

Ask yourself these questions with each piece, the rest can go by the time you're done with only the things you really need and the items you love

Make Space

If you look at the magazines for interior design, the rooms are stunning of course. One of the common themes that runs through these pictures is the sense of space, they're minimally styled. Look around your house, there's furniture you can do without (I didn't know you, my gran had four tiny side tables in her living room and the place was small!) What else can you take away that will allow more space?

If there is more room on the shelf, it will be easier for your child to take off from the job and the same applies to books. Children often find it easier to return work/books when there is plenty of space in the shelf for doing so. You may need to take some things off and bring them into the rotation to achieve space. Less is certainly better, with less on the shelf, your child can spend more time with every item that develops focus skills in turn.

## Set an Example

If your own looks like a bomb has struck it, you can hardly trust your kids to keep their room clean. If you're guilty of leaving stacks of papers and "stuff" mountains all across the room, then expect your kids to follow suit.

We not only follow your lead, but they will also be rubbed off by the chaotic environment. Now, I'm not a naturally clean person (as my mother will testify) but when I

discovered the Montessori way, I desperately wanted my son to have that kind of environment in which to grow, so I trained myself to be cleverer. I narrowed my piles of

confusion to a small side table and set out on a quest to get rid of anything that we didn't really need. It's an ongoing process, since new things are always coming into the building. The house just looks so much bigger, lighter and cleaner after a big DE clutter session and I feel less depressed. Which really is worth the effort.

## 5.13 QUESTIONS FREQUENTLY ASKED

What is the Montessori Approach and what is it?

Were Montessori religious schools?

What are the differences between a traditional classroom

Should kids like other kids get to play Montessori?

Why are different age groups brought together by Montessori classes?

Can I do my child's Montessori at home?

Are Montessori good for learning disabled children? What about gifted kids?

Following Montessori, do kids have trouble adjusting to the public school?

How well do Montessori pupils do in non-Montessori schools relative to students?

Are the children of Montessori successful later in life?

What's the Montessori Approach and what's it?

Are the Montessori religious schools?

What are the differences between a traditional classroom and a Montessori environment?

Must teachers at Montessori follow a curriculum?

Will kids from Montessori play like other kids?

Why do different age groups group Montessori classes together?

Can I get my child to do Montessori at home?

Are Montessori good for kids with cognitive impairments? What about the gifted kids?

After Montessori school, do children have trouble adjusting to public school?

How well do students at Montessori do compared to students at non-Montessori schools?

Were children effective in Montessori later in life?

What's the Montessori Approach and what is it?

Montessori education (pronounced MON-tuh-SORE-ee) was founded in 1907 by Dr. Maria Montessori, the first woman to become a physician in Italy. She based her instructional approaches on scientific observation of the learning processes for children.

Guided by her discovery that children are teaching themselves, Dr. Montessori created a "prepared environment" in which children can choose freely from some development-friendly activities.

Today, almost a century after the first Casa Dei Bambini ("children's house") by Maria Montessori in Rome, Montessori education is found all over the world, spanning ages from birth to adolescence.

Are Montessori religious schools?

Some are, but this is not Children's Manor. Many Montessori schools work under the auspices of a church, synagogue, or diocese, just like other schools but most are independent of any religious affiliation.

What are the differences between a traditional classroom and a Montessori environment?

At the six-level underage, Montessori puts emphasis on learning through all five senses, not just listening, viewing, or reading. During Montessori classes children learn from hundreds of possibilities at their own, individual speed and according to their own choice of activities. Children are not involved to sit and listen to a teacher speaking with them as a group, but are involved in their own individual or group activities, with resources presented to them1:1 by the teacher who understands what each child is prepared to do this.

Learning is an exciting discovery process which leads to concentration, motivation, self-discipline and a love of learning. Kids learn to do independent research after age 6, arrange field trips to gather information, interview specialists, create group presentations, dramas, art exhibits, music productions, science projects etc.

In this kind of intelligently driven independence, there is no limit to what they make. There no textbooks or adult-directed group lessons and daily schedules.

Montessori classes place children in groups of three years or more (3-6, 2.5-6, 6-12, and so on), creating communities where the older children naturally share their knowledge with the younger ones. Montessori stands for a completely different approach to education.

Do the teachers at Montessori follow a curriculum?

Montessori schools teach the same basic skills and offer a rigorous academic curriculum as traditional schools. Most of the subject areas are familiar — like math, science, history, geography, and language — but are introduced through an integrated approach that brings together different curriculum strands.

For example, students can explore the art, history, and inventions of various African nations while studying a map of Africa. This may lead them to look at ancient Egypt like hieroglyphs and their role in writing history. Naturally the study of the pyramids is a natural bridge to geometry. This approach to the curriculum reveals how all aspects are interrelated. It also allows students to get deeply immersed in a topic — and give full rein to their curiosity

Should kids like other kids get to play Montessori?

Needless to say! They explore new things playfully every day in addition to traditional recesses. With a new open mind, they are seeing something of interest. We love treasured grown-ups and other kids' business. They are shaping myths. They're dreaming. They just imagine. This impression comes from parents who don't know what to do with the amazing concentration, order, and self-discipline we often see among Montessori kids.

Montessori students are also inclined to take very seriously the activities they do in school. Responding, "This is my work" is normal for them, when adults question what they are doing. They work hard and expect respect from their parents for handling them and their jobs. But it's cheerful, playful and incredibly enjoyable.

**Why do different age groups come together** in Montessori classes?

Often parents worry about getting one category or the other shortchanged by having younger children in the same class as older ones. We worry that younger children will consume the time and attention of the teachers, or that the value for the five-year-old of covering the kindergarten curriculum will keep them from offering the emotional support and encouragement we need for the three-and four-year-old. They are both misguided.

- Montessori programs are designed at each level to address the developmental characteristics which are normal for children at that stage.
- Montessori classes are designed to cover a period of two to three years, enabling younger students to inspire older children, who in turn benefit from acting as role models. Each child is learning at their own pace, and will be ready in their own time for any given lesson, not on the lesson schedule of the teacher. Children can always find peers in a mixed age class who work at their specific class.

- The children normally stay for three years in the same class. Despite two-thirds of the class usually returning every year, the atmosphere in the classroom tends to remain fairly stable.
- Learning for two or three years in one class means students can build a strong sense of community with their classmates and teachers. The age range also provides the encouragement of academic peers to particularly gifted children, without forcing them to miss a grade or feel emotionally out of place.

Can I do the Montessori for my child at home?

Sure, you can use the Montessori child development principles at home. Look through your child's eyes into your home. Kids need a sense of belonging and they get it by fully participating in daily activities. "Help me do this by myself" is the theme of life for the pre-schooler.

Do you find ways to include your child in preparing meals, cleaning, and gardening and would you think about clothing, shoes, and toys? Providing independence opportunities is the best way to build the self-esteem of your child.

Most home schoolers and other parents at the school level use Montessori's concept of pursuing the child's interest and not interrupting attention to educate their children. At school, only a qualified Montessori teacher can effectively incorporate Montessori education using the Montessori "prepared space" advanced learning equipment. Social development here comes from being with other children in a supportive and particular atmosphere— an integral part of Montessori education.

Are Montessori good for kids with learning difficulties? What about gifted kids?

Montessori aims to help all children achieve their full potential at their own unique pace. A classroom where kids have different skills is a culture in which everyone learns from each other and contributes. In addition, multi-age grouping helps each child to find their own speed in comparison to peers, without feeling "ahead" or "behind."

After Montessori school do kids have trouble adjusting to the public academy?

Montessori kids are usually curious, self-confident learners who look forward to going to school by the end of age five. Usually, they're active, enthusiastic learners who want to know honestly and who ask excellent questions.

Montessori children aged six have spent three to four years in a school where they received honest and respectful care. Although there were specific standards and ground rules, their views and concerns were taken very seriously within that structure.

Unfortunately, there are still some teachers and classrooms where children are seen as challenging authority as they ask questions. It's not hard to imagine an autonomous Montessori child asking his new teacher, "But why do I have to ask each time I need to use the bathroom?" or, "Why do I have to interrupt my work right now?"

One child may be very responsive, or may have special needs that may not be well served in a traditional classroom focused on teachers. Other kids could be successful at any academy.

There is nothing inherent in Montessori that makes it difficult for children to be transferring to traditional schools. Some are going to get bored. Others may not understand why at the same time, everybody in the class has to do the same. But most adapt fairly quickly to their new setting, making new friends, and succeeding within the definition of success their new school has understood.

If a Montessori child moves to a traditional school, there will of course be trade-offs. Montessori school curriculum is often more complex than that learned in other US classrooms.

There may also be very different values and attitudes of the children and teachers. Learning is often more focused on tasks assigned to adults that are done more by rote than with enthusiasm and comprehension.

How well do Montessori pupils do in non-Montessori schools as contrasted with students?

There is a little but growing body of well-designed studies contrasting students at Montessori with those in traditional schools. Results show that Montessori students perform as well or better in academic subjects than their peers who are not from Montessori

For example, in one study, children who had attended preschool and elementary Montessori schools earned higher scores on standardized math and science tests in high school. Another study found that the self-writing of 12-year-old Montessori students were more imaginative than those created by the non-Montessori community and used more complex sentence structures.

The research also shows that students at Montessori have greater social and behavioral competencies. For example, they demonstrate a greater sense of fairness and justice and are more likely to pick positive responses to address social dilemmas.

Montessori students seem to do quite well, too, by less stringent measures. Many Montessori schools say that their students are usually accepted into their chosen high schools and colleges. And many **successful grad**es, reflecting on important influences in their lives, cite their years at Montessori.

Are children successful at Montessori later in life?

Research studies show Montessori children are academically, socially, and emotionally well prepared for later life. In addition to scoring well on customize tests, Montessori children are ranked above average on criteria such as following directions, timely work, careful listening, basic skills, accountability,

**To pick Montessori?**

While looking at your child care choices, it's important to consider why you choose Montessori over other methods of education. For many families, this decision merely "makes sense," because they have seen Montessori's benefits through their own children's achievements and happiness.

To understand why parents are choosing Montessori, you need to really see the Montessori approach in action to see the impact. Montessori has so many real-life advantages that are difficult to explain in just a few short sentences. To give you a very detail overview of these advantages, a concise description of the top ten reasons parents choose Montessori is given below.

**1. Child-Centered, Guided Teacher**

First, each child learns in a different way, and at its own pace. Our teachers at Montessori Academy develop a learning program which is unique to each child's needs and interests. Our prepared classroom environments are designed specifically to encourage children to take an active part in their learning. Some parents choose Montessori for their child, for this reason.

**2. Learning Holistic Experience**

The **Montessori Curriculum** also covers five key areas focusing on the child's full development. Key areas of the curriculum include: practical life, sensory life, math, language, and culture. The Montessori Curriculum, while teaching them real-life skills, correlates with the educational programs that children will learn at school.

**3. Human Learning and Collaboration**

Kids within a three-year age range are often paired together in a Montessori classroom. This framework promotes the role sharing of adolescents, collaborates with others and facilitates imitative learning. Kids thus learn to respect each other, develop skills in team building and create a sense of community. Parents recognize that these soft skills are important to the full development of their children. As a consequence, parents prefer Montessori this is one of the main reasons why.

## 4. Confident Lifelong Learners

Self-correction and self-assessment are also an integral part of Montessori education. When children advance through the Montessori Curriculum, they learn to look at their work objectively and correct their mistakes. Students learn to become positive and independent learners by giving children the right to challenge and make connections.

## 5. Highly skilled and Passionate Staff

Dedicated workers All teachers at the Montessori Academy undergo extensive instruction and treatment in Montessori and early childhood. Montessori Academy also provides staff with regular training and development programs in addition to the relevant qualifications and extensive experience. As a result, teachers at Montessori Academy are constantly updating their knowledge and skills to run a Montessori classroom of best practice.

## 6. Well Resourced Learning Environments

Our primary focus in developing our learning programs, services, and classrooms is to create a learning environment that meets the desires and development needs of children as they grow up. A passion for learning flourishes in this nurturing environment and sets strong foundations for a lifetime.

## 7. Best Practices

Montessori Academy Best Practices adheres to best practice practices for early childhood education and early learning in Montessori. Our belief is that education should prepare children for the success of later schooling and life. When our founder, Dr. Maria Montessori, puts it: "Learning should no longer only express knowledge, but should take a new direction, aiming to unleash human potentialities."

## 8. Learning Fosters

Equality everything about the classroom at Montessori encourages equality. The environment is ready to allow the child to learn to do things for itself that an adult would otherwise do. Over time, children begin to develop a sense of pride in doing things independently. These tasks include washing dishes, caring for plants, and folding child-sized washcloths. As a consequence, this not only empowers the child but also gives them a sense of trust and personal accomplishment.

## 9. Parent Satisfaction

Parents at Montessori Academy are extremely satisfied with the learning experience of their children. Many credits receive the strong educational foundations which their children receive with their later school and success in life.

Since June "My son Benjamin has been attending Montessori Academy of last year and I couldn't be happier with his growth! He couldn't write or sound letters when he began at Montessori Academy. Now, he can write capital letters and lower-case letters, spell small words, read and write his name. The center is always constantly looking for ways to make learning fun every day with the show and showing, dress-up days and giving the kids something new and challenging. The teachers of my son are amazing and I really appreciate their help and support in influencing the education of my son."~ Heather, Condell Park. Click to read more parent testimonials.

## 10. Learning is Enjoyable

In a Montessori classroom, you learn about all aspects of the curriculum by engaging actively in activities that involve many senses.

Why choose Montessori for your child ultimately, one of the most important decisions a parent makes is to choose an early education program. Make the right choice for your kids, and for your family. If you think education should be hands-on, foster independence and teach kids to love learning, Montessori is for you.

The best thing about the Montessori curriculum is that your child will be studying more than just the math and language core subjects. Students will also learn soft communication skills, self-motivation, individuality and problem-solving skills.

Dr Maria Montessori created Montessori's educational theory because she wanted to create a better world for future generations.

You'll see why Montessori works, and why parents chose Montessori with a little study into the advantages of Montessori education, and a tour of a Montessori preschool.

# 6: Conclusion

Setting up a Montessori space at home is something that any parent can do – because it can suit any household and any family. A Montessori room is particularly helpful to children and pre-schoolers, but it is also helpful at the elementary level.

The tasks of Practical Life are naturally fascinating experiences for the child because they are things, he/she has seen grown-ups do. Practical Life sequencing starts with scooping and spooning, rolling and folding, twisting, squeezing, grasping and controlling, stringing and lacing, pounding and pushing, self-care, environment-care, grace and courtesy, and finishing with the preparation of food. Products are sequenced by the following progressions: use of hands to arms, large to small, left to right, top to bottom, gross motor to fine motor, no transition to move, two handed to two handed in opposition, size and shape of a medium used, dry materials to liquid, basic operations to complicated, few materials to many, short operations to long, insulation skills

Children benefit from all facets of the world of Practical Life. We hear about the basic goals of liberty, focus, teamwork, and order as well as the indirect goals of the actual skills being practiced. Practical Life is the cornerstone of the classroom at Montessori and helps the child to become a well-adjusted adult.

When parents are educated on Montessori and child development, it is beneficial to the child in their continuance of independence while at home. Parent education is the first step to the 11 progression of child independence

When parents can slow down and enjoy their time with their children, their lives are often less stressful and filled with more joyful family moments. Overall, independence may help lessen the frequency of frustration, emotional outbursts, and support a child's development of emotional skills that will be beneficial for adulthood.

When children are given a routine to follow each day, it helps them remember what is coming next, and can do their tasks without being asked. Children thrive with consistency which is why a routine or schedule is essential

# References

Should You Send Your Kid to a Montessori School? [Online] Available at: **https://www.verywellfamily.com/how-a-montessori-education-will-shape-your-child\**

Easy and Practical Montessori Tips to Help Kids Practice Mindfulness - Raising-independent-kids. [Online] Available at: **https://raising-independent-kids.com/easy-practical-montessori-tips-help-kids-practice-mindfulness\**

Montessori at Home | How to Create a Montessori-Friendly Home. [Online] Available at: **https://sapientiamontessori.com/montessori/montessori-at-home\**

Mind-minded parenting: Does attuned "mental talk" help kids thrive?. [Online] Available at: **https://www.parentingscience.com/mind-minded-parenting.html.**

6 Montessori parenting habits to practice every day. [Online] Available at: **https://www.mother.ly/child/6-key-ways-to-be-montessori-with-your-kids-every-day**.

Tips for Spending Quality Time With Your Child | NAEYC. [Online] Available at: **https://www.naeyc.org/our-work/families/spending-quality-time-with-your-child**.

Frequently Asked Questions | Children's Manor Montessori School. [Online] Available at: **https://childrensmanor.com/faq/**

Montessori Parenting Tips & Ideas. [Online] Carrots Are Orange. Available at: **https://carrotsareorange.com/montessori-parenting/**

# References

- O'Keeffe, A. (n.d.). *The Danish Way of Parenting review – how to raise the world's happiest kids*. [online] the Guardian. Available at: https://www.theguardian.com/books/2016/aug/06/danish-way-of-parenting-review.

- HARDING, N. (n.d.). *UK couple change family routine as they adopt The Danish Way of Parenting*. [online] The Sun. Available at: https://www.thesun.co.uk/living/1501594/uk-couple-change-family-routine-as-they-adopt-the-danish-way-of-parenting/.

- HealthyWay. (n.d.). *Want To Raise Happier Kids? Parent Like The Danish*. [online] Available at: https://www.healthyway.com/content/want-to-raise-happier-kids-parent-like-the-danish/.

- Sandra M. Bell - Hypnotherapist. (n.d.). *Raise Happy Kids, The Danish Way | Sandra M. Bell - Hypnotherapist*. [online] Available at: **https://www.sandrambell.com/raise-happy-kids-the-danish-way/.**

- Psychology Today. (n.d.). *Can Parenting the Danish Way Be Applied Elsewhere?*. [online] Available at: **https://www.psychologytoday.com/us/blog/neuro-behavioral-betterment/201705/can-parenting-the-danish-way-be-applied-elsewhere.**

# References

The Brain before Birth: Using fMRI to Explore the Secrets of Fetal Neurodevelopment. from https://ehp.niehs.nih.gov/doi/10.1289/EHP2268

Fetal Brain Development - Nervous System. Retrieved from https://www.whattoexpect.com/pregnancy/fetal-development/fetal-brain-nervous-system/

5 Stages of Human Brain Development. Retrieved, from https://nancyguberti.com/5-stages-of-human-brain-development/

Cold, F., Health, E., Disease, H., Disease, L., Management, P., & Conditions, S. et al. Cynicism Starts Early in Children. Retrieved from https://www.webmd.com/parenting/news/20050527/cynicism-starts-early-in-children#1

Child Has a Negative Attitude - Focus on the Family. Retrieved from https://www.focusonthefamily.com/family-qa/child-has-a-negative-attitude/

Retrieved from https://www.who.int/maternal_child_adolescent/child/nurturing-care-framework-first-draft.pdf

Lightning Source UK Ltd.
Milton Keynes UK
UKHW021029271220
375899UK00014B/1652